The Jesus
of
Christian History

Donald J. Goergen, O.P.

D0169819

A Michael Glazier Book
THE LITURGICAL PRESS
Collegeville, Minnesota

A THEOLOGY OF JESUS
Volume 3

A Michael Glazier Book published by The Liturgical Press

Cover design by Mary Jo Pauly

1 2 3 4 5 6 7 8 9

Library of Congress Cataloging-in-Publication Data

Goergen, Donald.
    The Jesus of Christian history / Donald Goergen.
        p.   cm. — (A Theology of Jesus ; v. 3)
    "A Michael Glazier book."
    Includes bibliographical references and index.
    1. Jesus Christ—History of doctrines. I. Title. II. Series:
Goergen, Donald.   Theology of Jesus ; v. 3.
    BT198.G585   1991
    232'.09—dc20   91-26663
ISBN 0-8146-5605-6   CIP

Contents

To the students
I have taught

Preface

This is the third volume in an effort to construct a theology of Jesus for pastors, preachers, and teachers. This volume addresses the second of four tasks which I set for myself—the task of historical retrieval, an interpretation of the history of Christology. The first two volumes in this series, *The Mission and Ministry of Jesus* and *The Death and Resurrection of Jesus,* were concerned with the first task—an interpretation of the Jesus of historiography, an effort to understand the earthly Jesus of Nazareth via the methods of contemporary historical biblical research. (For further elucidation of these four tasks, see the introduction to vol. 1.)

As indicated toward the close of volume 2, there is more to the earthly Jesus than scientific historiography can provide by its own methods. And there is also more to Jesus than the earthly, pre-resurrection Jesus. Thus our pursuit of an ecclesially, professionally, and socially responsible theology of Jesus cannot be content with a historiographical interpretation alone. There is more to Jesus and we must carry our pursuit further.

As data for an eventual construction of a theology of Jesus itself (which will comprise vol. 4), we have responded to the following questions in volumes 1 and 2: With the aid of contemporary critical biblical methods, what can we say about Jesus of Nazareth? What kind of picture emerges? Now, for the sake of further data, we must also ask, how has Jesus been understood, portrayed, or interpreted within the Christian tradition itself, within the history of the Christian movement? This is in no way an effort to set a biblical, historical Jesus over against a Jesus of the Christian faith or a Jesus of the Christian Churches. Rather, it is simply the effort to seek more data before we attempt to construct a theology of Jesus for our period of history. Biblical, historiographical research itself led us to conclude that a historiographical interpretation alone, while necessary, is inadequate. Thus we inquire in this volume into what Christian faith has had to say. What does the historical Christian faith say about Jesus Christ?

I want to make it clear that this volume is not a history of Christology as such. One should turn to the work of Aloys Grillmeier for that, or to other competent histories of doctrine and theology. What I present here is rather seven interpretative essays and a concluding reflection on some lessons we learn from a historical inquiry. I have chosen seven points in the history of Christian theology that will give us a further perspective on Jesus and access to the historical Christian faith and tradition. These seven points of departure for further theological reflection are: (1) the particular understanding of Jesus toward the end of the first century manifest in the Johannine community, (2) the effect of the spread of Christianity in the second century on Christian interpretations of Jesus, (3) the conflictual and contrasting approaches to Jesus elaborated within the concerns and methods of Alexandrian and Antiochene Christianity, (4) the role, constructive contributions, and failures of the great councils as East and West took similar and yet different historical paths, (5) Byzantine and medieval mystical theology as a way of speaking about Jesus Christ, (6) the philosophical theology of Thomas Aquinas as another way of speaking about Jesus Christ, and (7) the reformation of theology inaugurated by Martin Luther that articulated another way of proclaiming Jesus Christ.

My hope is that these essays on various aspects of Christian history and its theology will give us further data and help us to understand more adequately Jesus of Nazareth.

As with each of the previous volumes, there are many to whom I am grateful, in particular, Fran Cogan, Diana Culbertson, Stanley Drongowski, Thomas McGonigle, Suzanne Noffke, Margaret Ormond, Frances Plass, Boniface Ramsey, the late James A. Weisheipl, and Ann Willits.

As in the two previous volumes, I have used inclusive language. With quotations from primary sources, however, I have been cautious, ordinarily retaining earlier translations of Greek or Latin sources rather than doing my own. Given subtle but significant differences of meaning in the history and development of Christological language, I have refrained from retranslating a text to favor inclusive language where a specific theological meaning could be jeopardized, or I have only retranslated when such could be easily and justifiably done on the basis of the original text. Ordinarily, questions of translation are made clear in the text or notes. Biblical quotations ordinarily follow the Revised Standard Version.

Since some technical terms are not thoroughly explained upon first use, I have included a limited glossary of terms to which someone may wish to refer before reading further.

1

The Christology of the Johannine Community

Johannine research in the past twenty-five years manifests wide agreement on several issues: (1) Behind the Gospel of John there was a body of tradition which was inherited by the evangelist and which formed the basis for the Gospel. The form in which this tradition was received remains uncertain. (2) The evangelist, whose identity remains unknown to us, was a formative figure, both in shaping the tradition received into a Gospel and in shaping the first century of Christian history. (3) The evangelist was addressing and wrote the Gospel for a particular and distinctive Christian group. The needs of the community contributed to the shaping of the Gospel. It was a particular community with its own set of problems. Robert Kysar terms the Fourth Gospel an "occasional writing,"[1] one produced for a particular occasion and situated in a particular setting in the history of the Church. (4) The distinctive problem confronting the Johannine community was tension between itself and Judaism, between Church and synagogue. The Johannine community included a large body of Christian Jews affected by the growing hostility between an emerging orthodox Judaism and the Christian movement. The synagogue's eventual expulsion of Christians from its membership affected

---

[1]Robert Kysar, *The Fourth Evangelist and His Gospel: An Examination of Contemporary Scholarship* (Minneapolis: Augsburg, 1975) 171, 270. An excellent survey of modern Johannine research prior to 1975 and a delineation of areas of consensus or lack thereof.

the future and very existence of the Johannine Christians. The evangelist wrote to strengthen the community in the midst of its struggle. (5) Finally, and perhaps most significantly, the character and context of the Gospel was Jewish, particularly marginal Judaism, not Hellenism or Gnosticism. The Johannine Christian Jews were not necessarily the more normative Jews.

The "making of the Fourth Gospel" as we now have it remains a disputed issue. The majority of scholars would suggest a process that extended over many years and stages of composition. Not only did the evangelist inherit a tradition and creatively shape a Gospel, but the evangelist's Gospel itself underwent further redaction. A tradition preceded the work of the evangelist and redaction followed it. Simply by way of exemplification, we can examine one of the current theories concerning the formation of the Gospel and the history of the Johannine community.[2]

Raymond Brown posits five stages in the composition of the Gospel: (1) a body of traditional material, the origins of which were independent of the synoptic tradition; (2) the development of this material over perhaps several decades as it took distinctive shape through oral preaching and teaching, and even eventually through some written forms, under the influence of a dominant preacher and theologian; (3) the organization of this material into the first edition of a distinct Gospel by the same preacher and theologian, whom we can refer to as "the evangelist," the dominant influence in the shaping of the tradition; (4) re-editing, or perhaps several further editings, by the evangelist; and (5) the final redaction by someone other than the evangelist, perhaps a disciple of the evangelist, who added further "Johannine" material, including material that did not come from the preaching and teaching of the evangelist, such as the prologue. The tradition ultimately behind the Gospel (stage 1) goes back to an eyewitness, the Beloved Disciple.[3] The evangelist (stages 2–4) was an unknown disciple of this figure whose genius developed

---

[2]See Raymond Brown, *The Gospel According to John, I–XII,* Anchor Bible 29 (Garden City, N.Y.: Doubleday, 1966) xxxiv–li, lxxx–civ; R. Brown, *The Community of the Beloved Disciple* (New York: Paulist, 1979); and R. Brown, *The Epistles of John,* Anchor Bible 30 (Garden City, N.Y.: Doubleday, 1982) 69–115. See *The Community of the Beloved Disciple,* 171–182, for a summary of other reconstructions of Johannine history.

[3]In *The Gospel According to John, I–XII,* lxxxviii–xcviii, Brown identifies the Beloved Disciple as John, son of Zebedee, one of the Twelve. Later, in *The Community of the Beloved Disciple,* 31–34, he prefers to leave the identity of the Beloved Disciple unknown.

and shaped the Johannine tradition into a Gospel. The Gospel was most probably composed at Ephesus. The final form of the Gospel (stage 5) was written most probably between 90 and 100 C.E.

The history of the Johannine community was not precisely the same as the history of the composition of the Gospel, and Brown outlines the community's history in four phases: its origins and history prior to the writing of the Gospel (mid-50s to late 80s); the community at the time of the writing of the Gospel (ca. 90); the community at the time of the writing of the epistles (ca. 100); and the community after the writing of the epistles (second century).

Phase One. The originating group of Johannine Christians were Jews, and not particularly heterodox or marginal Jews. Some had been disciples of John the Baptist. These were Christian Jews; they had accepted Jesus as the awaited Davidic Messiah. Within this group was someone who had known Jesus and who would later be known as the Beloved Disciple. Thus far, there was no severe conflict between these Christian Jews and other Jews. At some point there entered into the Johannine community another group, Samaritans and Jews of a more anti-Temple bias, the assimilation of whom led both to conflict with Judaism and to a more developed or "higher" Christology. During the latter part of this phase, about 85, the Christians were expelled from the synagogue. At this point, after the break with Judaism, the Johannine community gained Gentile converts as well. Thus the pre-Gospel community comprised fairly standard Jews, disciples of the Baptist, more marginal and anti-Temple Jews, Samaritans, and Gentiles in the midst of an open hostility with "the Jews."

Phase Two. The Johannine community had originated in Palestine. By the time of the writing of the Gospel, it may have moved. The community solidified as it defined itself over against outsiders and attempted to understand more deeply its own faith in Jesus. In this context the evangelist wrote the Gospel. Eventually, however, dissent arose within the community, and it had to cope with internal struggles.

Phase Three. Division within the community led to schism between the "secessionists" and "the adherents of the author of the epistles." Both groups were familiar with the Gospel; they interpreted it, however, differently. For the secessionists, the humanity of Jesus became less and less a significant reality. Brown suggests that the author of the epistles was someone other than the evangelist responsible for the Gospel. The epistles had to face a different crisis from that of the Gospel, internal schism in contrast to rejection and persecution from outside.

Phase Four. After the phase of schism and the composition of the epistles, each group went its own way. The secessionists, who may have been the majority, continued down the road toward Docetism and Gnosticism, taking the Fourth Gospel and their interpretation of it with them. Those who remained with the author of the epistles, with their high but non-Docetic Christology, were swallowed up by "the Great Church."

In the history of the Johannine community, Brown posits three significant figures without identifying them: the Beloved Disciple (the source of the tradition spoken of in stage one of the Gospel's composition), the evangelist (stages two through four of the Gospel's composition), and the author of the epistles (phase three of the community's history).

A new commentary on the Gospel According to John, soon to appear, is that by Thomas Brodie.[4] It relies heavily upon literary analysis, and from that basis it proceeds to deal with theological and historical concerns. Due to its emphasis on the final text of the Gospel and a literary analysis thereof, it both offers creative insights and also challenges some presuppositions in the mainstream of contemporary Johannine scholarship.

Among its contributions will be its perspective on the three ages of interpretation in the history of Johannine studies: theological interpretation, which was dominant until the eighteenth century and which Brodie prefers to emphasize as "theological" rather than as "pre-critical"; historical interpretation, which has dominated nineteenth- and twentieth-century discussions; and finally literary interpretation, which has more recently emerged and in

---

[4]Thomas Brodie, *The Gospel According to John, A Literary, Theological and Historical Commentary* (New York: Oxford University Press, forthcoming). References to Brodie rely on a draft of part of his work. As does Brodie, Peter Ellis also argues for the unity of the Gospel and that it stands now as it came from the hand of the author. See P. Ellis, *The Genius of John, A Composition-Critical Commentary on the Fourth Gospel* (Collegeville: The Liturgical Press, 1984). Ellis acknowledges his indebtedness to John Gerhard, *The Literary Unity and the Compositional Methods of the Gospel of John,* unpublished dissertation (Washington: The Catholic University of America Press, 1975). Also see Eugen Ruckstuhl, *Die Literarische Einheit des Johannesevangeliums* (Freiburg, Switzerland: Paulus, 1951).

the face of which some of the modern historical emphases can appear as "pre-critical" as well. Yet Brodie's contention is that all three approaches or skills, which have been dominant at different periods in the history of interpretation, are incomplete by themselves alone and that there is the need to integrate these three diverse emphases. Thus Brodie's own approach is to give due regard to each emphasis while he judges the best starting point to be that of literary analysis and thus to not pose or judge historical issues prematurely. Hence, Brodie's starting point is a literary analysis of the finished text and only after that a discussion of the Gospel's background and sources.

By a literary analysis of the final text's structure, Brodie argues for a greater unity to the text than is ordinarily acceptable to historical critics and also for a complex, multi-level artistry, which manifests a subtle unity that is the work of a master literary artist. Brodie is not inclined to suggest stages in a history of composition but rather the Gospel as a unified whole that contains literary ambiguity.

Johannine Christology

We now turn to the Christology of the Gospel. The evangelist concluded the Gospel (if we consider ch. 21 as added later by someone other than the evangelist) with a statement of purpose: "Now Jesus did many other signs in the presence of the disciples, which are not written in this book; but these are written that you may believe that Jesus is the Christ, the Son of God, and that believing you may have life in his name" (20:30-32). In this final statement, the evangelist indicated that he had written (1) to enable the Johannine Christians to see and thus believe that Jesus was the Messiah expected by the Jews, (2) to impress upon them who this Messiah was, not simply the Jewish Davidic Messiah but one who uniquely deserved to be called the Son of God in the full sense of Johannine theology, and (3) that their faith in this Messiah, this Jesus, would bring life, for such faith had salvific consequences.

The second of these statements will concern us here. The other evangelists also wrote out of their conviction that Jesus was the awaited Messiah, but John's Gospel presents the most theologically developed understanding of this messiahship. More than the others, the Fourth Gospel took Christology beyond any understanding within Judaism and thus contributed significantly to the Christian understanding of who the Messiah was as applied to Jesus. John began to formulate the later Christians' Christology of Jesus. His distinctive understanding of Messiah made the Fourth Gospel distinct from the Synoptic tradition and affected the history of Christian theologies of Jesus. This Johannine theology of Jesus was (1) a Christology from above, (2) in which the "glory" of Jesus shone through on earth, (3) and thus made for a new type of Christology, (4) in which the word "logos" was used, (5) and thus helped to flesh out the Johannine understanding of Jesus' unique sonship. This statement is elaborated in what follows.

In the Synoptic Gospels, Jesus is God's agent here on earth. In the Fourth Gospel, the heavenly world is woven into earthly scenarios here below. To describe this Christology as a theology of Jesus "from above" is to use Johannine language itself. "He who comes from above is above all; he who is of the earth belongs to the earth, and of the earth he speaks; he who comes from heaven is above all" (3:31). "For I have come down from heaven, not to do my own will, but the will of him who sent me" (6:38). "You are from below, I am from above; you are of this world, I am not of this world" (8:23). Johannine Christology is expressed by a descending and ascending motif. "No one has ascended into heaven but he who descended from heaven, the Son of Humanity" (3:13). In its contrast between the heavenly sphere and earthly sphere, it invites us to be born again (see 3:3-15), and it distinguishes between one who is of God and the one who is of this world (see 8:47). Jesus was with the Father but has come down from heaven. He was sent by the Father. He knows the Father. To understand Jesus, one cannot abstract him from this heavenly sphere; it is his natural habitat. He lives there even while living on earth. Jesus' origins, his roots, are with God in the beginning. Jewish wisdom helps us to understand this background of Johannine Christology.[5]

---

[5]Concerning the contrast between the heavenly and earthly spheres in the Fourth Gospel, the descending/ascending motif, and the background in the Wisdom tradition, see Brown, *The Gospel According to John, I-XII*, lii–lxvi, cxv–cxxviii; Kysar, *The Fourth Evangelist and His Gospel*, 111-119; Edward Schillebeeckx, *The Christ*, trans. John Bowden (New York: Seabury, 1980) 321-331.

The Johannine theology of "glory" *(doxa)* links the glory that properly speaking is the Father's (7:16-18) very closely with Jesus' mission on earth (5:21, 36; 11:40; 17:1-4). The Father's glory, which has been shared with the Son (5:20-23; 8:50, 54; 17:22-24), manifests itself in the "signs" *(sēmeia)* Jesus works. Although Jesus expressly subordinates himself to the Father (5:19, 30; 8:28; 12:49; 14:28), Jesus and his Father are for all practical purposes equal (5:17-18; 8:16-18; 10:30; 14:9-11). He who hears one hears the other; he who rejects one rejects the other (3:17-21; 5:22-23; 8:19; 14:7).

The first "sign" that Jesus performs at Cana links Jesus' works with revelation and faith. Jesus' miracles, or signs, manifest the Father's and his own glory to those who can see and who believe. "This, the first of his signs, Jesus did at Cana in Galilee, and manifested his glory; and his disciples believed in him" (2:11). "Signs" *(sēmeia),* "glory" *(doxa),* and "believing" *(pisteuein)* weave heaven and earth together in Johannine Christology. And although the Gospel is readily divided into two parts (1:19–12:50 and 13:1–20:31),[6] glory manifests itself in the seven signs, which form the basis of the first part, and also the sign par excellence, which forms the basis of the second part, the passion and resurrection of Jesus, which is but a manifestation of the glory that the Father has shared with the Son. Sign and glory are woven together as are earth and heaven throughout the entirety of the Gospel. This beauty and complexity in the Fourth Gospel leads Brodie to speak of literary ambiguity[7] and Kysar to speak of elements in the Gospel as intentionally paradoxical.[8]

It can be argued that Johannine Christology either "blurs" the distinction or "integrates" the relationship between faith and history. The theologian behind the Fourth Gospel would probably argue that heaven and earth have come together in Jesus of Nazareth. To fail to "see" this is to not yet "know" Jesus. Thus, as J. Louis Martyn points out, Johannine Christology is a drama operative on two levels.[9] From the Johannine theological perspec-

[6]Brown, *The Gospel According to John, I–XII,* cxxxviii–cxliv.

[7]Brodie, see n. 4 of this chapter.

[8]Robert Kysar, *John's Story of Jesus* (Philadelphia: Fortress, 1984) 16.

[9]J. Louis Martyn, *History and Theology in the Fourth Gospel,* rev. ed. (New York: Abingdon, 1979).

tive, one simply cannot know Jesus and still contrast faith and history. Only faith understands history, sees God's presence in this Jesus, and sees this same Jesus (of faith) as still with the community. To distinguish between a Jesus of history and a Jesus of faith is a faithless perspective. There is only Jesus as he truly is (sent by God), the perspective of those who know him in truth. A superficial understanding of Jesus as only a child of Abraham or Moses is the perspective of those who have not been born of the Holy Spirit, and it represents a false Jewish understanding of Jesus.

We can call the Johannine Christology a "higher" or "high" Christology. Perhaps it is better called a "deep" or "deeper" Christology. (Some would say a vertical [ontological] in contrast to a horizontal [historical] Christology.) The Johannine Jesus can comfortably say, "I proceeded and came forth from God" (8:42), and "Before Abraham was, I am" (8:58). This is certainly a new Christology, not the same as that of the Synoptics. But it need not necessarily be pictured as "much later." It may simply manifest distinctiveness rather than lateness in the Johannine community's history.[10]

The first Johannine Christians had been Christian Jews who believed that Jesus was the Messiah. As the Johannine Christian Jewish community became more complex (the influx of more marginal Jews, Samaritans, Gentiles), their Christology was affected. The Temple in Jerusalem became less significant. The stage is set for Jesus to be God's *shekinah,* or presence on earth, and the door is opened to a new insight. Jesus as Son is not simply prophet, sage, and servant but one who has been in the very presence of God and has come down to earth. The Johannine community's theology of Jesus' sonship underwent development. The Samaritan element in the community brought with it its emphasis on the expected prophet-like-Moses, a teacher and revealer who would surpass Moses, and this influence could account for the Mosaic elements in Johannine Christology.[11] These trends within the Johannine community's Christology set it even further at odds with a Judaism faced with its own problems in the post-70 C.E. world.

---

[10]Kysar, *The Fourth Evangelist and His Gospel,* 275-776.

[11]Concerning the Moses typology, see Martyn, *History and Theology in the Fourth Gospel,* 102-228; and Wayne Meeks, *The Prophet-King: Moses Traditions and the Johannine Christology* (Leiden, Netherlands: E. J. Brill, 1967).

The Jews' charge against the Johannine Christian Jews[12] was that they were making Jesus into a god (5:16-18; 10:31-39). The community's history and conflicts were intimately bound up with this developing insight. The unique aspect of the Fourth Gospel's Christology in contrast with the Christologies of the Synoptic Gospels was the pre-existence of Jesus. This was also one of the Johannine community's major contributions to later Christian history and theology.

In the Gospel of John we find, within the community's Christology itself, the tension between a "lower" Christology and a "higher" Christology, the emphasis on Jesus as not equal to the Father (14:28) and as equal to the Father (10:30). These insights are not necessarily incompatible. As I suggested above, the earthly Jesus sees the Father as greater, and yet *for all practical purposes* Jesus and the Father are one: To know the one is to know the other.[13] Yet this tension manifests two strains within Johannine Christology, the subordination of Jesus to the Father and the equality of Jesus with the Father. Brown argues that the Gospel is open to various interpretations.[14] The adversaries of the author of the Johannine epistles, the secessionists, developed the Johannine emphases in a Docetic, Gnostic, and heterodox (from a later Christian viewpoint) direction, whereas the author of the epistles and their adherents preserved the salvific importance of *both* the human bodiliness of Jesus *and* his pre-existence and preserved these for the larger Christian Church of which they eventually became a part. Hence the epistles emphasized Jesus' com-

[12]Martyn distinguishes between Christian Jews and Jewish Christians in order to elaborate more clearly Johannine community development. See J. Louis Martyn, *The Gospel of John in Christian History* (New York: Paulist, 1978) 90–121, esp. 107.

[13]The most thorough recent exploration of the theme of Jesus' equality with God in the Fourth Gospel is that of Jerome H. Neyrey's *An Ideology of Revolt: John's Christology in Social-Science Perspective* (Philadelphia: Fortress, 1988). Neyrey examines the confession that Jesus is "equal to God," and also what he considers its corollary, that Jesus is "not of this world," and how this confession functioned or what purpose it served for the community, namely, as an ideology for revolt against synagogue and other Christian groups. I do not agree with Neyrey that "equal to God" is equivalent to "not of this world," that Jesus' heavenliness is valued over his humanity. Neyrey's analysis of Jesus' equality with God, however, is excellent, pp. 9–112. Jesus' equality with God is rooted in Jesus' participation in God's two basic powers: God's creative power and God's eschatological power.

[14]See Brown, *The Community of the Beloved Disciple*, 26–54, 81–88, 109–123, 151–162; and *The Epistles of John*, 49–68, 73–79, 104–115. These reconstructions are always hypotheses.

ing in the flesh (1 John 4:2; 2 John 7) and represented an "orthodox" interpretation of the Gospel.

The Prologue of the Fourth Gospel

The Gospel of John does indeed manifest layers of Christology. What is unique, however, is the theology of the Word and the particular theology of the Son. We begin with the Johannine prologue.

> [1]In the beginning was the Word, and the Word was with God, and the Word was God. [2]He was in the beginning with God; [3]all things were made through him, and without him was not anything made that was made. [4]In him was life, and the life was the light of humankind. [5]The light shines in the darkness, and the darkness has not overcome it.
>
> [6]There was a man sent from God, whose name was John. [7]He came for testimony, to bear witness to the light, that all might believe through him. [8]He was not the light, but came to bear witness to the light.
>
> [9]The true light that enlightens everyone was coming into the world. [10]He was in the world, and the world was made through him, yet the world knew him not. [11]He came to his own home, and his own people received him not. [12]But to all who received him, who believed in his name, he gave power to become children of God; [13]who were born, not of blood nor of the will of the flesh nor of human will, but of God.
>
> [14]And the Word became flesh and dwelt among us, full of grace and truth; we have beheld his glory, glory as of the only Son from the Father. [15](John bore witness to him, and cried, "This was he of whom I said, 'He who comes after me ranks before me, for he was before me.' ") [16]And from his fullness have we all received, grace upon grace. [17]For the law was given through Moses; grace and truth came through Jesus Christ. [18]No one has ever seen God; the only Son, who is in the bosom of the Father, he has made him known (John 1:1-18).

Much recent Johannine scholarship supports the hypothesis that the prologue (1) is based on an independent Logos hymn, (2) which may have been composed in Johannine circles, and (3) which was edited and added to the Gospel.[15] The dissimilarities between the prologue and the rest of the Gospel incline one to postulate its original independence; for example, the central Christological expression in the prologue is that of *Logos,* but Logos as such, as a title, never occurs again in the rest of the Gospel. Similarities between the prologue and the Gospel, however, urge us to postulate that the hymn had its origins in the Johannine circle even if originating independently of the Gospel (for example, pre-existence, or Jesus' eternity in the past, is a theme present in both prologue and Gospel). Yet it is difficult to separate the original hymn from the later editorial additions. Rudolf Schnackenburg concludes to verses 1, 3, 4, 9, 10a, c, 11, 14a, b, c, and 16 as an original hymn.[16] I translate these verses as follows:

> [1]In the beginning was the Word, and the Word was with God, and the Word was God. [3]All things were made through it, and without it was not anything made that was made.
>
> [4]In it was life, and the life was the light of humankind. [9]The true light that enlightens everyone was coming into the world.
>
> [10]It was in the world, yet the world knew it not. [11]It came to its own home, and its own people received it not.

[15]Those who argue for the unity of the Gospel as a literary whole also argue for the unity of the prologue, for example, Brodie, Ellis, Gerhard, n. 4 of this chapter. Brodie, unlike most contemporary Johannine scholars, argues in favor of the unity of the prologue as a literary text and its unity with the Gospel as a whole, that the prologue is not, in other words, a pre-existing hymn to which other material has been added and thus edited and added later to the Gospel. Brodie accepts the final form of the text as a coherent literary unit, including vv. 6–8, 15, those most often seen as later interpolations. Although I have followed Schnackenburg's reconstruction of a pre-existing hymn, accepting the unity of the text would not significantly alter my interpretation of the text as the history of the Logos in creation and salvation. The hymn as a whole in its final form (whether such was its original form or not) is a Logos theology in which the entire hymn presupposes the intimate relationship between the Logos and Jesus explicitly stated in v. 14. But to see the Logos as both distinguishable from Jesus and as incarnate in Jesus only reflects a multi-leveled understanding on the part of the literary artist or poetic genius. Brodie's commentary on the prologue is sensitive to the Word's history in creation, in Hebrew salvation history, and in the incarnation or New Testament.

Peder Borgen also argues that John 1:1-18 in entirety can be treated as a composition of the evangelist. See especially "Logos Was the True Light," *Novum Testamentum* 14 (1972), 115–130, also contained in *Logos Was the True Light, and Other Essays on the Gospel of John* (Trondheim, Norway: Tapir Publishers, 1983) 95–110.

[16]Rudolf Schnackenburg, *The Gospel According to St. John,* trans. Kevin Smyth (New York: Herder and Herder, 1968) 1:224–229. In disagreement with Schnackenburg are some authors listed in n. 15 above.

¹⁴"And the Word became flesh and dwelt among us, full of grace and truth. ¹⁶And from his fullness have we all received, grace upon grace.

The original hymn was edited when incorporated as a prologue to the Gospel; the material on John the Baptist, for example (vv. 6-8, 15), was added. There is no consensus on whether the final redactor who incorporated the prologue into the Gospel was the evangelist (stages 2-4 of Brown's theory of composition) or a later redactor (the one who added ch. 21 to the Gospel). Brown suggests the later redactor; Schnackenburg maintains that the evangelist was responsible.[17]

One of the more disputed issues has been that of the background for the expression "Logos" as used in the prologue. It is generally accepted today that neither Gnosticism nor Philo provide the immediate background; rather, it is provided by the concept of the word of God as found in the Hebrew Scriptures (Isa 55:10) and, even more so, by the Hebrew sapiential tradition and its concept of wisdom.[18] The hymns to wisdom in Job 28; Wisdom 9:9-18; Proverbs 8; and Sirach 24:3-21 are suggestive. Wisdom was divine (Wis 7:25-26), had a role to play in creation (Wis 9:9), was sent into the world (Wis 9:10), and is not recognized by the world (Sir 15:7). Practically speaking, *logos* (word) is equivalent to *sophia* (wisdom).

If the Johannine Logos so well reflects Hellenistic Jewish speculation on *sophia,* why did the Johannine school or evangelist not incorporate a hymn to wisdom incarnate? What prompted the selection of the word "logos" rather than "sophia"?[19] What seems most likely is that the word "logos" would establish a point of contact with the wider Hellenistic world, a suitable function

¹⁷Brown, *The Gospel According to John, I-XII,* xxxviii, also 18-23. Schnackenburg, *The Gospel According to St. John,* 1:223.

¹⁸See M.-E. Boismond, *St. John's Prologue* (Westminster, Md.: Newman, 1957) 73-76, 82-101; and James D. G. Dunn, *Christology in the Making: A New Testament Inquiry into the Origins of the Doctrine of the Incarnation* (Philadelphia: Westminster Press, 1980) 215-239. Also Brown, *The Gospel According to John, I-XII,* cxxii-cxxviii, 519-524; Kysar, *The Fourth Evangelist and His Gospel,* 107-111, 144-146; Schillebeeckx, *The Christ,* 353-362; Schnackenburg, *The Gospel According to St. John,* 1:229-232, 481-493.

¹⁹See T. E. Pollard, *Johannine Christology and the Early Church* (Cambridge: University Press, 1970) 6-15; Schnackenburg, *The Gospel According to St. John,* 1:486, 493. I consider it less likely that the choice of "Logos" over "Sophia" had something to do with their masculine or feminine gender as Brown suggests in *The Gospel According to John, I-XII,* 523.

for a prologue; the Gospel does not refer to the concept of logos again, not even when stating the purpose for which it was written (20:31). One could also suggest the revelatory function of Jesus in the Gospel and the revelatory connotation of the word "logos."

The logos of the Johannine prologue is with God in the beginning; it pre-exists its activity in creation and its incarnation in our world. The Logos is not only with God, but is God; the divine nature or character of the Logos is affirmed. With John's Gospel we now have the full story of Jesus' life, a story that unfolds in three stages. We clearly have a three-stage Christology (in contrast to the two-stage Synoptic Christologies), an understanding of three stages in the life of Jesus: pre-existence, earthly existence, risen and exalted life. Using "Word" enabled the evangelist to complete his story of Jesus by integrating the stage of pre-existence into it. Jesus is the pre-existent Word made flesh. In addition to the Johannine interpretation of a pre-existence of Jesus as God's Word, the word "God" applies to all three stages in the life of Jesus: the pre-existent Word (1:1), the incarnate Word (1:18), and the risen Lord (20:28).

Verses 1-2. In the beginning or at the beginning was the Logos. The Logos is eternal; it pre-exists creation; there was no time when the Logos was not. It was already with God at the beginning. The first words of the prologue *(en archē)* reflect the first words of Genesis: "In the beginning God created the heavens and the earth" (1:1). The prologue goes back further, prior to creation, when the Word was and creation was not yet. "The Word was with God" implies a distinction between God and the Word; the Word was in the company of God. "The Word was God" implies an identity with God, *theos* is what God and the Logos have in common. Yet the distinction between God and the Word is still maintained. In the Greek text, the definite article is used when referring to God *(ho theos)* and not when describing the divinity of the Logos *(theos ēn ho logos)*. This usage may reflect the Johannine consciousness that the Son is not equal to the Father. The Logos is divine and for all practical purposes equivalent to God; yet a distinction is maintained. I have translated "Logos" prior to verse 14 with a neuter pronoun. This is the way we would ordinarily translate it into English, although its grammatical gender in Greek is masculine. Perhaps its identity with God would suggest that it be translated with the same gender with which God is translated (who is beyond gender), or perhaps masculine gender is more appropriate given the climax of the prologue's identification of the Logos with Jesus.[20] Yet prior to verse 10 nothing necessitates attributing gender to the Logos. It is simply with God and in some sense is God.

Verses 3-5. The Logos plays an active role in creation. All things *(panta)* come to be through its instrumentality; without it nothing *(oude hen)* would exist. Translators are divided as to whether *ho gegonen* goes with verse 3 (thus, "All things were made through it, and without it was not anything made that was made"), or with what follows (thus, "All things were made through it, and without it not anything was made. What was made in it was life . . . "). The arguments for either of these translations are not conclusive. If we take the second reading ("What was made in it was life, and the life was the light of humankind"), life, natural life, created life, is the meaning of the first reference to *zōē* (life). What came to be through the creative action of the Logos was life. This does not imply that all of creation is alive. The action of the Logos reaches its height in verse 14 when the Logos becomes flesh. All is created through the Logos, but even more significant is a particular reality or creation which came to be through it, namely, life.

The second reference to life ("and the life was the light of humankind") could be taken in two ways. (1) The meaning of the word "life" shifts; it now refers to the life of the Logos. What was made through the Logos was life. And the life of the Logos (which is an even fuller life) is light for humankind. By association, the first reference to life (natural life) echoes a reference to another kind of life, which is the light for humankind. (2) There is continuity between the two uses rather than contrast. Just as the greatest among the created works of the Logos was life, so

---

[20]Does Logos throughout the prologue imply "the Word enfleshed"? If so, as de Ausejo argues, then translating it with a masculine pronoun is more justified. See Serafin de Ausejo, "¿Es un himno a Cristo el prologo de San Juan?" *Estudios Biblicos* 15 (1956) 223–277, 381–427. Such, however, does not necessarily seem to be the case to me. It is difficult to determine. Borgen, *Logos Was the True Light,* 20, suggests that Jesus Christ is being referred to three times, in vv. 9, 11, and 14. My inclination would be to go with expressions like literary ambiguity and intentional paradoxicality (nn. 7 and 8 above) and suggest that "Logos" can legitimately be read *both* as the pre-incarnate Logos *and* as the incarnate Logos, whether one postulates the unity of the prologue by the evangelist or whether one speaks of the theology of a redactor.

the greatest among the living works was humankind. Creation follows the Genesis pattern. And life (created life), as it manifests itself in the human order, is even more. It is light, a natural light. It is even fuller life, akin to eternal life or divine life, the very life that is the life of the Word. Here, however, life (eternal life, the life of the Word) is not seen in contrast to natural life but in continuity with it. All life is analogous, we might say. This is in keeping with a Johannine perspective that eternal life is the fullness of life. There is more life in life than biological life alone. Thus, the verse is something of a history of life—which extends from the life created through the Logos to human life to the divine and eternal life in which humankind shares to the very life of the Logos. What was created in it was life. And this life is also light. It does not appear as if these verses necessarily refer to Jesus as the Word incarnate, for it is verse 6 that moves us in that direction with the testimony of John. Rather, so far we have: What comes from the Logos is life, and this life, which comes to be through the Logos, is light for us.

The light of verse 4 is not yet the light of verse 9. It is the light in us that is in conflict with the powers of darkness. But darkness has not been able to overcome it or extinguish it. Light shines in darkness and darkness cannot destroy it. The Logos has brought light into the world of darkness through its creation of life.

Verses 6-8. These verses may be intrusive and indicate redaction. Verse 9 begins to introduce Jesus of Nazareth into the prologue, to whom the prologue has thus far not referred directly. Verses 6-8 are introduced as a preface to the career of Jesus, the Word made flesh. John was sent by God to give witness or testimony to Jesus. The meaning of "light" *(phōs)* in these verses is to be read back from the meaning in verse 9, for which they are an introduction. Jesus is the true light; John is not. The point corresponds to the evangelist's subordination of John to Jesus. M.-E. Boismond has suggested that these verses may at one time have preceded verse 19 and served as an introduction to the Gospel and the work of John the Baptist.[21]

Verse 9. This verse could follow directly after verse 4 or 5, if one does not accept the compositional unity of the prologue and depending upon how one reconstructs the pre-Johannine hymn.

[21]Boismond, *St. John's Prologue,* 24–25.

All has been created through the Logos. Through the power of the Logos, life and light have entered the world, especially the human world. The introduction of the theme of light now enables a connection. The light of verses 4 and 5 is not the fullness of light, or the true light. Just as life appears in the world of creation, and human life (and with it light) in the world of life, so in the midst of the human world will come the true light. This light is not simply a created light or enlightenment but a light that more truly enlightens everyone. This true light is about to enter the world. This true light is the Logos.

Verses 10-13. The true light, the Logos, was in the world. The fact is that the world did not recognize it. The Logos had created the whole world. Yet the world, here the human world, did not take note of it. So the Logos came to "its own," a special people. But its own people did not listen to it. We are now shifting from the role of the Word in creation to the Word in human and salvation history. As the *Letter to the Hebrews* had said, God spoke through the prophets. But the Word's presence in history is unheeded, although not completely. To those who heard and heeded the Word, it gave power, the power to be God's very own offspring, of whom it can truly be said that they are born of God more than of flesh and blood. The Word's activity in the world had divided the world into those who did not receive the Word and those who did and who were thus empowered to be reborn. These verses need not yet refer to the Word as incarnate, to Jesus' earthly ministry. The pre-incarnate Word (prior to Jesus) empowers people to be born from above; such an understanding is consistent with Johannine theology.

Verses 14-16. Verse 15 may be intrusive, paralleling verses 6-8 above. It assigns John the function of giving testimony to Jesus as the greater of the two. Reflecting very closely verse 30, which it may be copying, it may have been inserted by the redactor. Thus, verses 14 and 16 can be read together.

Verse 14 is the first clear affirmation of the incarnation of the Logos. It is the next chapter in the history of the Logos, which was present in creation (vv. 1-5), in human history (vv. 9-13), and now in the flesh as Logos incarnate (vv. 14, 16). The Word became flesh, a concrete historical individual. This is the fullest or closest expression of the Logos in relation to us. The Logos, which was and is in the presence of God, and is God, has now also come to dwell in our midst. We can now behold no longer *its* but *his* glory. We can begin to speak of the Logos as a person. For the first time, the evangelist implies the word "Son." The Word incarnate is the unique Son of the Father.

Although I have interpreted verses 9-13 as the Logos' presence in salvation history, these verses anticipate the incarnate manifestation in verse 14. They can be read (and ought to be) with the twofold sense of the pre-incarnate Logos and the incarnate Logos.[22]

The Logos became *sarx* (flesh). The word *sarx* denotes the whole person, full humanness, the human being as fragile and perishable—"the human mode of being."[23] It means incarnation and denies Docetism. The word *sarx* as relevant to a theology of Jesus is also found in Paul (Rom 1:3; 8:3) as well as in the interpreter of the Gospel of John, the author of 1 John (4:2-3).

In becoming *sarx,* the Logos pitched his tent in our midst, made his home with us, came to dwell with us, to be the one-who-is-with-us *(eskēnōsen).* The Greek verb implies the history of God's presence with God's people. In Exodus 25:8-9, Israel is instructed to make a tent (tabernacle) so God can dwell with the people. The Temple had been the tent of divine dwelling, the localized presence of God. Now Jesus is seen as the new tent, the new temple, the locus of God's presence on earth. The Word incarnate is the *shekinah* (God as present).

Prior to verse 14, the prologue had spoken only of God and God's Logos. Now, in verse 14, God becomes Father. The adjective *monogenēs* means "only," or "unique."[24] The incarnate Word is a unique child of the Father, like an only son of a father, the beloved son. (See John 3:16, 18; 10:30-38; 14:11, 20; 16:32; 17:21.)

In verse 16, the Incarnate Word, Jesus, is described as a fullness, a fullness that overflows and from whom we all benefit.

Verses 17-18. Schnackenburg lists these verses with the later redaction of the hymn. Verse 17 contrasts Jesus and Moses. There

---

[22]See n. 20 of this chapter.

[23]Schnackenburg, *The Gospel According to St. John,* 1:267.

[24]"Monogenēs" as such does not mean "only begotten." See D. Moody, "God's Only Son: The Translation of John 3:16 in the RSV," *Journal of Biblical Literature* 72 (1953) 213-219; Brown, *The Gospel According to John, I-XII,* 12-14.

is textual variation among the manuscripts for verse 18. The two more significant readings are *monogenēs theos* (God the only Son) and *monogenēs huios* (the only Son). In either case, the reference is to the Son "who is in the bosom of the Father." The unique one, who is in the bosom of the Father, has revealed God to us. This revelatory function is implicit in the concept of Logos, and its revelatory action has become complete in its becoming God's unique and beloved Son. In verse 1 the Logos is in the presence of God; and now the Son, the Logos incarnate, is in the bosom of the Father. God and God's Word have become Father and Son for us.

The prologue has presented Jesus' life on earth as a work of the Word of God, and thus has brought the life and history of Jesus into the very inner being of the life of God. The two are intimately, functionally, and ontologically connected. The Word's activity is creative, revelatory, and salvific.[25] Jesus cannot be separated from his inner connectedness to God's Word. In fact, in the deepest sense, Jesus, as incarnate, is this Word. Jesus is one instance of the work of the Word, and Jesus can in no way be separated from that Word. Nor can the Word any longer be separated from its incarnation as Jesus. In this action God has become our Father.

Jesus is the eternally existing Logos of God enfleshed in human history, the only explicit affirmation of incarnation in the New Testament.[26] There is dispute about whether the word "functional" or "ontological" more appropriately describes the relationship between the Word and God, and between Jesus and the Word in the prologue. Yet cannot both apply? The very being of the Son, Jesus, is woven into that of the pre-incarnate, preexistent Logos, and the Logos *is,* in some sense, God. Yet this identity is primarily functional, as in Johannine Christology in general: *Practically speaking* the Father and the Son are equivalent, yet John is careful to have Jesus recognize the Father as greater. One way of seeing the thought of the prologue as both functional and ontological is to follow the suggestion of R. G. Hamerton-Kelly. Taking advantage of the widely accepted distinction between an

---

[25]See M.-E. Boismond, *St. John's Prologue,* 79–95; Pollard, *Johannine Christology and the Early Church,* 14–22.

[26]Dunn, *Christology in the Making,* 239–247.

earlier, independent form of the hymn and the later redacted prologue, he suggests that the thought of the earlier, independent hymn is ontological, whereas the thought of the evangelist or redactor is historical.[27] It may well be that such could account for the dual and rich associations in the final form of the prologue. Or one may wish to appeal again to literary ambiguity or intentional paradoxicality.

It is difficult to overemphasize the importance of the Johannine prologue's Logos Christology for the history of Christian theology. In identifying Jesus with the Logos, and the Logos with God, the prologue puts in focus the Christologies of the New Testament, for it says quite clearly that in dealing with Jesus one has to do with God. As we will see shortly, Logos Christology shapes the theologies of Jesus in the next four centuries. It will take general councils of the Church to clarify the twofold problem in the theology of the prologue: the relationship between the pre-existent Logos and God (what will be the theology of the Trinity), and the relationship between the man Jesus and the divine Logos (what will be the central focus of Christology). The Johannine circle's faith, decision, and wisdom, in using the concept of preexistent Logos in articulating a theology of Jesus, manifested extraordinary theological creativity.

Important as the Logos concept is to Christian theology, it was not the Fourth Gospel's primary way of understanding Jesus. After the prologue, the Logos concept (in the sense of the divine, pre-existent Word) never occurs again in the Gospel! The Gospel's Christology is primarily articulated in terms of the expression "Son," and the Father/Son relationship.[28] T. E. Pollard writes, "The regulative Christological concept of the Gospel is not *Logos,* but *the Christ, the Son of God.*"[29] Because the redacted and once independent hymn is used as a prologue to the Gospel, the prologue must be interpreted in the light of the Gospel and not vice versa. For the Gospel, the Logos concept is secondary. It es-

[27]R. G. Hamerton-Kelly, *Pre-Existence, Wisdom and the Son of Man* (Cambridge: Cambridge University Press, 1973) 200–215.

[28]Pollard, *Johannine Christology and the Early Church,* 6–18. For a list of all the titles applied to Jesus in the Fourth Gospel, see Schnackenburg, *The Gospel According to St. John,* 1:507–514.

[29]Pollard, *Johannine Christology and the Early Church,* 6–7.

tablishes contact with the wider world and enables a clear statement to be made about Jesus' divine status by the affirmation of a theology of incarnation. But the incarnate Word, the Son, Jesus, is the Gospel's primary concern. The sonship of Jesus is unique *(monogēnes)*. We have here to do with God's very own Son come in the flesh. It is not accurate to read Docetism into the Gospel of John.[30] Just as surely as Jesus is one with the Father (and the Logos of God), so he has come "in the flesh." Jesus was a real human historical individual. This does not deny that the Gospel is open to ambiguous interpretation; hence, according to Raymond Brown's thesis, the epistles express the "orthodox" interpretation of the Gospel.

We observed in volume 2 of this series that the titles used to interpret or proclaim Jesus served different functions or that one expression might convey analogous but still varied meanings. We can look back at some of the New Testament expressions thus far used. "Prophet," "sage," and "servant" were particularly applicable to the earthly Jesus; they tell us how he would have been perceived. They were our starting points for understanding Jesus. But there is more to the history of Jesus than his earthly career alone. He survived death, entered into his eschatological life, and was given an exalted status. To convey this fuller understanding of the destiny of Jesus as well as his earthly history, the evangelists used the expression "Lord." "Lord" had a flexibility to it that "prophet" and "servant" seem not to have had. "Lord" can and did refer to both the pre-resurrection history of Jesus, who was both teacher and Lord, and to the post-resurrection destiny: He was and is risen Lord. No wonder "Lord" came to play such a prominent role in the Christian proclamation. It was flexible and able to convey the continuity of the one Jesus in two phases of his mission. The titles "risen prophet" or "risen servant" do so less adequately. Both on earth, however, and in heaven, Jesus is Lord. The expression "Lord" is being used analogously but is capable of carrying both levels of meaning. Nor do we need to go outside Judaism to understand it in its full sense, even though it was later affected by a Gentile milieu.

---

[30]See Marianne Meye Thompson, *The Humanity of Jesus in the Fourth Gospel* (Philadelphia: Fortress, 1988), for her repudiation of Käsemann's thesis that Johannine Christology is "naively Docetic."

Just as "Lord" was able to convey the reality and continuity of Jesus in his earthly and exalted conditions, so within the circle of Johannine Christians, the word "Logos" or "Word" was able to do so for the pre-historical reality of Jesus as well as for his historical, earthly career. "Word," again analogously, describes both the eternal Word and the incarnate Word. The flexibility of the term and its adaptability to two phases in the life of Jesus made it particularly valuable to Christians. Jesus is both Lord and Word, the eternal as well as incarnate Word, the earthly as well as exalted Lord. Whereas "Lord" focuses on the "ascent," "Word" focuses on the "descent."

Of all the expressions thus far, however, "Son" may be most helpful because most flexible.[31] As a term, it is able to describe all three phases in the story of Jesus as the Christian faith came to understand him. He is eternal Son, incarnate Son, and exalted Son. Sonship points to a reality in all three stages and expresses the perduring identity of Jesus. But the word "Son" when applied to the three stages in the life of Jesus is clearly being used analogously. The most useful titles are useful *because* they can be applied analogously. To say that Jesus is the eternal Son of God, or to use Son to describe the eternal Word, to say that Jesus is the historical Son of God, God's prophet, sage, and servant, and to say that Jesus is the Son of God, exalted to the right hand of the Father as risen Lord, is to use "Son" in three varied but related ways. Yet "Son" may be the most adequate way for talking about Jesus. "Son of God" says it all. It gives us a theology of three stages in the life of Jesus as Christian tradition came to understand him. In the Johannine circle we have the fullest Christology in the New Testament, a three-stage Christology. The emphasis, however, is on the earthly stage, in which the glory of God breaks through. Prophet, sage, servant, Christ, Lord, Word, Son, and also Son of Humanity in its post-resurrection milieu: All were expressions for articulating an understanding of Jesus. Johannine Christology, especially, was a springboard for further development.

The Gospel of John is a unique work of sacred literature. It is a Christian literary masterpiece, and it is quite distinctive from

[31]See Donald Goergen, *The Death and Resurrection of Jesus,* A Theology of Jesus 2 (Wilmington, Del.: Michael Glazier Inc., 1988) 174–179. Also Martin Hengel, *The Son of God,* trans. John Bowden (Philadelphia: Fortress, 1976).

the other three Gospels, although we classify all four Gospels together with the same genre. Although the Fourth Gospel was a later literary compilation (between 90 and 100 c.e.), its passion narrative, as we have seen, is historiographically significant. The Fourth Gospel had contact with reliable sources. Yet the Gospel's theology so affected the first portion of the Gospel that this "Book of Signs" provides less an access to a historiographical portrait of Jesus than to a profoundly developed Christology of Jesus, a penetrating interpretation and understanding of the man rather than objective data about him. The Jesus of John's Gospel is very much a Jesus of faith.

The "glory" of Jesus underlies John's insight and presentation and, in fact, holds together the two dimensions of the Gospel. The "signs" in the first part are intimations or revelations or glimpses of this glory shining through in the ministry of Jesus. Like the other Gospels, John gives us an account of Jesus' ministry and Jesus' passion. But the evangelist's theology informs his presentation of Jesus' ministry. Here are all the necessary "signs" of what Jesus truly is and who he is to become. But just as the marvels from the ministry of Jesus reveal his glory, so does Jesus' passion. These are two sides of a coin. The coin is glory, a glory that manifests itself in the *sēmeia* of part 1 and in the "sign of Jonah," or passion, of part 2. John's theology or understanding provides a unified picture of both ministry and passion—both are signs, and both are glory.

John's theology or interpretation of Jesus is thus a "high" Christology. The emphasis is on Jesus as one from above. This is indeed the first Christology from above, and a Logos-Christology that will affect the future history of Christian theology.

A Concluding Theological Reflection

What about Jesus stands out most prominently in the Gospel According to John? Who does the evangelist say that Jesus is? What in the evangelist's theology of Jesus distinguishes it from the theologies of Jesus presented in the other three Gospels?

Practically speaking, Jesus is, from the perspective of his revelatory mission, God. More specifically, Jesus is Son of God, with a new and distinctive theology of that divine sonship. For all practical purposes, Jesus and the Father are one.

The Fourth Gospel does present the gospel of Jesus Christ in a theologically distinct and unique way. There is no other theology quite like it in the New Testament.

The Christology of the Fourth Gospel begins "from above." This is the language of the Gospel itself. Jesus comes from above; others come from below, although we too can be born again, born from above, through the power of the Spirit. Jesus comes from God and is God's unique Son.

The Johannine theology of Jesus' sonship is distinctive. Jesus and his heavenly Father are not only intimate, they are one. Jesus' sonship has a revelatory function and yet is more than functional. Jesus is in the Father and the Father is in Jesus. They are not who they are apart from each other. There are some complications or difficulties in the Gospel's theology of sonship that do not get completely worked out within the Gospel itself. It will take several centuries of theological reflection to do that. In the Gospel, Jesus is both subordinate to his Father and also equal to the Father. There is no denying that the Johannine theology of Jesus is a very "high" or "deep" or "developed" theology of sonship distinct from that of the Synoptic Gospels. The Johannine "Son" is all that God is.

All that we have said thus far is true even apart from the prologue. The prologue captures, makes succinct, highlights, the Christology of the Gospel. It presents nothing new other than that it articulates the theology of the Gospel in terms of the Logos or Word rather than in terms of the Father/Son relationship in which it culminates. Yet the Word is clearly the Son, and vice versa. The language of the prologue, however, does imbed itself in history: The prologue presents the first Christian theology of the Logos, and Logos-Christology is the dominant shape that Christology will take in Christian history. Yet, even apart from the prologue, the Fourth Gospel is a Christology from above, expressed in terms of a divine Son, within a descending/ascending pattern. Jesus descends from above, and after his mission and ministry on earth he returns to the Father. Jesus is both a divine Son and a heavenly man who has descended from heaven and who consciously speaks as one sent from heaven. One cannot abstract Jesus from his heavenly sphere or his relationship to the

Father. This is of the essence of who Jesus is. Jesus is defined in the Gospel relationally—in relationship to the Father, and also in relationship to the Spirit. The Father sends Jesus. Jesus sends the Advocate. I think it true to say that apart from the Fourth Gospel, the eventual Christian theology of the Trinity would have been quite different, and apart from the prologue, there may have been no theology of incarnation as we know it. Certainly the prologue is a unique affirmation of incarnation —a theological notion that is absent in the Synoptics.

The Johannine theology, however, is a beautifully, mysteriously, poetically, paradoxically constructed articulation of the faith of the Johannine Christians. It weaves together heaven and earth, Jesus' "glory" and "humanity," God and human history. For the Johannine Christian, for the one who has eyes to see, there is no dichotomy between faith and history. One only reads or understands history through the eyes of faith. The Jesus of history is the Jesus of faith: the real Jesus of Nazareth whose true home was with the Father in the beginning, the Word who became incarnate, God's very own Son. To distinguish too strongly the Jesus of history and the Jesus of faith is to verge on a false understanding of Jesus.

The Christology of the Fourth Gospel presents clearly a three-stage Christology. To do full justice to Jesus requires a narrative in three parts: the story of the pre-incarnate Word, the incarnate Word or Son, and the risen Lord. Johannine Christology makes an irreversible imprint on Christian theologies of Jesus. The Jesus of Christian history is the Jesus of the Johannine Christian's faith.

The Johannine Christology, for all its "height" or "depth," in no way resembles Docetism. It is truly "incarnational." Incarnation implies two poles in terms of which Jesus is understood— both the divine (Word) and the human (Jesus). These two poles will eventually be defined as both essential for any Christology to do justice to Jesus. Incarnation implies equal emphasis on both—the real divinity of the Word, and that the Word became *sarx* (flesh). *Sarx* implies the humanness of Jesus in all its earthiness. In the Johannine Jesus, God's glory shines through as does Jesus' very human solidarity and identity with humankind: his relationship to the Beloved Disciple, his tender affection for his friends in Bethany, his appearance to Mary Magdalene, his washing the feet of the disciples and final farewell, the weaknesses of his chosen followers—Peter, Judas, Thomas. The Fourth Gospel presents some of the most moving images of an earthly Jesus. Jesus is the Logos, and Jesus is also *sarx*. Johannine Christology is incarnational.

One must ultimately interpret the prologue in the light of the Gospel as a whole, and the theology of the Gospel is a theology of the Son, and the Father-Son relationship is at the center of the story of Jesus. Yet the prologue provides a clear backdrop for the theology of Jesus and the Christian communities who believe in him. The Logos/Son is related to all of creation and to the whole history of salvation. There is more to the Word than Jesus alone, and there is more to God than the Word alone. In and through the incarnation, God and the Word are revealed as Father and Son—another way of expressing their relationship. The Son in the Fourth Gospel is always the divine Word of the prologue. And the Father in the Gospel is always the Father of Jesus Christ. In and through Jesus, God is revealed as having become our Father too. The central title for Jesus is Son of God, with a highly developed theology of sonship that made Johannine theology unacceptable to what became Orthodox Judaism. Jesus is also Son of Humanity, the heavenly teacher, the Messiah. But primarily, he is the one who is sent and the one who reveals. Johannine Christology is a theology of revelation. The Logos/Son reveals the one who sends it/him.

Earlier, we spoke of Robert Kysar's analysis of the Gospel in terms of intentional paradoxicality and Thomas Brodie's reference to literary ambiguity. One clearly cannot penetrate any Gospel without literary analysis and criticism. The Gospel is both literature and theology—a unique form of theological or sacred literature. And the Fourth Gospel makes us face the mystery it longs to disclose, the inadequacy of language to do so, and the value of paradox in any attempt. With the Gospel According to John, we find ourselves confronted by the reality of mystery, the necessity and limitations and beauty of language, and the function of paradox in mediating the rational and the mystical. Christian theology will be facing these over and over again. With the Gospel According to John, the Christian communities will eventually find themselves very much at home.

SUGGESTED READINGS

Ashton, John, ed. *The Interpretation of John.* Philadelphia: Fortress, 1986. An anthology of significant articles.

Boismard, M.-E. *St. John's Prologue.* Trans. Carisbrooke Dominicans. Westminster, Md.: Newman, 1957.

_____. *Moïse ou Jésus: Essai de Christologie Johannique.* Leuven: University Press, 1988.

Borgen, Peder. *Logos Was the True Light, and Other Essays on the Gospel of John.* Trondheim, Norway: Tapir Publishers, 1983. A collection of essays by Borgen.

Brodie, Thomas. *The Gospel According to John: A Literary, Theological and Historical Commentary.* New York: Oxford University Press, forthcoming.

Brown, Raymond. *The Gospel According to John,* 2 vols. Anchor Bible 29 and 29A. Garden City, N.Y.: Doubleday, 1966–1970. A significant commentary with an introduction to crucial questions. Contains extensive bibliography.

_____. *The Community of the Beloved Disciple.* New York: Paulist, 1979. The best single introduction to contemporary Johannine research into the history of the Johannine community.

_____. *The Epistles of John.* Anchor Bible 30. Garden City, N.Y.: Doubleday, 1982.

Bruns, J. Edgar. *The Art and Thought of John.* New York: Herder and Herder, 1969.

Bultmann, Rudolf. *The Gospel of John: A Commentary.* Trans. G. R. Beasley-Murray, R. W. N. Hoare, and J. K. Riches. Philadelphia: Westminster Press, 1971.

Collins, T. A. "Changing Style in Johannine Studies." *The Bible in Current Catholic Thought.* Ed. J. L. McKenzie, 202–225. New York: Herder and Herder, 1962. A survey of literature.

Cullman, Oscar. *The Johannine Circle.* Trans. John Bowden. Philadelphia: Westminster Press, 1976.

Dodd, C. H. *The Interpretation of the Fourth Gospel.* Cambridge: University Press, 1953/1968.

_____. *Historical Tradition in the Fourth Gospel.* Cambridge: University Press, 1962.

Duke, Paul D. *Irony in the Fourth Gospel.* Atlanta: John Knox, 1985.

Ellis, Peter F. *The Genius of John: A Composition—Critical Commentary on the Fourth Gospel.* Collegeville: The Liturgical Press, 1984. An introductory study and new approach based on the hypothesis of the unity of the Fourth Gospel as the work of one author.

Feuillet, André. *Johannine Studies.* Trans. Thomas E. Crane. Staten Island, N.Y.: Alba, 1964. A collection of previously published articles.

Haenchen, Ernst. *A Commentary on the Gospel of John,* 2 vols. Trans. Robert W. Funk. Philadelphia: Fortress, 1984. Volume 1 contains excellent introductory and bibliographical materials, pp. 1–97.

Kysar, Robert. *The Fourth Evangelist and His Gospel: An Examination of Contemporary Scholarship.* Minneapolis: Augsburg, 1975. Does exactly what the subtitle says.

_____. *John's Story of Jesus.* Philadelphia: Fortress, 1984.

_____. *John.* Augsburg Commentary on the New Testament. Minneapolis: Augsburg, 1987.

Marsh, John. *The Gospel of Saint John.* Pelican New Testament Commentaries. New York: Penguin Books, 1968.

Martyn, J. Louis. *The Gospel of John in Christian History.* New York: Paulist, 1978. A collection of three creative and significant essays.

_____. *History and Theology in the Fourth Gospel.* Rev. ed. Nashville: Abingdon, 1979.

Meeks, Wayne. "The Man from Heaven in Johannine Sectarianism." *Journal of Biblical Literature* 91 (1972) 44–72.

_____. *The Prophet-King, Moses Traditions and the Johannine Christology.* Leiden: E. J. Brill, 1967.

Neyrey, Jerome H. *An Ideology of Revolt, John's Christology in Social-Science Perspective.* Philadelphia: Fortress, 1988.

Pollard, T. E. *Johannine Christology and the Early Church.* Cambridge: University Press, 1970.

Richard, Earl. *Jesus: One and Many, the Christological Concepts of New Testament Authors,* 187–231. Wilmington, Del.: Michael Glazier, Inc., 1988.

Schillebeeckx, Edward. *Christ: The Experience of Jesus as Lord,* 305–432. Trans. John Bowden. New York: Seabury, 1980.

Schnackenburg, Rudolf. *The Gospel According to St. John,* 3 vols. New York: vol. 1, Herder and Herder, 1965/1968; vol. 2, Seabury, 1971/1980; vol. 3, Crossroad, 1975/1982.

Thompson, Marianne Meye. *The Humanity of Jesus in the Fourth Gospel.* Philadelphia: Fortress, 1988.

2

The Second Century

The Christian movement in the first century was inseparable
from its relationship to Judaism. The earliest Christians were
Jews, and the earliest interpretations of Jesus were Judeo-
Christian interpretations. The Christians were one among several
Jewish groups; they were Jews who believed in Jesus as having
been sent by God, Jews who accepted Jesus as the Messiah or
Christ. Eventually Christianity, that is, Jewish Christianity, incorporated more and more Gentiles into its midst, and eventually
Gentile Christians predominated. Later "Christians" and "Jews"
parted company and went their own ways. In its origins, however, and therefore still today, Christianity implies Judaism.

In the first century Judaism was diverse, pluralistic, sectarian:
Judaism was not simply one thing. So, likewise, Christian Jews
could not be expected to be monolithic either; Jewish Christianity
would be as diverse as the Judaism from which the followers of
Jesus came. Christians could number in their midst more normative Pharisaic Jews; more marginal, less Temple-centered Jews;
followers of the Baptizer; am-ha-aretz; Judeans, Galileans, and
Samaritans; Diaspora Jews.

J. Louis Martyn introduced a distinction between Christian
Jews and Jewish Christians to alert us to the fact that the first
Christians were truly Jews.[1] In time, especially after 70 c.e. and

---

[1] J. Louis Martyn, *The Gospel of John in Christian History* (New York: Paulist, 1987)
93–107; *History and Theology in the Fourth Gospel,* rev. ed. (Nashville: Abingdon, 1979)
64–100.

the destruction of the Temple, and after the expulsion of the Christians from the synagogue about 85 C.E., the Jews who were also Christians became Christians who were still Jewish, a move from being a Christian group comfortable within the synagogue to being a Christian group separated from and even alienated from the synagogue.

Eventually it became necessary to distinguish Judaism from Jewish Christianity and Jewish Christianity from Gentile Christianity.[2] Although Jewish-Christian theology survived in varied forms, Gentile Christianity was the form of Christianity that predominated in the second century and thereafter. Raymond Brown's fourfold typology of Jewish-Gentile Christianity is really a specification of four varieties of Jewish Christianity.[3] To the degree, however, that the Gentile was assimilated into the Jewish-Christian structure and thought, we are talking about Jewish Christianity; to the degree that Gentile membership so predominated that the Christian life was less and less Jewish, we have Gentile Christianity. Paul, even though his preaching was first directed to the synagogue, tried to bridge the gap, to translate the gospel into the Gentile world. Pauline Jewish Christianity facilitated the birth of a Gentile Christianity.

Jewish Christianity in its varied forms, as it may have existed in Jerusalem, Antioch, or Alexandria, as in a Pauline community or a Johannine community, can be contrasted with Gentile

[2]See Raymond Brown, "Not Jewish Christianity and Gentile Christianity but Types of Jewish/Gentile Christianity," *Catholic Biblical Quarterly* 45 (1983) 74–79. Although Brown's point is well taken, it is still valid to distinguish Jewish Christianity and Gentile Christianity once membership in the Churches becomes predominantly Gentile. Christianity in the second century is no longer primarily Jewish, although Jewish forms of Christianity continued to survive.

[3]Ibid. The four strands of Jewish/Gentile Christians to which Brown refers are (1) Jewish Christians and their Gentile converts who practiced full observance of the Mosaic Law, including circumcision; (2) Jewish Christians and their Gentile converts who did not insist on circumcision for Gentile Christians but did require them to keep some Jewish purity laws, a movement associated with Jerusalem and James and Peter; (3) Jewish Christians and their Gentile Christian converts who did not require circumcision or the observation of Jewish purity laws for Gentile Christians, associated with Antioch and Paul; (4) Jewish Christians and their Gentile converts who saw no abiding significance in the cult of the Jerusalem Temple, non-Law-observant, Hellenist in the sense of Acts 6. As Brown describes these, he is talking about four types of "Jewish Christians" (including their Gentile converts), not invalidating the distinction between Jewish and Gentile Christianity. In fact, he even has to use "Jewish Christians" and "Gentile Christians" in order to construct the typology. The value of Brown's typology is its further elucidation of the multiform character of Jewish Christianity.

Christianity. To some degree the contrast is temporal as well: first-century (Jewish) Christianity and second-century (Gentile) Christianity. Yet we do find a truly Gentile Christianity in the Pauline Churches of the first century as well. Membership in the Christian Churches of the first century was generally mixed. A radical distinction between Jewish Christianity and Gentile Christianity in the concrete is not helpful for a study of the first century. These forms are capable of being distinguished only because of what they later became.

The expression "Jewish Christian" is itself not precise. It refers to:

1. Ebionites and related groups who acknowledged Jesus as a prophet or a messiah but not more.[4] From a later Christian perspective these Jewish Christians would be considered heterodox. The Ebionites themselves were a fairly clearly defined group. Their mode of life reflected that of the Essenes. Although they believed in Jesus, which distinguished them from non-Christian Jews, they denied the virginal conception. They believed that the power of God descended on Jesus at his baptism, that he was a true prophet who came to reform Judaism. The Ebionites observed the Law carefully and did not believe that Jesus came to do away with it. For these reasons, they rejected Pauline Christianity;

2. Christian Jews who held a "higher" Christology than did the Ebionites but who considered the Mosaic Law to be obligatory and to be binding on Gentile converts;

3. the Jewish-Christian community of Jerusalem, and those who looked to it for leadership. The Jerusalem Church was a united entity but also diverse, with tension existing between the "Hellenists" and the "Hebrews" (see Acts 6) and conflicts about the Gentile mission.[5] Its apostolic authority was James, but also Peter. After the "Apostolic Council" of 51 c.e., it did not require circumcision and full observance of the Law by Gentile converts.[6] The relationship between James and Paul

[4]See Jean Daniélou, *The Theology of Jewish Christianity*, trans. John A. Baker (Chicago: Henry Regnery Co., 1964) 55–85. J. A. Fitzmyer, "The Qumran Scrolls, The Ebionites and Their Literature," *Theological Studies* 16 (1955) 335–372.

[5]C. F. D. Moule, "Once More, Who Were the Hellenists?" *Expository Times* 70 (1958–1959), 100–102.

[6]See Robert Jewett, *A Chronology of Paul's Life* (Philadelphia: Fortress, 1979) 95–104.

has been the subject of much discussion.[7] The least that can be said is that after 51 Paul relinquished the Jewish mission to the Jerusalem Church and they entrusted the Gentile mission to him. The Jerusalem community, of course, was dramatically affected by the destruction of Jerusalem in 70 c.e. When we begin to talk about Jewish Christians who are no longer Law observant, we are talking about Gentile Christianity, even if it still includes former Jews. Paul's communities were mixed, but Pauline theology helped to create the basis for a fully Gentile Christianity;

4. in a final sense, Jewish Christianity does not refer so much to a specific Christian group or mission but rather to a way of conceptualizing Christian thought, a type of Christian theology characterized by Semitic imagery and thought, whether that be the Hebrew Scriptures or early Judaism or rabbinical Judaism. This is the sense in which Jean Daniélou uses the expression "Jewish-Christian."[8] In this vein Paul reflects Jewish-Christian thought. Jewish-Christian theology was not a conscious formulation of a particular theology but, rather, manifested certain images and patterns. One prominent feature of Jewish-Christian Christology was the variety of expressions with which Jesus was designated. He was "the Name of God," "the Law" *(nomos)*, "the Beginning" *(archē)*, "the Day" *(hēmera)*, "the Righteous One" *(dikaios)*, "the Shepherd."[9] Although Jewish-Christian theology and Jerusalem Christianity are diverse within themselves, they are nevertheless distinguishable from both Judaism and Gentile Christianity.

The proclamation, "Jesus is the Messiah, the Christ," was central to Jewish-Christian theology and the historical starting point for Christological interpretation, the reason that early Christian theology was primarily Christology.[10] The earliest application of

---

[7]E.g., Walther Schmithals, *Paul and James,* SBT 46, trans. Dorothea M. Barton (Naperville, Ill.: Alec Allenson, 1965).

[8]Daniélou, *The Theology of Jewish Christianity,* 7–11. Longenecker, *The Christology of Early Jewish Christianity* (London: SCM, 1970) 1–4, uses the expression in a combined sense of both numbers 3 and 4 in the text. Also see pp. 4–11 for Longenecker's five theses, which I accept.

[9]Daniélou, *The Theology of Jewish Christianity,* 147–172. Longenecker, 39–58.

[10]Oscar Cullmann, *The Christology of the New Testament,* rev. ed., trans. Shirley C. Guthrie and Charles A. M. Hale (Philadelphia: Westminster Press, 1963) 2–3.

christos to Jesus was not as a proper name but a proclamation: This Jesus was the Christ. The proclamation "Jesus is the Christ" was not distinctive of Jewish Christianity, however, even if central to it. It was part of Pauline preaching and Gentile-Christian faith as well. Yet its most immediate meaning came from Jewish-Christian circles.

In addition to this Christology, which was central to any orthodox Jewish-Christian theology and to the Jerusalem Church, there were other images or concepts distinctive of Jewish Christianity. We can mention (1) a Mosaic theme, Jesus as the eschatological prophet-like-Moses, a Mosaic in contrast to a Davidic Messiah; (2) a priestly understanding of Jesus as mediator, Jesus as the new high priest; (3) an angelic interpretation, that is, Jesus as the angel of great counsel, and the general borrowing of vocabulary from Jewish angelology to designate both the Word and the Spirit (e.g., Jesus Christ identified with the archangel Michael and the Spirit with Gabriel); (4) the theme of descent/ascent, of the descent of Christ from heaven at the moment of the incarnation and of the ascension of Christ; (5) the hiddenness of Christ's descent at the incarnation, hidden even from the angels; (6) a descent of Christ into Hades after his death to liberate or preach to the righteous saints of Israel, at times accompanied by faith in a resurrection for them already; (7) a theology of the cross that is a theology of glory, an accent on the victory of Christ and the glorious or victorious cross, and also that the return of Christ would be preceded by his glorious cross; (8) millenarian eschatology.

Not all of these beliefs were accepted by all Jewish Christians. These emphases do indicate, however, a Christological core (Jesus is the Messiah) as well as extensive pluriformity, some elements of which (the descent/ascent theme, descent into hell) were retained in later theology. The Jewish-Christian community at Jerusalem came to an end in 70. Yet Jewish Christians and Jewish Christianity continued to influence the Christian Church into the second century, and Judeo-Christianity, in Daniélou's use of the expression, continued to exert an influence even into the fourth century in the region of Antioch. Indeed, Judeo-Christian theology has permanently influenced Christianity, even though, before the turn of the century, Judaism and Christianity had taken separate paths of development. The story of the second century is more and more the story of Christianity's encounter with the wider Roman world and with Greek ways of thinking.

A marked characteristic of Christianity in the second century was its variety, geographically and theologically. The New Testament itself had manifested great diversity, and this tendency toward diversification continued. It was a part of Christian history from its beginnings. Aloys Grillmeier writes, "No epoch of Christology displays such numerous and different currents of thought as the second century."[11] We are now talking about more than a Palestinian Christianity: Egyptian, Syrian, the wider Asiatic, and Roman Christianity were all present on the scene. Christianity experienced a widespread growth at the same time that it experienced rejection by Rome. Christianity found itself outside the Jewish synagogue and outlawed by the Roman state. Persecution posed a threat to survival, yet Christianity spread throughout the Empire. Variety also posed a threat to Christian self-identity and self-definition. Orthodoxy is not a word that can be used early in the second century; the dividing line between it and heterodoxy or heresy was still to be worked out. And this was another significant factor in the development of early Christianity—its encounter with what a later perspective could call great heresies, which included the many variations of Adoptionism, Docetism, and Gnosticism.

Christianity continued the literary activity that the New Testament had begun, and its literature continued to manifest the variety that marked the age. Many apocryphal Christian writings manifested popular interest in the life of Jesus: his birth, childhood, baptism, temptation, transfiguration, death, and resurrection.[12] From the turn of the century and after came the *Didache* and the writings of apostolic Fathers, such as Clement of Rome, Ignatius of Antioch, Polycarp of Smyrna, the Letter of Barnabas, and the Shepherd of Hermas.[13] Prominent in the second century were Christian apologists like Aristides, Justin Martyr,

---

[11]Aloys Grillmeier, *Christ in Christian Tradition: From the Apostolic Age to Chalcedon (AD 451)*, trans. John Bowden (London: Mowbrays, 1975) 37.

[12]Ibid., 64–76.

[13]See *The Epistles of St. Clement of Rome and St. Ignatius of Antioch*, Ancient Christian Writers 1 (Westminster, Md.: Newman, 1946); *The Didache*, and others, Ancient Christian Writers 6 (New York: Newman, 1948); and John Lawson, *A Theological and Historical Introduction to the Apostolic Fathers* (New York: Macmillan, 1961).

Tatian, Athenagoras, Theophilus of Antioch, and Melito of Sardis.[14] The Christian apologies, or defenses of the Christian faith, attempted to refute the intellectual attacks against the faith; in them Christian thought reached a new level in its encounter with Hellenistic and Roman culture. Apologists directed their efforts not so much to the Jewish world but to the wider Roman world. New categories of thought were necessary, and we see a step in the direction of "the Hellenization of Christianity." In this the Logos concept played an important role.[15] The apologists manifested a new point of departure for Christian thought: a philosophical, systematic, or learned theology in which the "Greek mind" held sway. In the second century Christianity encountered the Greek world in a new way. In addition to the apostolic Fathers and apologists, Irenaeus of Lyons manifested the literary activity, struggle for self-clarification, and need for defense present in the second century. Christianity was clarifying, developing, and forming itself over against Judaism, Gnosticism, and cultured Greco-Romans. I have chosen Ignatius of Antioch, Justin Martyr, and Irenaeus to represent second-century Christology.

Ignatius of Antioch

The second bishop of Antioch, Ignatius, left the Christian Church seven letters, which he composed en route to martyrdom in Rome, where he was put to death about 107, during the reign of Trajan. His seven letters are not a systematic treatment of Christian thought but a witness to his existential theological concerns shortly before he was to be put to death. During the second century there was as yet no canonical New Testament, although Ignatius certainly knew the Gospel of Matthew and Paul's First Letter to the Corinthians.

In Antioch, one of the more significant centers of early Christianity, where followers of "the Way" first came to be called Christians, Ignatius was the first writer, as far as we know, to describe the Church as Catholic: "Just as where Jesus Christ is,

[14]See the bibliographical references to the major histories of theology at the end of this volume.

[15]Grillmeier, *Christ in Christian Tradition,* 108-113; J. N. D. Kelly, *Early Christian Doctrines,* 2nd ed. (New York: Harper & Row, 1960) 95-104.

there is the catholic church" (Ign. *Smyrn.*, 8). Ignatius had a strong ecclesial sense, and his theology was a Catholic theology.

One of the major objectives of Ignatian Christology was the repudiation of Docetism—a heresy that remained a prime enemy of Antiochene theology. Ignatius wrote that Jesus Christ "was really *(alēthōs)* born and ate and drank . . . was really crucified and died" (Ign. *Trall.*, 9).

At the same time that Ignatius affirmed so clearly the full and real humanity of Jesus, he also recognized Jesus' unity with God. Already in the Gospel of John, the word "God" was used of Jesus three times. This usage was even more frequent in Ignatius. "Our God Jesus was conceived by Mary" (Ign. *Eph.*, 18) anticipated the explicitation of this *theotokos* doctrine (Mary as mother of God) at Ephesus in 431. We find in Ignatius an "exchange of predication" *(communicatio idiomatum)* in which divine attributes are predicated of Jesus, as above, and human attributes of the divine Logos, as in Ignatian expressions like "my suffering God" (Ign. *Rom.*, 6) and "the blood of God" (Ign. *Eph.*, 1). Ignatius affirmed both the humanity of Jesus and the divinity of Jesus, or Jesus' oneness with God. The understanding of the unity and duality of Jesus Christ, that he is both "God" and "human" is expressed in an Ignatian formula (Ign. *Eph.* 7, 2):[16]

There is one physician

fleshly	yet spiritual
begotten *(gennētos)*	yet unbegotten *(aggenētos)*
having come in the flesh	yet God
in death	true life
both from Mary	and from God
first capable of suffering	then incapable of it

Jesus Christ our Lord.

The silence of God, or the silence that God is, was broken by God's Word, God's Son who reveals God and opens up the mystery (Ign. *Eph.*, 15; Ign. *Mag.*, 8). Jesus, God's Word, is revelation. Although Ignatius used the Johannine expression "Logos," he more frequently used the more common Johannine expression

---

[16]Grillmeier, *Christ in Christian Tradition*, 87, for the parallel arrangement. Translation my own.

"Son." The word "Logos" appears only three times (Ign. *Rom.,* 2; Ign. *Mag.,* 8; Ign. *Smyrn.,* preface).

Ignatian spirituality, or his concept of discipleship, followed upon his Christology. We are called upon to imitate Christ (Ign. *Rom.,* 6; Ign. *Phil.,* 7); we most perfectly conform ourselves to Christ in martyrdom (Ign. *Smyrn.,* 4); yet Christ dwells within us and we are his temples (Ign. *Eph.,* 15). God and Christ are so immanent in the lives of Christians that we are *theophoroi* (God bearers), *christophoroi* (Christ bearers), and *naophoroi* (temple bearers), (Ign. *Eph.,* 9).

In Ignatius we already see the firm rejection of Docetism, an affirmation of the oneness between Jesus and God, a theological way of speaking that exchanges divine and human qualities, consciousness of the divine indwelling in us, and Jesus as one who reveals God.

Justin Martyr

Justin exemplifies another theological tradition of the second century, that of the apologists, who manifested an early effort on the part of the Christian Church to reconcile faith and reason. Justin was martyred in Rome, about 165. Born in Palestine in Samaria at Flavia Neapolis, the ancient Shechem, today's Nablus, he was a philosopher and became a convert to Christianity only after he had first turned in search of truth to the Stoics, Aristotelians, Pythagoreans, and Platonists. Both Stoicism and Middle Platonism continued to influence him as a "Christian philosopher." After his conversion he traveled as an itinerant teacher, and later he founded a school in Rome. Only three of his many writings are extant: two *Apologies,* which were originally probably one work, and the *Dialogue with Trypho.* The former shows Justin in dialogue with Hellenistic philosophy, the latter with Judaism. Justin was a millenarian in his eschatology. He also expressed belief in deification in his interpretation of Psalm 81 (*Dialogue,* 124). And he was the first Christian theologian to introduce the Mary-Eve contrast as a counterpart to the Pauline Christ-Adam contrast (*Dialogue,* 100).

Justin's Logos-Christology enabled him to be open to the truth in Greek philosophy and in Judaism and also to establish the supremacy of Jesus Christ. For the Logos is present as the principle of rationality in all humankind; thus Greek philosophy and Judaism had access to the truth. "Everything that the philosophers and legislators discovered and expressed well, they accomplished through their discovery and contemplation of some part of the Logos" (*Second Apology,* 10, also 13). These, however, did not have a full knowledge of the Logos. Only Jesus Christ embodied the Logos in its totality. Thus, the Logos concept provided a bridge between Christian thought and pre-Christian philosophies; the difference is between the whole and a part. The partial understanding of pre-Christians was due to the *Logos spermatikos,* the seminal or germinal Logos, the Logos as present in Judaism and in Greek philosophy. The Logos was the rational principle in the universe, the seeds of the Logos were the rationality of the universe available to all people of intelligence, and the seminal Logos the reason in which each individual participates. Because of the seeds of the Logos in the world, every intelligent creature, due to the *Logos spermatikos* of each of us, can grasp accurately a part of the truth. Only Christ, however, is the fullness of the Logos.

The Logos concept was not only a bridge between philosophy and Christianity, the Logos was also the intermediary or bridge between God and world. God is utterly transcendent but is self-communicating and self-revealing through the Logos. Justin's understanding of the divine Logos is subordinationist. The Logos is divine but subordinate to the Father (*Dialogue,* 61).

We can see the importance of the Logos concept to Justin's theology. The divine Logos is the mediator between God and the world. This Logos created the world and appeared in its fullness in Jesus Christ. But in addition to the divine Logos, there is the *Logos spermatikos.* Seeds of the Logos are planted in the world and in our human minds to know whatever truth was present in philosophy and Judaism. It was the Logos who was at work among the prophets and in the Hebrew Scriptures and gave Judaism its validity.

Justin also contributed to later theology the typological interpretation of the Scriptures (*Dialogue,* 116), and he was "one of the first exegetes to use belief in Christ consistently as a basic hermeneutical principle in expounding the Old Testament."[17] In a

[17]Ibid., 90.

typological interpretation, Old Testament events point to events in the life of Jesus; the former events are types *(typoi)* of what is to come, just as the Old Testament prophecies do in fact find their fulfillment in Christ. Only a Christian interpretation of the Old Testament fully grasps its meaning and truth; Judaism only partially grasps it. Typological exegesis is not the same as allegorical interpretation, which may find hidden and imaginative meanings. In typology the real historical event prefigures an event to come for which it was a sign. In the Gospel of John one already sees the raising of the brazen serpent in the Hebrew Scriptures interpreted as a type of the cross of Christ (John 3:14).

According to Justo Gonzalez, "Justin's theology . . . is an attempt to achieve a Christian interpretation of Hellenism and Judaism. Both have a place within the divine plan."[18] This concept of the divine plan or economy *(oikonomia)* will be a central reality for Irenaeus as well. Justin wrote and died in Rome. Yet he was not a Western theologian. His background was Hellenism and Hellenistic Judaism. The tradition in theology that he established will find its closest parallels in Alexandria in "Christian philosophers" like Clement and Origen. Justin had already emphasized a Logos theology, a concept of deification, and a typological interpretation of Scriptures (which at that time meant the Old Testament, or Hebrew Scriptures).

Irenaeus

Irenaeus (ca. 130–200) was a native of Asia Minor, probably Smyrna, but he later moved to Gaul, where he became bishop of Lyons after the martyrdom of Photinus, the previous bishop.[19] It is not clear whether Irenaeus himself died a martyr's death. Having come from Smyrna, he may have had contact with Polycarp, and later, as bishop and theologian in Lyons, he became a bridge between East and West. His theology is closer to that of Antioch than Alexandria, and Theophilus of Antioch has been suggested as a precursor of Irenaeus.

[18]Justo Gonzalez, *A History of Christian Thought* (Nashville: Abingdon Press, 1970) 1:110.

[19]In addition to the references in the chapter bibliography, A. Benoit, *Saint Irénée, Introduction a l'étude de sa théologie* (Paris, 1960); John Lawson, *The Biblical Theology of Saint Irenaeus* (London: Epworth Press, 1948); L. S. Thornton, "St. Irenaeus and Contemporary Theology," *Studia Patristica* 2 (1957) 317-327.

Irenaeus' major task as a writer and theologian was the refutation of Gnosticism. Of his many works, we have only two, the primary one being the five books of his *Detection and Overthrow of Gnosis Falsely So Called,* better known as the *Adversus Haereses (AH);* and the second work, *The Demonstration of the Apostolic Teaching.* His Christology, centered around Christ as the Second Adam, and a biblical theology of history, of the "economy of salvation," were at the center of Irenaeus' theology.

Much in Irenaean Christology can be seen as a reflection on Ephesians 1:9-10, the text that speaks of recapitulation *(anakephalaiōsis)* of all things in Christ: "For he has made known to us in all wisdom and insight the mystery of his will, according to his purpose which he set forth in Christ as a plan for the fullness of time, to unite all things in him, things in heaven and things on earth."

As in Paul, Jesus is another Adam (Rom 5:12-21), yet Irenaeus also develops the Adam parallel and the concept of recapitulation beyond what they were in Paul. In Christ we have a restoration of what was lost through the first Adam; not only a restoration, however, for the work of Christ goes beyond what was lost. Christ's obedience is a contrast to Adam's disobedience. Christ relived, so to speak, the life of Adam, but with a different outcome. Christ went through experiences parallel to those of Adam and even shared in developmental experiences. "Therefore he passed through every stage of life, restoring to each age fellowship with God" (*AH* 3, 18, 7; also see 1, 10, 1; 3, 16, 6; 3, 18, 1; 5, 14, 2). Death itself was an event necessary to this recapitulation that Jesus undertook:

> He came to save all through himself; all, that is, who through him are born into God, infants, children, boys, young men and old. Therefore he passed through every stage of life: he was made an infant for infants, sanctifying infancy; a child among children, sanctifying those of this age, an example also to them of filial affection, righteousness and obedience; a young man amongst young men, an example to them, and sanctifying them to the Lord. So also amongst the older men; that he might be a perfect master for all, not solely in regard to the revelation of the truth, but also in respect of each stage of life. And then he came even unto death that he might be "the firstborn from

the dead, holding the preeminence among all" [Col 1:18], the Prince of Life, before all and preceding all (*AH* 2, 22, 4).

In his opposition to heretical Gnosticism, Irenaeus firmly opposed Docetism. "If he [Christ] did not really suffer, there was no grace" (*AH* 3, 18, 6). He recognized the full humanness of Jesus, but he acknowledged that Jesus was also the Son of God. "He is truly the good and suffering Son of God, the Word of God the Father made the son of man" (*AH* 3, 18, 6). There is a real incarnation. The Word becomes flesh, or an even more Irenaean phrase, becomes a human being [*homo factus est*] (*AH* 3, 18, 17; 3, 22, 1; 5, 1, 1). Like Ignatius of Antioch, Irenaeus saw both Jesus' humanity and his oneness with God. An Irenaean phrase, "Christ, one and the same," was important for later Christology.

Irenaeus' Christology was integrally related to his anthropology. He was aware that the human person is created in the image and likeness of God (Gen 1:26-27), but Irenaeus made a distinction between the "image of God" and the "likeness of God" (*AH* 5, 6, 1–2). Although the distinction is not always clear, image connotes our human nature, rationality, and freedom. The likeness is what has been lost through the Fall, through sin: our divine destiny or union with God.

Anthropology now becomes linked to soteriology, or the doctrine on salvation. The incarnation has enabled us to restore our likeness to God, to be God's children by adoption, and to become one with God. One side of salvation is the restoration of the likeness to God that is possible for us, this assimilation to God. The human person, in the image of God, is to become the likeness of God, daughters and sons of God, gods by adoption. "For it was for this end that the Word of God was made man, and he who was the Son of God became the son of man, that man, having been taken into the Word, and receiving the adoption, might become the Son of God" (*AH* 3, 19, 1; also 4, 38, 4; 5, 32, 1). Irenaeus did not use the word "deification," but his anthropology was open to it.

Another feature of the theology of Irenaeus was his understanding of Adam before the Fall as more akin to a child than an adult. Irenaeus offers an alternative to Augustine in Latin theology and to an Augustinian understanding of the Fall.[20] Adam before the Fall possessed a likeness to God and the gifts of the Holy Spirit, but there was still room for growth because he was not perfect in understanding. He was not the fully rational human being of Augustine's theology. Adam was created as a child whose destiny was to develop. There are three main texts referring to the childhood of Adam (*AH* 4, 38, 1; *Demonstration,* 12 and 14). Some conception of the childhood of Adam was also present in Theophilus of Antioch (*ad Autolycum,* II, 25).

There are thus two kinds of growth envisioned in Irenaean anthropology, that which Adam and Eve would have had to undergo apart from the Fall, and the growth incumbent upon us as a result of the Fall. The possibility of this growth into oneness with God has been restored to us through Christ. Irenaeus' theology of the Fall was obviously affected by his understanding of the childhood of Adam. The effects of the Fall were serious, but the effect was not so much the guilt that we see later in Augustine's theology. In Irenaeus' theology, Adam was not mature enough in understanding to incur the guilt Augustine attributed to him.

In addition to the anthropological side of redemption, union with God, Irenaeus discussed the work of Christ conceived as a ransom. Jesus Christ "gave himself as a ransom for those who have been led into captivity" (*AH* 5, 1, 1). This ransom was not conceived in a strictly legal way, as if the blood of Christ is a payment due the devil, but rather a manifestation of the justice of God: God wins humankind back *fairly.* God's victory is persuasive rather than coercive; through Christ, God rightly and justly wins humankind back and the devil is properly defeated, not by some feat of divine omnipotence but by the redemption won or ransom paid willingly by Christ.

> Therefore, the Word of God, mighty in all things and not lacking in his own justice, acted justly even in the encounter with the Apostasy itself, ransoming from it that which was his own, not by force, in the way in which it secured sway over us at the beginning, snatching insatiably what was not its own; but by persuasion, as it became God to receive what he wished; by persuasion, not by the use of force, that the principles of jus-

---

[20]For a development of this contrast, see John Hick, *Evil and the God of Love* (London: Macmillan, 1966).

tice might not be infringed, and at the same time, that God's original creation might not perish (*AH* 5, 1, 1; also 4, 37, 1).

Like Justin, Irenaeus was also millenarian in his eschatology. Against Gnosticism, the one true God is the Creator. The Son and the Spirit are like two "hands of God" (*AH* 4, 19, 2; 4, 20, 1; 5, 1, 3; 5, 5, 1; 5, 28, 1). The Spirit is a hand of God equal with the Son. Irenaeus uses the expression "Word" but like previous authors uses "Son" even more frequently. The Word or Son is eternal with the Father (*AH* 2, 13, 8; 2, 25, 3; 2, 30, 9; 3, 18, 1; 4, 6, 2; 4, 14, 1; 4, 20, 7; *Demonstration,* 30, 43, 52). "The Father is Lord, and the Son is Lord, and the Father is God and the Son is God" (*Demonstration,* 47).

Irenaeus, as well as Ignatius, had a strong sense of Church and contributed to a theology of tradition. Reminiscent of Justin, he showed the continuity between Hebrew Scriptures and the New Testament with typological exegesis. He began to refer to the apostolic writings, or New Testament, as Scriptures. Previously Scripture would have meant the Hebrew Scriptures or Old Testament. He saw the apostolic writings as having authority equal to the Hebrew Scriptures. These specifically Christian Scriptures comprised for Irenaeus the four Gospels, Paul's epistles, the Acts, the Johannine epistles, the Apocalypse, 1 Peter, and the writing of the Shepherd of Hermas. He quotes Matthew more than any other Gospel, then Romans and 1 Corinthians. Scripture and tradition give witness to the faith of the apostles. Scripture and tradition are not two witnesses but one.

In his struggle with Gnosticism and heresy, Irenaeus had to determine what was consonant with the faith of the apostles as it had been handed down. Irenaeus maintained that the apostolic teaching continued to live in the Church, and that this apostolic tradition was a norm for faith. That tradition was safeguarded in the apostolic Churches, those founded by the apostles, and with an uninterrupted succession that went back to the apostles. This apostolic succession gave them an authority. The apostolic tradition continued to live and was at one with the apostolic writings, which Irenaeus called Scripture. Among the apostolic Churches, that of Rome was preeminent for Irenaeus.

In his typological exegesis and millenarianism, Irenaeus can be compared to Justin. In his sense of Church, his understanding of God, Son, and Spirit, his refutation of Docetism and appreciation of the oneness of Christ, he was closer to Ignatius and Theophilus of Antioch. Coming as he did at the close of the century, he had a strong appreciation of tradition. He has been called the greatest theologian of the second century.

A Concluding Theological Reflection

The Church's later Christology or understanding of Jesus was already present in the second century, although in a less technical form. Jesus is fully human. Jesus is one. Jesus is one with God. Jesus is God's Word and Son. This second-century understanding was already present in the theology of the Johannine community at the end of the first century. From the Johannine community to Ignatius to Irenaeus we see continuity in the Church's understanding.

Not only continuity, however, but also diversity: A hallmark of the second century is its variety, and we see the tendency of Christian thought toward diversification. Already in the New Testament period we spoke of one faith but many theologies. So in the second century, we observe one tradition, but many Christologies. Continuity in the tradition ultimately reflects the fact of one historical Christ. Diversity reflects the varied cultures in which that one Jesus will be proclaimed. In the first and second centuries we already see the reality and tension that will be with the Christian self-understanding through the centuries—both gospel and culture will demand their due.

The *tendency toward diversification* will manifest itself over and over.

One Faith	{ Jewish Christian theology { Gentile Christian theology
Gentile Christian Theology	{ The Greek East { The Latin West
The Greek East	{ Alexandrian theology { Antiochene theology

The story will repeat itself: continuity and unity accompanied by diversity and change. Just as we find the tendency toward diversification, so we can detect a complementary *tendency toward con-*

solidation. Docetism, Adoptionism, and Gnosticism were perhaps pathways that had to be tried, but they would not be the paths to the future, no matter how often they continued to reassert themselves. They were dead ends as far as the development of Christian thought was concerned, which is not to say they had no purpose to serve. Indeed, they did help the Church define itself and its faith. Thus we find in the Christian movement of the second century a rich variety coupled with the sense of catholicity (Ignatius) and tradition (Irenaeus).

It is fatal when Christian believers lose a sense of their history, for the Christian faith is always a historical Christian faith. We can lose this sense of history by identifying authentic Christian faith with one particular historical expression of it. We can also lose it by ignoring it as if we could return to the faith in some pure (ordinarily conceived as early) form, often proclaimed as the faith of the New Testament. Christian faith never existed in some pure, non-historical, unenculturated form. Its "essence" can never be abstracted from the concrete forms of its historical existence. We violate this historical character of the Christian faith when we sever Scripture and tradition, or fixate on one tradition to the exclusion of others: Christian faith is not an "ism" but an appreciation of the catholicity, diversity, and individuality of Christian thought.

One can find the gospel enfleshed in all periods of history. One can read the second century and find there the Catholic tradition and the historical Christian faith. It is problematic to define any one century of Christian thought as paradigmatic or normative. Each century was simply a different period of history with its own struggles, peoples, questions, needs, opportunities. When God's Word entered space-time, it meant that God's Word thereafter could not be encountered outside of space (a concrete culture) and outside of time (a period of history).

This does not mean that anything that would pass itself off as Christian would be accepted as a valid expression of the tradition. But it does mean that the effort to remain faithful to the gospel and its Catholic tradition would involve historical struggles, issues, and decisions. The Holy Spirit would be with the Christian people but only in and through their ongoing history.

There always has been more to the historical Christian faith than Jesus alone. This was already true in the New Testament itself. Faith and history, or gospel and culture, while distinct, can never be separated. They never were, not even in Jesus himself, and never will be. This is the "nature" of Christianity; it never comes disincarnate. This evidently is the only way the Word could reach us—through the media of culture, history, language, and art.

We already find in the second century of the gospel's history (1) many elements which are later considered essential to orthodox Christian faith; (2) diverse theological expressions of that faith, from the "existential theology" of Ignatius and the apostolic Fathers to the "philosophical theology" of Justin and the apologists to the "biblical theology of history" of Irenaeus; (3) the conscious need for catholicity, continuity, and consolidation, as the Christian movement had learned from experience that it would need to define itself over against what was perceived to be a falsification of the faith and gospel, and the second century had learned to repudiate Docetism, Adoptionism, and Gnosticism; and (4) a recognition of not only cultural diversity but also the individuality of particular theologians. Not only are Justin and Irenaeus distinct but no two apologists were exactly the same either. All of these facets of the history of Christian theology, so apparent in the second century, were already present in the first century of Christian history as well—the New Testament world. While the varied expressions of the Christian faith always have much in common, no effort at complete harmonization can do justice to orthodox Christian diversity. The Word cannot be abstracted from the flesh that makes it present on earth.

Jaroslav Pelikan has not only given us a first-rate multi-volume history of the Christian tradition, but also an exploration of the images of Jesus as they became dominant in the history of culture.[21] We have not only the prominent New Testament "images" and "titles" for Jesus, but also twenty centuries of Christian efforts to image and name Jesus, as well as our own varied contemporary Christological expressions. Some of the historical images to which Pelikan refers include those of the rabbi (Jesus the Jew, the first-century rabbi Jeshua bar-Joseph), the Lord of history (as in Augustine's *City of God,* and by the sixth century

[21] Jaroslav Pelikan, *Jesus Through the Centuries: His Place in the History of Culture* (New Haven: Yale University Press, 1985). For his 4-volume history of Christian tradition, see the bibliography at the end of this volume.

Jesus Christ had become the turning point for reckoning time), the light to the Gentiles (Justin had found Hebrew prophecy as well as Greek philosophy fulfilled in Jesus Christ, as did many who followed him), the king of kings (closely related to the political theology and theological politics of Constantine and the emergence of a Christian Roman Empire), the cosmic Christ (pantocrator of the Greek East and Greek iconography), the image of the invisible God (which lay underneath the Eastern theology of deification as well as its theology of the icon and Christian art), the perfect monk (the inspiration through many centuries of Christian monasticism, as later for mendicants like Dominic and Francis), the lover or bridegroom of the soul (the inspiration for many centuries of Christian mysticism, East and West), the universal human being (the model and the inheritance of the Renaissance), the prince of peace (even though Jesus has just as often been the cause of war), to the Jesus of common sense of the Enlightenment to the Jesus as poet of the spirit of Romanticism to Jesus the liberator in contemporary theology.

As Pelikan says of the history of the images of Jesus, "It is not sameness but kaleidoscopic variety that is its most conspicuous figure."[22] And yet the struggle to know the selfsame Jesus persists—diversification and consolidation, discontinuity and continuity. And the search for truth emerges at its best from within "the conflict of interpretations," to borrow an expression from Paul Ricoeur.[23] It is indeed the selfsame Jesus, the risen Lord, the Spirit of the risen Christ who continues to interact as grace in our midst as the gospel is proclaimed.

A fact of history is the diversity, pluriformity, or variety in the world of Christian theology. We saw this in the New Testament world. We have also seen this just within the world of Judeo-Christianity. And Aloys Grillmeier has noted the numerous currents of thought in the second century alone. There is the historical tendency toward diversification as gospel encounters diverse cultures. Theology is formed where gospel and culture meet. Even the character of theology varies according to method and

[22]Ibid., 2.

[23]Paul Ricoeur, *The Conflict of Interpretations,* ed. Don Ihde (Evanston: Northwestern University Press, 1974). Also see the introduction to the work of Ricoeur and bibliography prepared by Loretta Dornisch in *Semeia: An Experimental Journal for Biblical Criticism* (1975) 4:1-26.

purpose, for example, from the more existential theology of Ignatius to the learned philosophical theology of Justin to Irenaeus' biblical theology of history.

The move from orality to textuality in the first century was irreversible. The literary productivity of the first century continued into the second century. Yet, for Irenaeus, in theory, written word and oral word, Scripture and tradition, were still able to be held together as one apostolic tradition. Yet even here Christianity had given birth to a literary, literate culture as well as a more popular, oral culture.

Following closely upon the heels of diversification, there was the complementary tendency toward self-definition, catholicity, consolidation, and orthodoxy. Some interpretations of the Christian message were judged by the Catholic tendency to be unfaithful to the apostolic faith: Adoptionism, Docetism, and Gnosticism were rejected by the Catholic tradition.

Already by the close of the second century, certain theological realities became clarified (the humanity of Jesus and Jesus' oneness with God), and other theological insights emerged that would be significant throughout Christian history (the divine indwelling as the basis for the future doctrine of deification, the exchange of predicates in the theology of Jesus, Ignatius' emphasis on Jesus as revelation, Justin's hermeneutics rooted in typology, Irenaeus' appropriation of the Pauline doctrine of recapitulation and understanding of redemption as ransom, and Justin's theology of the Logos as the basis for a theology of Judaism and Christian appreciation of Greek philosophy). Among the theological emphases of the century was the continued attention to Jesus as the Word or Logos, even if Jesus as Son was more prominent. Nevertheless, the basis for the continuing development of a theology of the Logos was in place.

SUGGESTED READINGS

Daniélou, Jean. *The Theology of Jewish Christianity*. Trans. John A. Baker. Chicago: Henry Regnery Co., 1964.

Davies, J. G. "The Origins of Docetism." *Studia Patristica* 6 (1962) 13–35.

Donovan, Mary Ann. "Alive to the Glory of God: A Key Insight in St. Irenaeus." *Theological Studies* 49 (1988) 283-297.

Farrer, Austin. "Gnosticism." *Interpretation and Belief,* 138-148. Ed. C. C. Conti. London: SPCK, 1976.

Grant, Robert M., ed. *Gnosticism and Early Christianity.* New York: Columbia University Press, 1959.

_____. *Gnosticism: A Source Book of Heretical Writings from the Early Christian Period.* New York: Harper and Brothers, 1961.

_____. *Greek Apologists of the Second Century.* Philadelphia: Westminster Press, 1988.

Jonas, Hans. *The Gnostic Religion: The Message of the Alien God and the Beginnings of Christianity.* 2nd ed. Boston: Beacon Press, 1963.

Lawson, John. *A Theological and Historical Introduction to the Apostolic Fathers.* New York: Macmillan, 1961.

_____. *The Biblical Theology of Saint Irenaeus.* London: Epworth Press, 1948.

Little, V. A. S. *The Christology of the Apologists.* London: 1934.

Longenecker, Richard N. *The Christology of Early Jewish Christianity.* Studies in Biblical Theology, Second Series. London: SCM, 1970.

Perkins, Pheme. *The Gnostic Dialogue: The Early Church and the Crisis of Gnosticism.* New York: Paulist, 1980.

The Didache. Ancient Christian Writers 6. New York: Newman, 1948.

The Epistles of St. Clement of Rome and St. Ignatius of Antioch. Ancient Christian Writers 1. Westminster, Md.: Newman, 1946.

Thornton, L. S. "St. Irenaeus and Contemporary Theology." *Studia Patristica* 2 (1957): 317-327.

3

Alexandria and Antioch

Classical Christology emerged, developed, and was primarily shaped in the Greek-speaking East. Its early history was inseparable from communities and conflicts in Egypt, Syria, and throughout the Byzantine world. Alexandria, Antioch, and Constantinople were the historical focal points. The West, too, made a significant contribution, but one will never understand the Jesus Christ of Christian history without some appreciation for the challenges, struggles, and insights of the first five formative centuries in the Greek East.

The historical tendencies toward diversification and consolidation continued to make themselves known. As Logos Christologies developed, they moved in two primary directions exemplified in the theological methods and Christological emphases of Alexandria and Antioch. Both schools of thought were incomplete by themselves alone. Both contributed significantly to the great experiment and synthesis consolidated in a preliminary way at Chalcedon.

The intriguing history of classical formulae was the story of a complex, conflictual, and faith-filled search for an unattainable precision and clarity incapable of being separated from politics, economics, personalities, and cultures. Classical Christology can neither be abstracted from its history nor completely identified with it. Like Jesus, the story is one of history and also more than history: of historiography and faith, of the contingencies and particulars of which history is made as well as the activity of the Spirit of which history is also made.

In order to get a feel for this history, we will focus on individual exemplifications of the Alexandrian and Antiochene directions in Christological thought. In this way we may come to see what God and human beings were trying to say through these two great and formative centers of Christian intellectual life.

Alexandrian Christology

The city of Alexandria had been founded in 331 B.C.E. by Alexander the Great and had become a center of Hellenistic civilization. Hellenism and Judaism had met each other there in a unique way. At Alexandria the Hebrew Scriptures were translated into Greek. This Septuagint version was completed in the second century B.C.E. Alexandrian Hellenistic Judaism reached a peak with Philo (ca. 20 B.C.E–50 C.E.), who was born in Alexandria and taught there. A prolific writer, Philo had begun to apply the allegorical methods of Hellenistic exegesis, which were being applied to Homer and Hesiod, to the Hebrew Scriptures.

Alexandria became an equally important center for Christian civilization. In the second and third centuries C.E. the Coptic language developed, an Egyptian language with a Greek alphabet. According to Eusebius (ca. 260–340), bishop of Caesarea and "Father of Church history," John Mark the evangelist had gone to Alexandria and become its first bishop. Christian literature in the second century, in the face of heresy, persecution, and polemic against Christianity, had taken a defensive, apologetic character. In the third century, especially at Alexandria, with converts from educated, Hellenistic circles, Christian literature began to develop learned theology. In the third and fourth centuries Alexandria became the center of Christian culture and Christian Hellenism. Here Christianity encountered Greek philosophy and put it at the service of the faith. In this regard, Plato was preeminent and remained so during the patristic period. It was not until the thirteenth century that Aristotle assumed an equivalent importance for Christian thought.[1] Although Aristotle was known in the second and third centuries, he was only known through some

---

[1]Concerning the earlier use of Aristotle, see Jean Daniélou, *Gospel Message and Hellenistic Culture,* trans. John Austin Baker (Philadelphia: Westminster Press, 1973) 129–135. Concerning the influence of Plato, see 107–127, 303–322.

writings, such as the *Protreptikos*, not through his major philosophical works. Middle Platonism provided the major background for the encounter between Christianity and Hellenism. This encounter, however, was neither the Hellenization of Christianity nor the Christianization of Hellenism. It was rather a struggle with the questions of whether and how to put Greek philosophy at the service of the faith. Justin had already seen a place for it, but it was Clement of Alexandria who gave explicit attention to the nature of the task, and not without opposition. In that sense he was one of the founders of Christian theology, certainly of philosophical theology and Alexandrian theology. The allegorical method had been used by philosophers, had been applied to the Scriptures by Philo, and was now used by the Christians as well.

In third-century Alexandria, one of the earliest and most significant Christian catechetical and theological schools developed. We read in Johannes Quasten: "The school of Alexandria is the oldest center of sacred science in the history of Christianity. The environment in which it developed gave it its distinctive characteristics, predominant interest in the metaphysical investigation of the content of the faith, a leaning to the philosophy of Plato, and the allegorical interpretation of Sacred Scriptures."[2] We already had "schools" in the second century in Rome. Philosophically educated converts such as Justin and his pupil Tatian had taught publicly a small circle of students. These schools were not, however, established by the Roman Christian community. They were instituted by the individual Christian philosophers. Alexandria had a strong intellectual and philosophical tradition going back to the times of the Ptolemies. Educated Alexandrian converts also established their schools, but these too were Christian teachers and philosophers with a private following. The first of these teachers known to us was Pantaenus (d.ca. 190). His "school," however, was not an ecclesiastical or catechetical school, although it was Christian education. Clement of Alexandria was in some fashion his successor. Clement was not yet the head of an ecclesiastically instituted Christian school; his teaching had the private character of his predecessors. Only later, with

[2]Johannes Quasten, *Patrology*, vol. 2, The Ante-Nicene Literature after Irenaeus (Westminster, Md.: Newman Press, 1964) 2.

Origen, when Origen assumed responsibility for the instruction of catechumens at the request of the bishop, can we speak properly of a catechetical or theological school at the service of the Church in Alexandria. Yet with Clement we have the beginning of Alexandrian Christian theology.

Clement of Alexandria (ca. 150–215).[3] Clement seems to have been an Athenian by birth. After his conversion to Christianity, he traveled to Italy, Syria, Palestine, and eventually ended up in Alexandria as a student and associate of Pantaenus. Johannes Quasten writes: "What was of the greatest importance for his scholarly education was that his journeying brought him in the end to Alexandria. Pantaenus' lectures had such attraction for him that he settled down there and made that city his second home."[4] Clement became a Christian teacher in Alexandria in his own right. About 202, he was forced to flee Egypt because of the persecution under Septimus Severus, never to return.

Many of Clement's writings have been lost, such as his commentary on the Scriptures. Of his extant writings, we ought take note of three in particular: the *Protreptikos,* or *Exhortation,* the first of an intended trilogy, directed toward conversion; the *Paidogogos,* or *The Tutor,* the second of the trilogy, taking the task of Christian instruction beyond the *Protreptikos* for those who have been converted; and *Stromateis,* literally *Carpets,* or *Miscellanea,* not the intended third of the trilogy, which was to have been *Didaskolos,* or *The Teacher.*

Clement stands in the tradition of Justin in his respect for philosophy. Yet he goes beyond Justin's understanding of the seeds of the Logos, arguing that philosophy was for the Greeks what the Law was for the Jews, that philosophy, too, came from God, as did the Law. The Greeks, too, had their inspired prophets. They were the ancient philosophers.

Clement, in the tradition of Irenaeus, was in conflict with Gnosticism. For Clement, the Christian faith was "the true gnosis." Christianity is a gnosis, and the Logos is the teacher of this gnosis, a secret tradition in Christianity in addition to the com-

---

[3]See S. R. C. Lilla, *Clement of Alexandria: A Study in Christian Platonism and Gnosticism* (London: Oxford University Press, 1971); and E. F. Osborn, *The Philosophy of Clement of Alexandria* (Cambridge: Cambridge University Press, 1957).

[4]Quasten, *Patrology,* 2:5.

mon Christian tradition, both of which came from Jesus Christ via the apostles. Clement thus distinguished two groups of Christians: the ordinary Christians, and the gnostic Christians, who were different from heretical Gnostics. Christian gnostics were true gnostics. They achieved both ethically and intellectually a higher or deeper understanding than the ordinary Christian (*Stromateis,* 4, 21, 23; 6, 9, 10; 7, 3 15). Clement's theology at this point had an aristocratic and esoteric character, which ought not be considered as representative of the Church in Alexandria as a whole. T. E. Pollard writes, "Clement's appeal was primarily to educated, wealthy, cultured pagans in Alexandria."[5]

Clement's perception of gnosis is related to his allegorical interpretation of the Scriptures. With both Justin and Irenaeus we encountered typological exegesis; with Clement we encounter much more.[6] His view of various levels of meaning in Scripture reflected the methods of Greek exegesis and of Philo as well as a Platonic conception of the world. According to Clement, there are two meanings in Scripture, the literal and the spiritual. The first or literal level of meaning is that directly contained in the text; the spiritual levels of meaning are more hidden and uncovered through allegorical interpretation. Allegorical exegesis reflected a theology in which God communicates with both the simple and the wise, in which God's meaning in Scripture is inexhaustible and not narrowly circumscribed, in which the Scriptures are truly seen as a work of divine art, providence, and wisdom.

For Clement, God is utterly transcendent, far removed from the world, incomprehensible (*Stromateis,* 2, 6, 1; 2, 21, 5; 5, 12, 82; 5, 65, 2; 5, 78, 3; 5, 81, 3). God, that is the Father, can only be known by means of the Word, who is inseparable from the Father, whose generation from the Father is without beginning (*Protreptikos,* 98, 3; *Paidogogos,* 1, 24, 3; 1, 53, 1; 1, 62, 4; 1, 71, 3; 3, 101, 1; *Stromateis,* 4, 162, 5; 5, 1, 3; 5, 12, 83; 5, 16, 3; 7, 2, 2; 7, 5, 5). Clement's *Logos* is akin to the *Nous* of Middle Platonism. The Spirit is the power of the Logos which pervades the world (*Stromateis,* 7, 9, 4; 7, 79, 4). There is a Trinity (*Paidogogos,* 1, 42, 1; 3, 101, 2); its character is Platonic.

[5]T. E. Pollard, *Johannine Christology and the Early Church* (Cambridge: Cambridge University Press, 1970) 77.

[6]See Daniélou, *Gospel Message and Hellenistic Culture,* 237-255.

Since "the bosom of the Father" (or the "abyss") is unknowable and inaccessible, "it is only by his own Logos, issuing from him, that one can know the unknowable" (*Stromateis,* 5, 12, 81). Thus Clement's theology focused on the Logos and became a theology of the Logos, and not just in the Johannine sense of Logos.

The Logos for Clement had a history, or different stages of existence.[7] It is essentially one with God, in the bosom of the Father, the mind of God but identical with God. Then, and this can be seen as a second stage in the story of the Logos or as the first of a triple incarnation of the Logos, "The Word became flesh not only in becoming human at the moment of its descent into this world, but in the very beginning, when the Logos, remaining constant in its identity [*en tautotēti*], became Son by delimitation [*perigraphē*] and not by essence [*ousia*]" (*Excerpta ex Theodoto,* 19). The Logos is begotten as the image of the Father. Creation and the delimitation of the Logos as Son is the first of "a triple incarnation." Jean Daniélou writes: "This text contains a number of noteworthy points, especially the assertion that the Son and the Father are identical in essence but distinct by 'delimitation.' The latter term is the most precise usage to be found in theological language for indicating distinction of Persons in the Trinity, until the standardization of the Greek *hypostasis* and the Latin *persona* for this purpose."[8]

"Again he became flesh when he acted through the prophets" (*Excerpta,* 19). This is another stage in the story of the Logos, a second incarnation. The first incarnation accompanied creation, by which God was already revealed, and now by the continua-

[7]Ibid., 364–375; Aloys Grillmeier, *Christ in Christian Tradition: From the Apostolic Age to Chalcedon (AD 451),* trans. John Bowden, (London: Mowbrays, 1975) 134–135; Lilla, *Clement of Alexandria,* 199–212; Pollard, *Johannine Christology and the Early Church,* 80–86. Grillmeier, in accord with Lilla, speaks of three different stages of existence of the Logos. These would be its eternity in the bosom of the Father, its becoming Son through delimitation, and its manifestation through the prophets and Jesus. Pollard speaks of a triple incarnation. This is not the same as the three stages above. Pollard distinguishes between the essential Logos and the child of the essential Logos. The first incarnation is the delimitation, which is also associated with creation. Stage one above is not yet an incarnation of the Logos. Stage two is the first of the incarnations. The second (through the prophets) and third (Jesus) incarnations belong to stage three. Thus one could speak of four stages: being in the bosom of the Father; becoming Son through delimitation; the theophanies and activities in the "Old Testament"; and the incarnation in Jesus.

[8]Daniélou, *Gospel Message and Hellenistic Culture,* 367.

tion of that revelation, among the Hebrew prophets and in Greek philosophy.

Finally, there is a third incarnation of the Logos in Jesus of Nazareth, the child of the Logos, the fullness of the incarnation. "The incarnation of the Logos in Jesus Christ does not differ from his activity in the prophets in kind, but only in degree."[9]

Through the Logos, God is made known. There remains the contrast between the unknowable abyss, the Father, and God as knowable through the Logos-Son. Clement's theology of the Word undergirded his interpretation of the Scriptures and his doctrine of true gnosis. A theology of the Word is a theology of revelation. The Word is revealer and educator. Clement's Christology emphasizes Jesus as the teacher, because teaching is what the Logos would quite naturally be doing. "Not long ago the pre-existent savior appeared on earth; he who exists in God [because 'the Word was with God'] appeared as our teacher" (*Protreptikos,* 1). But Christ is also our father, mother, guardian and nourisher (*Paidogogos,* 1, 42, 1–3).

Clement's theology is so much a theology *of the Logos,* a theology from above, with a Philonic, Platonic, and Gnostic background, that the inner psychic life of the human Jesus seems nonexistent. It seems as if Jesus is "taken over" by the Logos, is essentially the Logos and that is all. His Christology is simply a part of the theology of the Logos. This tendency to fail to see or find a significant place for the inner *human* workings in the life of Jesus, what is later seen as the reality of a human soul in Jesus, will characterize Alexandrian Christology. It will be an aspect of a Logos-dominated Christology, and its weakness is that it will not do full justice to the humanity of Jesus, to his (what will later be called) human nature as well as his divine nature. Some have seen in Clement for this reason an element of Gnosticism or Docetism, but such labels are inaccurate. Clement saw himself as rejecting the false Gnostics with true gnosis, and he never consciously denied a human soul in Christ. He simply manifested what would be a weakness in Alexandrian Christology.

The Logos had "attached" himself to human flesh. He had "clothed himself" with humanity (*Protreptikos,* 11, 111, 2; 11, 112, 1; *Paidogogos,* 1, 2, 4; *Quis dives salvetur?* 37, 3). It would

[9]Pollard, *Johannine Christology and the Early Church,* 82.

be inappropriate to demand in these statements what we can only reasonably associate with later theology. Christological thought and language develop; they are not all there from the beginning.

Yet, for Clement, Jesus was no ordinary human being. We have the beginning of a tradition that will not always see Jesus as "one like us *in all things,* except for sin." Although we cannot expect of Clement a clarity of language about the humanity of Jesus that will only become clear later, and although Clement is no Docetist in a heretical sense, we do have a picture of Jesus in which Jesus becomes less like us and in which his fleshly existence is robbed of its human qualities. Clement writes, for example:

> In the case of the Savior, it were ludicrous (to suppose) that the body, as a body, demanded the necessary aids in order to endure. For he ate, not for the sake of the body, which was kept together by a holy energy, but in order that it might not enter into the minds of those who were with him to entertain a different opinion of him just as some afterwards supposed that he appeared in phantasmal shape. But he was completely impassible, inaccessible to any movement of feeling, either pleasure or pain (*Stromateis,* 6, 9, 71).

In this picture of Jesus, "the flesh which the Logos assumes is human flesh stripped of what makes it specifically human."[10] But, at the same time, it reflects Clement's view of ideal humanity and the life of the true gnostic, the Hellenistic ascetical ideal of *apatheia,* or freedom from passion. Clement simply saw Jesus as *truly* human. His anthropology as well as the theology of the Logos influenced him. Christ is no ordinary human being because he was *the* true gnostic. From our perspective, Clement had spiritualized the human reality. From Clement's perspective, however, Jesus was like us, in that we are to be like him. The passions of the soul are to be subdued or controlled in the true Christian gnostic; thus they are unthinkable in Christ, and not because Christ has no soul.

Origen (ca. 185–254).[11] Unlike Justin and Clement, Origen was not a convert; he was born of Christian parents, probably in Alex-

---

[10] Ibid., 84.

[11] See C. Bigg, *The Christian Platonists of Alexandria* (Oxford: Clarendon, 1913); Jean Daniélou, *Origen* (New York: Sheed and Ward, 1955); Rowan Greer, *Origen,* Classics of

andria about 185. His father died a martyr during the persecution of Septimus Severus, the persecution that had forced Clement to leave Alexandria. With Clement's absence, Origen, who was then only eighteen, was asked by Bishop Demetrius to assume responsibilities for the catechetical and theological school in Alexandria. Origen headed the school until 230–231, when conflict with the bishop forced him to leave. He then established a similar school in Caesarea in Palestine. The conflict with the bishop involved Origen's ordination to the priesthood by Palestinian bishops without the bishop of Alexandria's prior knowledge or consent. Two synods convoked by Bishop Demetrius at the time excommunicated Origen from the Church in Alexandria. Origen was head of the school in Caesarea for almost twenty years. During the persecution of Decius (250–251), he was singled out for special torture. Decius died in 251. Origen was released but died about 254, at the age of sixty-nine, in Tyre.

Origen's literary output witnessed to a love of both Scripture and Greek philosophy. He was a supreme representative of Alexandrian and Christian Platonism. Some of Origen's teachings (the eternity of the world, the pre-existence and reincarnation of souls, the final salvation of the devil) made his work suspect. Yet he was one of the greatest of the Alexandrian theologians. He influenced Athanasius and the Cappadocians (Basil the Great, Gregory of Nazianzus, and Gregory of Nyssa). Because of controversies concerning his orthodoxy, various synods condemned some of his opinions, even as late as 553 at the Second Council of Constantinople.

Of Origen's extensive literary output, much of which has been lost, we should mention the *Hexapla,* an elaborate edition of the Hebrew Bible consisting of the Hebrew text and Greek versions of the text arranged in six parallel columns; biblical writings of three sorts, the *scholia,* or short expositions of difficult biblical texts, homilies, and commentaries; an apologetic work, *Against Celsus;* a significant systematic and theological work, *First Principles (De Principiis);* other varied writings such as a work *On Prayer* and an *Exhortation to Martyrdom.*

One of Origen's major contributions to theology has been his contribution to the theology of the Trinity, which he discussed

Western Spirituality (New York: Paulist, 1979); and *Alexandrian Christianity,* Library of Christian Classics 2 (Philadelphia: Westminster Press, 1954).

both in the *First Principles* (I, 1–3) and in the *Commentary on John*. Origen knew the term "trinity" *(trias)* (*On John,* 6, 33, 166; 10, 39, 270). And the Father, Son, and Holy Spirit are three hypostases (*hypostaseis,* or persons) (*On John,* 2, 10, 75). Each is distinct from all eternity. A difficulty in previous Logos theologies (Justin, Clement) was that the generation of the Logos seemed to be for the purpose of creation, a theory that associated a kind of creaturely existence with the Logos. Clement had distinguished two fundamental stages in the coming to be of the Logos: the first, his being essentially with God, and the second, his becoming distinct through (de)limitation. Origen wrote: "Many of those who call themselves friends of God fall. . . . Either they deny the Son an identity [*idiotēs*] distinct from that of the Father . . . or they deny the divinity of the Son, making his individual identity [*idiotēs*] and essence [*ousia*] as distinct from those of the Father a matter of limitation [*perigraphē*]" (*On John,* 2, 2, 16). Origen assessed the situation well. How did he respond to it?

The Logos/Son is clearly eternal; this is Origen's main contribution to Trinitarian theology. The Father begets the Son by an eternal act. Almost refuting Arius in advance, Origen maintained that it cannot be said that there was time when the Logos/Son was not (*First Principles,* 1, 2, 4). The Logos/Son is clearly divine. "The only Son, our Lord and God, the only-begotten of the Father, is Son by nature and not by adoption"[12] (cf. *First Principles,* 1, 2, 4). Origen not only described the Logos as Son by nature but also used, perhaps coined, the word *homoousios* to describe the relationship between Son and Father (*On Hebrews,* frag.).

Although the Word/Son clearly implies divinity for Origen, the Word is not yet considered equal to the Father. There is a subordinationism in Origen. The Logos, although divine and uncreated, is intermediate between God and creation.

> As for us, who believe the Savior when He said: "The Father, who has sent Me, is greater than I," and who for that reason did not allow that the word "good" should be applied to Himself in its full, true and perfect sense, but attributed it to the

---

[12]Daniélou, *Gospel Message and Hellenistic Culture,* 379. The quote comes from Pamphilus, *Apology on behalf of Origen* (Patrologia Graeca 17:581).

Father and gave Him thanks, condemning him who would glorify the Son to excess—we say that the Savior and the Holy Spirit are without comparison and are very much superior to all things that are made, but also that the Father is even more above them than they are themselves above creatures even the highest (*On John,* 13, 25).

Origen drew another distinction (*On John,* 2, 2), based on the text of John's Gospel, between *autotheos* (God in an absolute sense, God in himself) or *ho theos* (God with the article) and all who are made God by participation (God without the article) *(ouk ho theos alla theos).* *Theos* (God without the article) belongs first and foremost to the "first born of all creation" (Col 1:15). *Ho theos* is God in the fullest and absolute sense. The Logos or Son, God by nature but also by participation, is *theos,* eternally *homoousios* with the Father, yet an image of God. The Holy Spirit, also truly divine, not a creature, ranks lower than the Son (*First Principles,* preface, 4). Then there are those who are gods by adoption, or images of the image of God: "God [*ho theos*] is the true God, then; the others are gods formed according to him as images of the prototype. But again, of the many images, the archetypal image is he who is with God, the Logos, who was in the beginning because he was God [*theos*] always dwelling with God, and who would not continue to be God, unless he existed in the perpetual contemplation of the depths of the Father."[13]

Origen was not only a biblical scholar, philosopher, and speculative theologian but also a mystic. The goal of human life for Origen was to perfect one's likeness to God (*First Principles,* 3, 6, 1). This involves true self-knowledge, complete freedom from the passions *(apatheia),* lifelong asceticism, the mystical assent, and the mystical union of the soul with the Logos—a mystical marriage. Origen's Christology is affected by his mystical interests. Jesus Christ is primarily the mediator and exemplar of the mystical union.

Nor is Origen's mysticism unrelated to his exegesis, which is both typological (as found in Justin and Irenaeus), with Christianity as the fulfillment of prophecy, and allegorical (as found

---

[13]Origen, *Commentary on John,* Die Griechischen Christlichen Schriftsteller (Leipzig: J. C. Hinrichs, 1903), on John 2:2, pp. 30ff. (See Pollard, *Johannine Christology and the Early Church,* 94.)

in Clement), which is typically Alexandrian.[14] Origen goes beyond Clement and systematizes the Alexandrian hermeneutics in *First Principles,* book 4. He distinguishes the three senses of Scripture: (1) the literal sense, including traditional typology, (2) the moral sense, and (3) the spiritual sense. It is the last that allows the use of allegory to flourish. And the three senses of Scripture are also related to the threefold classification of believers into beginners, those making progress, and the advanced in the spiritual life.

Origen taught that God had created a spiritual world that preceded this world, in which spiritual beings were free and equal. The Fall was pre-mundane; the spirits had turned away from God, and they became the souls that entered into this world. The depth to which pre-existent souls had fallen varied, and this variation accounted for inequalities in this world. This world is a process of returning to God, and it may take some a series of incarnations in order to effect the return (*First Principles,* 1, 6, 3; 1, 8, 1; 2, 11, 6). Salvation is the restoration of the spiritual order and the divinization of souls in their return to God.

Unlike Clement, and what we have referred to as an Alexandrian tendency, Origen clearly saw a human soul in Jesus. Yet his Christology was still a Logos-centered Christology, following upon his unique anthropology. His Christology followed upon his doctrine of the pre-existence of souls (*First Principles,* 2, 6, 3–5). "One of these souls, the one destined to be the soul of the man Jesus, in every respect a human soul like the rest, was from the beginning attached to the Logos with mystical devotion; it burned with love and desire for justice. All the other souls, by the misguided exercise of their free-will, fell away from the Logos, to whom they ought to have adhered; but this unique soul, as a result of its adoring contemplation, became inseparably united with Him."[15] There had been one exception to the Fall—the soul which was destined to become incarnate with the Logos.

Origen maintained a unity or oneness in Christ, and he was clear about the uncreated divinity of Christ, both hallmarks of Alexandrian Christology. As far as we can tell, Origen contributed the word *homoousios* to the theology of the Trinity. In Christology he contributed the word *theanthropos* (God-human), a word

---

[14]See Daniélou, *Gospel Message and Hellenistic Culture,* 273–288.

[15]J. N. D. Kelly, *Early Christian Doctrines,* 2nd ed. (New York: Harper & Row, 1960) 155.

that reveals a theology and insight that is a proper basis for the *communicatio idiomatum* (the communication of properties), another characteristic of Alexandrian Christology.

But the question remains whether Origen appreciated the humanity of Jesus Christ. The Alexandrian Logos Christologies in general did not. Practically speaking, the Logos had taken over as the operative principle *(hēgemonikon)* in Christ.

It seems as if the difference for Origen between Jesus and any other human being was a difference in degree and not in kind.[16] Aloys Grillmeier writes, "Christ is in danger of being still only a 'quantitatively' different exceptional case of the universal relationship of the 'perfect' to the Logos, however mystically deep Origen may wish to make the relationship between Logos and soul in the God-man."[17]

Origen's theology is intriguing in that he contributed to the development of orthodox Trinitarian and Christological thought at the same time that he was nonorthodox in his anthropology because of his Platonism. His eschatology is equally nonorthodox. His doctrine of *apokatastasis,* or the universal restoration of all things, implied the spiritual journey of the whole created order back to its origins, a universal salvation for all, even the demons and Satan (*First Principles,* 1, 6, 1; 2, 10, 6; 3, 6, 3–6; *Against Celsus,* 8, 72). Yet Origen remains one of the greatest Christian thinkers of all times.

Arius (ca. 250–336).[18] Born in Libya, Arius studied theology in Antioch in the school of Lucian, then moved to Alexandria, where he was ordained. Perhaps we ought not include Arius among the Alexandrians, except that he promulgated his thought as a priest in Alexandria, first came into conflict with the bishop of Alexandria, and was Origenist in his theology, representing a left wing of Origenism that emphasized Origen's subordinationism, such as is found in Dionysius of Alexandria (d.ca. 264, an earlier bishop of Alexandria and pupil of Origen). Yet there remains divided opinion about whether the roots of Arianism are

[16]Ibid., 156.

[17]Grillmeier, *Christ in Christian Tradition,* 147.

[18]C. Kannengiesser, "Arius and the Arians," *Theological Studies* 44 (1983) 456–475; Joseph T. Lienhard, "The 'Arian' Controversy: Some Categories Reconsidered," *Theological Studies* 48 (1987) 415–437.

only the Alexandrian tradition stemming from Origen or also the Antiochene tradition.[19]

Conflict between Arius and Alexander, the bishop of Alexandria, stems from either 318 or 323, the date being disputed. Alexander eventually convoked a synod of Egyptian bishops, which condemned Arius for his teachings and excommunicated him. Because dissension over the Arius affair continued, Constantine convoked the first ecumenical council at Nicea in 325, which confirmed the condemnation of Arius. Arius was exiled but later recalled.

Arius wrote little. The chief sources for his thought are the writings of Athanasius and Church historians of the fourth and fifth centuries. We do have three writings of Arius from the pre-Nicene period, a letter to Eusebius of Nicomedia, a letter to Alexander of Alexandria, and fragments of a work called *The Banquet*.

Arius and the history of Arianism were among the most significant episodes in the history of the Christian Church. The third-century, moderate, unclarified, acceptable subordinationism of the Church was pushed to a clear, extreme, and unacceptable subordinationism, the resolution of which resulted in the Nicene faith. Origen had been a predominant influence, and two types of Origenism had developed—a moderate wing, exemplified in Bishop Alexander of Alexandria, which emphasized the divinity of the Son/Logos in Origen; and a radical wing, exemplified in Eusebius of Caesarea, which emphasized the subordinationist element in Origen's thought. Arius carried the latter to a clear and unaccepted extreme. Thus the Arian affair culminated in what would be Trinitarian orthodoxy: it helped the Church to clarify its understanding for the future.

In our discussion of second- and third-century theologians, we have looked primarily at their thought, not their socio-political settings. The former, however, cannot be abstracted from the latter. The relationship between the two is quite apparent in the post-Nicene period. The fourth century is a new period, a new

---

[19]Justo Gonzalez, *A History of Christian Thought* (Nashville: Abingdon, 1970) 1:269-270, places Arius squarely in the Origenist tradition. Pollard, in *Johannine Christology and the Early Church*, 142-145, maintains the thesis that there are elements in Arianism that cannot be traced to the Alexandrian tradition. See also Grillmeier, *Christ in Christian Tradition*, 153-190. Origen's influence in Palestine and Syria must be recognized, given his many years with the school in Caesarea.

beginning, in the life of the Church. Persecution gave way to toleration. Church and empire moved closer together. We leave Diocletian (emperor 284–305) and find Constantine (emperor 306–337). Pre-Constantinian theology was set in the context of persecution and martyrdom as a reality for the Christian Church; the major enemy was without. With Constantine's conversion to the Christian faith and the increasing toleration of Christianity after 312, a general council of the Church of all of Christendom, convoked by the Roman emperor, became a possibility that contributed to the history of dogma.

What then was the teaching of Arius, which arose at such a moment in the life of the Church? The starting point for understanding Arius is his monotheism—the transcendence and uniqueness of God, the unbegotten source *(agennētos archē)*. This had implications for a theology of the Logos. According to Arius, the Logos or Son was God by grace, not by nature. This is the opposite of Origen's position. The Son is the primary participant in God for Arius. (This is not the Adoptionism of Paul of Samosata, whose frame of reference was the historical man Jesus. Arius is speaking of the preexistent Logos, not Jesus, although the nature of the Logos is determinate with respect to Jesus as well.)

Thus, Son and Spirit are removed from an existence on the uncreated side of the divine life; they are, in fact, then, creatures. This is not Origenism, in which Son and Spirit, although subordinate, were truly divine, *homoousioi* with the Father. Not so for Arius. The Logos for Arius is a creature *(ktisma, poiēma)*. He is a perfect creature, superior to the rest of creation, but a creature. From this the rest of Arian thought logically followed. As a creature, the Logos had a beginning, was not eternal, was begotten in time.

Prior to Nicea, we did not have an operative distinction between *agennētos (gennaō,* to beget), unbegotten, and *agenētos (gignomai,* to be born), unborn, uncreated. In Nicene theology, only the Father is unbegotten, and the Son is begotten, the only begotten one, but uncreated, distinct from the Father in being begotten, yet *homoousios* with the Father in being uncreated. For Arius, the Father is the unbegotten one, but without the above distinction, the Son is begotten, which is to say created. Origen earlier had spoken of an eternal begetting. For Arius, the Son became the created mediator of creation, preeminent in that he was directly created by God and all else was created by him. He was the mediator of all creation and intermediate between God and the rest of creation, an intolerable subordinationism which made the Son a creature in a Platonic hierarchy. Subordinationism is not necessarily Arianism (Origenism is not Arianism).

Since, for Arius, the Son is truly on this side of the creaturely divide, not truly God, he cannot fully know God. He is distinct from God's very essence, not *homoousios* with God, only God by grace, God in name only. For Arius the Holy Spirit is the first of the creatures of the Logos, as the Logos is the creature of the Father. God's transcendence remains protected and ultimately unbridgeable.

Certain slogans or propositions came to describe the Arian heresy: "There was once when the Son was not"; "He was not before he was begotten"; "The Son has a beginning"; "The Son is not like the Father according to essence [*ousia*]"; "The Logos is foreign and alien to and isolated from the essence of God"; "The Son is from nothing"; "The Son is a creature and thing made."[20] Not all of these are from the writings of Arius himself; some reflect the articulation of Arianism by opponents. Yet they express what was to be unacceptable at Nicea in 325.

Arius' theology was a seriously diminished or "low" theology of the Logos. It did not, however, do justice to the humanity of Jesus either. Arius' theology of the Trinity affected his understanding of the divinity of Christ—who would inevitably be less than fully divine. But this did not lead to a strong affirmation of the humanity of Jesus, as would be true for the Adoptionism of Paul of Samosata or for the Antiochenes. On both counts Arius was found wanting.

Arian Christology reflected what we have already seen as a weakness among Alexandrians, whose theology of the Logos eliminated for all practical purposes the human soul of Jesus as a self-functioning principle in the humanity. This theory is often referred to as a Logos-sarx Christology, the union between the Logos and *sarx* (flesh) being such that Christ has no human soul. Origen's thought, because it was partly related to his particular doctrine of pre-existent souls, was a clear exception to this. Not even Clement had eliminated explicitly the soul of Christ. Christ's

[20]See Pollard, *Johannine Christology and the Early Church*, 146-165.

human soul simply played no role in Christ's psychology. Thus, Arius was the first to deny explicitly a human soul in Christ; not only was Christ's divinity diminished, his humanity was impaired as well. Another Arian formula was "We believe in . . . the one Lord, the Son, . . . who became flesh, but not man. For he took no human soul, but became flesh so that God was revealed to us even through the flesh as through a curtain."[21] Here, in the actual wording of Eudoxius of Antioch, a post-Nicene extreme Arian, is a clear contrast between what is implied by a Logos-sarx Christology in contrast to a Logos-anthropos Christology.[22] The question of the human soul of Christ was not directly addressed at Nicea, and its role remained problematic in Alexandria until Apollinaris and the Council of Constantinople in 381. Nicea was concerned with Arius' false understanding of the Logos.

The divinity of the Logos, and thus also of Christ, was not simply a theoretical question, for it had practical implications for Christians in their liturgy, worship, and spiritual lives. The issue was whether Christ could be worshiped or not. We also see the significance of the Gospel of John in the development of Alexandrian Christology, the Johannine Father-Son relationship and the prologue's inclusion of the term "Logos." Alexandrian theology, heavily influenced by Middle- and Neo-Platonism, had its biblical basis in the Johannine prologue. A further observation can also be made. At the close of our reflections on the second century, we noted two tendencies in the history of Christian thought—diversification and consolidation. We can now mention a third—individualization. In Ignatius and Irenaeus we saw a strong awareness of Catholic theology. In the contrast between Antioch and Alexandria we will see diversification. We also will see individuality in each school of thought. Clement, Origen, and Arius were obviously quite distinct from one another. We will continue to see this individuality with Athanasius, Apollinaris, and Cyril. And we have already seen two Alexandrians (both probably Origenists) opposed to each other, Arius and Bishop Alex-

---

[21]Grillmeier, *Christ in Christian Tradition,* 244.

[22]Logos-sarx is an expression used to describe Alexandrian Christology, in which the union of the Word with flesh *(sarx)* lends itself to a lack of appreciation for the full humanness *(anthrōpos)* of Jesus. Logos-anthropos, descriptive of Antiochene Christology, emphasizes the total humanity *(anthrōpos,* human being, body *and* soul) of Jesus and not just the physical dimension. Antiochene Christology, however, has other limitations.

ander. Theology not only confronts culture, it is confronted by individual thinkers.

Athanasius (ca. 296–373). Born in Alexandria and educated there, probably at the famous catechetical school, Athanasius was ordained in 319 to the diaconate by Bishop Alexander of Alexandria, the opponent of Arius, whom Athanasius then served as secretary. He accompanied Bishop Alexander to the Council of Nicea (325), and succeeded him as the next Bishop of Alexandria in 328. Athanasius is known as the champion of Nicea, the father of Orthodoxy, and the enemy of Arianism. The life of Athanasius and the history of post-Nicene Arianism coincide. Arianism did not go away simply because it was rejected by the Council of Nicea.

In his struggle against the post-Nicene Arian party, which had a strong foothold in Alexandria, Athanasius was exiled five times, spending a total of more than seventeen years in exile. Yet he did not capitulate; he continued to be a defender of the Nicene faith and what had become Trinitarian orthodoxy. He was a major obstacle to the triumph of Arianism.

Athanasius bequeathed to history an extensive number of works. These include, among others, two short treatises that form one work, *Against the Heathen,* and the famous *On the Incarnation,* in the pre-Nicene period; three *Discourses Against the Arians,* his chief dogmatic work, which expounds the teaching of the Arians and defends Nicea; three apologies, *Apology Against the Arians* after his second exile, *Apology to the Emperor Constantine,* a very carefully written work, and the *Apology for His Flight;* the *History of the Arians;* several biblical commentaries; the significant *Life of St. Anthony,* the father of Christian monasticism; and a large number of letters, generally formal, significant for the history of the Arian controversy.

Athanasius' theology, influenced by Origenism, moved in a different direction. He was less speculative, less philosophical, less moved by Platonism. It is Alexandrian theology in a new key. His sources are Scripture and tradition. Although he used Greek concepts, he used them in the service of expounding the traditional faith of the Church. Faith has primacy over reason. He was a theologian in the best sense of the word, a pastoral theologian concerned with the faith of the people and the problems of his age. In the third century, Alexandria could rightly boast of Origen; in the fourth century its boast would be Athanasius. For Athanasius as well as for Arius, God is transcendent, but for Athanasius God did not need intermediaries to create or to have contact with creation (*Discourse Against the Arians,* 2, 25). The Word is not intermediate and subordinate, as in the Christian Platonism of Origen, or a creature, as in Arianism. The Logos is God, fully God, and there is but one God. With Athanasius, subordinationism came to an end. The one God is Father, Son, and Spirit; the Son is truly divine (against the Arians); and the Spirit is truly divine (against the Pneumatomachians). To protect the economy of salvation (which implies that *God* has truly saved us, and thus that the divine-human one is divine) and Christian monotheism (which insists that there is no second God, the expression *deuteros theos* having played a role in Origenism), Athanasius affirms the identity of the Logos with the divine nature, distinct from the Father but sharing the same divine nature, *homoousios.* The Son is of the Father's substance *(ek tēs ousias tou patros).*

Athanasius' understanding of the Logos is pretty much a simple reversal of Arius' understanding. For Athanasius the Logos is divine, not created but begotten, thus of the Father's essence, fully God, eternal. The Father and the Son have the same nature *(physis) (Discourse Against the Arians,* 3, 3–4). Father, Son, and Spirit share the one and same divine *physis* or *ousia.*

In defense of the Church's traditional monotheism, Athanasius allowed no subordinationism in God. There is *one God,* who is Father, Son, and Spirit. Athanasius' concern for salvation, that salvation had truly been effected in Jesus Christ, is an equal concern, and this means that God was involved as well as humankind, that Jesus was both truly God and truly human. Athanasius' understanding of salvation necessitated both, for salvation for Athanasius was a deification or divinization *(theopoiēsis).* As Athanasius wrote, "He was made one of us that we might be made God" *(On the Incarnation,* 54). In Jesus, God breaks through the sin of the world and a new creation is effected, in which we can once again be what we were created to be—images of God.

As far as the theology of the Word is concerned, as well as the divinity of Christ, Arius and Athanasius were opposed to each other. In their understanding of the humanity of Jesus, however, they are not as far apart. Both reflect the Logos-sarx framework of Alexandria. It is doubtful that Athanasius held that there was a human soul in Christ. This tendency to neglect the human soul of Christ reflects an emphasis on the unity in Christ: that Jesus Christ is one, not one thing as God and another as a human being.

Athanasius never explicitly denied a human soul in Christ. When speaking of the death of Christ, he never spoke about it as a separation of body and soul, a familiar concept, but rather a separation of body and Logos (*On the Incarnation,* 22; *Discourse Against the Arians,* 3, 57). In arguing against the Arians, he never refuted this aspect of their teaching. It would appear as if this were not a problem for him.

The question in Athanasian Christology is whether Athanasius simply ignored the soul of Christ while tacitly assuming it to be a reality or whether he regarded it as nonexistent. Grillmeier argues that the soul of Christ is certainly not "a theological factor," that it carries no theological significance in Athanasius' Christology. Grillmeier maintains that at least until 362, when Athanasius wrote the *Tomus ad Antiochenos,* a human soul in Christ was neither a theological factor nor a physical factor, and that after 362 it was still not a theological factor although it had become a physical factor.[23]

In 362, a synod in Alexandria had been held, which included the statement that "the Savior did not have a body lacking soul, sensibility, or intelligence." Athanasius chaired the synod and endorsed the formula. Thus it appears as if at this time he acknowledged the presence of a human soul in a purely formal or physical way. Yet Athanasius' *Tomus ad Antiochenos,* a letter written in the name of the synod, still conveyed no theological significance to the human soul of Christ.

Here we must also take note of a central Christological statement of Athanasius in his main work against the Arians: "[The Word] was made man and did not come into a man" (*Discourse Against the Arians,* 3, 30). This assertion helps to elucidate an

[23]A number of scholars maintain that there is no human soul in Christ within Athanasian Christology. Although this opinion may be nuanced, it is the opinion of Grillmeier, *Christ in Christian Tradition,* 308–328; Kelly, *Early Christian Doctrines,* 284–289; Johannes Quasten, *Patrology,* vol. 3, The Golden Age of Greek Patristic Literature (Utrecht: Spectrum Publishers, 1966) 73–74. Also see M. F. Wiles, "The Nature of the Early Debate About Christ's Human Soul," *Journal of Ecclesiastical History* 16 (1965) 139–151. For a different interpretation, see Pollard, *Johannine Christology and the Early Church,* 232–245, who argues that Athanasius moves out of the Logos-sarx framework into a Logos-anthropos Christology.

Alexandrian concern and sets up the contrast between two Christological approaches—a Logos-sarx Christology that we have seen in Alexandrian Christology and a Logos-anthropos Christology that will be seen in Antiochene Christology.

For Athanasius, the statement implied a rejection of Paul of Samosata's type of Adoptionism and an affirmation of the fundamental unity that Jesus Christ is. To emphasize too strongly the human being, as if complete in itself, would imply there was a human person already there before the incarnation that the Logos came into. "The Logos became flesh," that good, biblical, Johannine statement, avoids this danger and gives no impression that there was already a being there before the incarnation of the Word. Thus, Athanasius and Alexandria are identified with a Logos-sarx theology. A Logos-anthropos frame of reference was too easily suspect as Adoptionism in Alexandria.

On the other hand, with the emergence of the question of the soul of Christ, the Logos-sarx language can appear to deny the human soul and thus the full humanity of Jesus. At Antioch, the Logos-anthropos framework was the clear way of avoiding Docetism, and the Logos-sarx framework was suspect as Apollinarianism (see discussion below). We can see that each insight is to be respected, to preserve the unity of Christ and avoid Adoptionism and to preserve the humanity of Christ and avoid Docetism. The question will be how to do it! Even the language will give off different nuances in different locales. How can there be a universal language for the universal Church?

In Athanasian Christology we have the clearest statement thus far of both the unity of Jesus Christ and the full divinity of Christ. This provides us with the clearest theological basis thus far for the *communicatio idiomatum,* Christological language in which the human and divine properties are the property of one person, the Logos, or God. If Christ is the Logos enfleshed, and the Logos is truly divine, then it will be appropriate to speak about Mary as the mother of God, because she is the mother of the God-man. Athanasius had already used the expression *theotokos* (*Discourse Against the Arians,* 3, 14, 29). This, too, proved to be problematic language. But in Alexandria, and for Athanasius, to deny its truth was to be Arian or Adoptionist and to deny the unity or divinity that Jesus is. For Athanasius *theotokos* followed from the *homoousios* of the Nicene faith and the reality of the incarnation.

Athanasian Christology is a Logos-sarx Christology. Yet it is not simply a Logos Christology in the sense of preceding theories. It is no longer built upon Platonism. And the Logos is fully God. Thus, to distinguish Athanasius from Arius, one could speak here of a Theos-sarx framework.[24]

Apollinaris (or Apollinarius) (ca. 310–ca. 390). Born at Laodicea near Antioch in Syria, son of a Beirut grammarian, a close friend of Athanasius, a vigorous opponent of Arianism, Apollinaris became bishop of his native Laodicea around 360, a position he occupied until his death. A teaching resembling Apollinarianism had been rejected at the Council of Alexandria in 362, but it was only later that Apollinaris' Christology became known. Apollinarianism was formally condemned at the second ecumenical council held in Constantinople in 381.

Some of Apollinaris' theological works survived because they were preserved under false names. Among these are *A Detailed Confession of Faith (Quod unus sit Christus, De incarnatione Dei Verbi); a *Profession of Faith* addressed to the emperor Jovian *(De unione corporis et divinitatis in Christo, De fide et incarnatione);* and a letter to a Dionysius. His major dogmatic work was *Proof of the Incarnation of God According to the Image of Man.* Only fragments remain of his commentaries on Scripture and his thirty apologetic books against the Neoplatonist Porphyry.

A word should be said about our inclusion of Apollinaris here among the Alexandrians. He was not born or educated there; nor was he a teacher or bishop there. Thus he was not Alexandrian in the strict sense. What we are gradually coming to see as two directions in patristic Christology, however, the Logos-sarx and Logos-anthropos directions, associated with the Alexandrian and Antiochene traditions respectively, cannot always be geographically confined. This is especially true of "Alexandrian Christology." Alexandria never became a center for Antiochene thought, but the region around Antioch was at times a stronghold for Alexandrian thought, which is partially what makes some of the issues more volatile. Apollinaris was a defender of "Alexandrian thought" in the geographical region most predominantly in-

---

[24]Or one could follow Pollard, *Johannine Christology and the Early Church,* 232–245, and speak of a God-man framework. This, however, may distinguish Athanasius too little from Antiochene concerns and may reflect too strong an affirmation of the presence of a human soul in Athanasian Christology.

fluenced by Antiochene thought. Thus we include him as an Alexandrian, in the wider sense of that term. Apollinaris was dissatisfied with the Antiochene tradition and its inability to articulate to his satisfaction the closeness and unity between the divinity and humanity in Jesus—always a major concern of the Alexandrian school. Thus Apollinaris developed an Alexandrian mode of Christology. He was a close friend of Athanasius and a foe of the Arians. In fact, with Apollinaris, it can be said that the Alexandrian, Logos-sarx direction in Christology reached its logical conclusion. Apollinaris was perhaps a supreme, even if heretical, representative. Alexandrianism was not monolithic; it was Origenism, Arianism, Athanasian orthodoxy, Apollinarianism.

We have referred previously to the Alexandrian concern for the unity or union in Christ. For Apollinaris especially, one only has a true incarnation if the divine Logos and human sarx form a substantial unity. There can be no prior and independent person Jesus either ontologically or temporally; such temporal dissociation would make *one* (composite) entity impossible. Like Athanasius before him, Apollinaris argued that to become human is not the same as to enter into a human being. There is no human being before the incarnation. The Logos "enters into a real substantial conjunction with the sarx to make up a human being."[25] To have true unity, the two elements must be related as parts to a whole. One cannot begin with two wholes and try to make them one. Thus, for Apollinaris, the human nature of Christ must be incomplete—so that a true union might be constituted.

It appears as if Apollinaris held to a Platonic tripartite perspective; the human person is body, soul (the irrational or animal soul), and spirit or mind (the human, rational soul). The third is the specifically human element.[26] In Jesus Christ, for Apollinaris, there are the first two elements, body and irrational soul, but the third element is replaced by the Logos. Thus Christ is fully divine but not completely human: he is body, soul *(psychē alogos)*, and divine Logos. Christ is truly a unity. Just as the creature is one being composed of body and soul, so Christ is a being com-

[25]Grillmeier, *Christ in Christian Tradition*, 331.

[26]See Kelly, *Early Christian Doctrine*, 382; Grillmeier, *Christ in Christian Tradition*, 332, n. 13.

posed of body and Logos, except that Apollinaris seems to have begun with the trichotomous anthropology. Apollinaris (as is true of the Alexandrian approach in general) preserved the unity of Christ at the expense of his humanity. The Church was insistent that both the unity of Christ and the humanity of Christ must be preserved, even if the Church still did not have the language to do so. What it amounts to is that neither Adoptionism nor Docetism will do. The solution to the philosophical problems raised by Jesus Christ must lie somewhere between these two unacceptable extremes.

Apollinaris had substituted the divine Logos for the normal human psychology in Christ Jesus. Thus, Christ was truly one. He was one person, not a duality. In Christ, for Apollinaris, there was a "unity of nature" *(henōsis physikē);* Christ was one nature *(mia physis).* Any two-nature or Dyophysite way of speaking would destroy the unity of Christ, who was one person, and this meant one nature.

This *mia physis* formula would itself be a cause of much later discussion; yet it followed logically upon Apollinarian Christology. "Concerning Christ we hold that he is a created being in union with an uncreated being, an uncreated being in mixture with a created being; that he has a single nature compounded of those two parts, the Word supplying as its part the power for the forming of a whole with divine perfection."[27] The *mia physis* formula fit well a Logos-sarx, Alexandrian Christology. This formula was never the cause of consternation in Alexandria as it was in Antioch. For Apollinaris, Christ was one *physis,* or one *ousia* (equivalent expressions for Apollinaris): *Jesus Christ is one.*

This oneness was expressed in other ways by Apollinaris. Christ was not only one *physis,* one *ousia;* he was also a simple, undivided *prosōpon* (person).[28] Apollinaris also used *hypostasis.* In fact, he was the one to introduce the word into the Christological vocabulary that would be Christological language for centuries to come. For Apollinaris, however, the terms were all closely related, even if not exact synonyms. They were not distinguished. They all referred to Christ, who was one *physis,* one *ousia,* one

[27]Hans Lietzmann, *Apollinaris von Laodicä und Seine Schule, Texte und Untersuchungen* (Tübingen, West Germany: J. C. B. Mohr, 1904) 187.

[28]Ibid., 257 (also see Kelly, *Early Christian Doctrines,* 293).

prosōpon, one *hypostasis.* "The same is one physis, one hypostasis, one power *(energeia),* one prosōpon, fully God and fully human" *(De fide et incarnatione,* 6).[29] The unity in Apollinarian Christology was not so much what post-Chalcedonian Christology would call "personal unity" as much as it was a "natural unity."[30] It was a dynamic, vital unity. As in Alexandrian thought in general, there was in Apollinaris a theological basis for the *communicatio idiomatum.* This basis was the unity of Jesus Christ, always a first principle in Logos-sarx Christologies.

Arianism and Apollinarianism shared one problem in common —the denial of a human soul or complete human psychology in Christ. Yet they were worlds apart. The Logos was not truly divine for Arius; for Apollinaris the Logos was true God. This only illustrates the wide diversity or spectrum that can exist within a "Logos-sarx" or Alexandrian approach to Christology.[31] Between these extremes of Arius and Apollinaris was the more moderate and orthodox Athanasius, who defended the divinity of the Logos and did not explicitly negate the human soul of Christ.

Cyril of Alexandria (d. 444). Born and educated in Alexandria, Cyril became Patriarch in 412, succeeding his uncle Theophilus. Cyril was both ruthless and brilliant. His opposition to John Chrysostom was long lasting. He became prominent as the opponent of Nestorius, the bishop of Constantinople. The conflict between Cyril and Nestorius cannot be abstracted from the increasing estrangement between the two great theological centers of the East, Alexandria and Antioch, nor from the political rivalry between the two great patriarchal sees, Alexandria and Constantinople. The bitter quarrel between Nestorius and Cyril was only resolved by the emperor Theodosius II's summoning of the third ecumenical council, at Ephesus in 431.

Cyril's extensive writings as well as his theology can be divided into two periods, the pre-Ephesene period, which preceded the

---

[29]Apollinaris, De fide et incarnatione, 6 (in Lietzmann, *Apollinaris von Laodicea,* 199; also see Kelly, *Early Christian Doctrine,* 293). For the history of the word *hypostasis* in Christology, see M. Richard, "L'introduction du mot 'hypostase' dans la théologie de l'incarnation," *Mélanges de Science Religieuse* 2 (1945) 5-32, 243-270. Also Grillmeier, *Christ in Christian Tradition,* 330-340.

[30]See Grillmeier, *Christ in Christian Tradition,* 338.

[31]For a succinct summary of the Logos-sarx framework, see Grillmeier, *Christ in Christian Tradition,* 341-343.

conflict with Nestorius, extending until 428, and the period of the Nestorian controversy and anti-Nestorian writings. His commentaries on both the Old and New Testaments form the greater part of his writings, but of greater interest to the history of doctrine are his polemical works. During the pre-Nestorian period there were two treatises against the Arians, which follow in the tradition of Athanasius, the *Thesaurus de sancta et consubstantiali Trinitate* and the seven dialogues *De sancta Trinitate.*

Among the several anti-Nestorian works we can mention the five-volume *Adversus Nestorii blasphemias,* written in 430, and in the same year the famous *Twelve Anathemas Against Nestorius.* In addition there are letters, sermons, and an apologetic work against Julian the Apostate.

With Cyril, we move into the fifth century of Church history. Origen continued to have an impact, although we have not traced that influence here. Athanasius still exerted influence and had influence on Cyril. The pre-Ephesene Cyril was simply Athanasian. It was in his conflict with Nestorius that Cyrilline theology came into its own. Cyril was a contemporary of John Chrysostom (ca. 347–407), Theodore of Mopsuestia (ca. 350–428), and Nestorius (d.ca. 451) and thus the antagonist of the great Antiochene school.

Our concern here is only with the early, pre-Ephesene Cyril. For a consideration of the later Cyril we will wait until we discuss Nestorius and the Council of Ephesus, for these are too closely woven together for us to be able to treat them separately. The early Cyril was Athanasian in his Christology, a traditional Alexandrian Logos-sarx framework in which the soul of Christ was still not operationally apparent, not a "theological factor" although a "physical factor," and all this in spite of the whole Apollinarian history. Cyril's early enemy was still Arianism. He quoted the prominent Athanasian Christological statement: "The Word was made human and did not come into a human being" (*Discourse Against the Arians,* III). And the Word was made human still meant the Word became flesh. Christ is Logos (or God) and sarx.

Antiochene Christology

Another cultural region of Christendom, Syria and Asia Minor, was as important as Egypt for the history of the Church. We will see there as well what we have seen in the second through fifth centuries of Alexandrian thought: the diversity, individuality, and catholicity of Christian theology. We have seen that we cannot easily generalize about Alexandrian theology. The Logos is fully divine and equal to the Father (Athanasius), or fully divine but subordinate to the Father (Origen), or subordinate and not fully divine (Arius). And although the Logos Christology at Alexandria lay within a Logos-sarx framework, Origen clearly affirmed a human soul in Christ. Rather than describing the Alexandrian Christological tradition as a Logos-sarx framework, it would be better to say that Alexandrian theology was primarily a theology of the Logos, whether we go back to Justin, the Platonism of Clement and Origen, the heresy of Arius, or the orthodoxy of Athanasius. Alexandrian theology was an effort to work out a theology of the Logos. Theology in Antioch was also a Logos theology, but not in the same way.

Antioch (modern Antakya in Turkey) was a Hellenistic city in Syria founded by Seleucus I in 300 B.C.E. and named after Seleucus' father, Antiochus. It was the third most important city in the Roman Empire, ranking after Rome and Alexandria. A Christian community existed in Antioch from the earliest days of Christianity. It became a center for the Gentile mission, and the Jerusalem Church sent Barnabas there to observe developments. Barnabas then brought Paul there, and the two of them spent a year teaching in Antioch. It was in Antioch that the followers of the Way were first called Christians (Acts 11:18-26).[32]

By the beginning of the second century, the Church was well established there. We have already referred to Ignatius, either the second or third bishop of Antioch (depending upon how one evaluates the tradition that Peter was the first bishop there). Ignatius was the first writer to use the word "catholic" to describe the Church. In the fourth century, after the Council of Nicea, Antioch was ranked as the third patriarchal see, after Rome and Alexandria.

Earlier we referred to the theological complexity by which the Alexandrian tradition had established itself in Asia Minor, Syria,

---

[32]A helpful account of the first three Christian generations in Antioch has been provided by John Meier. See Raymond Brown and J. Meier, *Antioch and Rome* (New York: Paulist, 1983) 11-86. Also see the study by Wayne Meeks and Robert Wilken, *Jews and Christians in Antioch in the Four Centuries of the Common Era* (Missoula, Mont.: Scholars Press, 1978).

and Palestine, whereas the Antiochene tradition never had such an influence in Alexandria. Part of the explanation for this situation can be traced to Origen, who had been so favorably received by bishops in Palestine; they in fact were the ones who ordained him. After his exile from Alexandria about 231, Origen had established a similar school in Caesarea in Palestine, where he taught for about twenty years. After his death his works became the basis for a significant library, which one of his pupils enlarged—Pamphilus, who became the head of the school. Thus the influence of Origenism was not confined to Egypt.

A school in Antioch was founded in the early fourth century in opposition to the school at Caesarea and in opposition to the excesses of the allegorical interpretation of Scripture. The Antiochene tradition became known for its textual, straightforward, and historical approach to Scripture. Caesarea had followed the traditions of Origen and Alexandria. Alexandria's bent owed much to Plato; Antioch's owed much to Aristotle.

Each tradition in the Church had orthodox as well as heretical representatives. Each tendency worked itself out and gave rise to dead ends for doctrine along the way, although even these contributed to the development of the Church's understanding. At Alexandria we encountered Athanasius and Cyril, the Church's theologians for the future, especially in regard to Trinitarian and Christological orthodoxy. Arius and Apollinaris led the way to Trinitarian and Christological heterodoxy. An extreme representative of an otherwise valid framework can force the faith along a false path. At Antioch it was Paul of Samosata who hung over the Antiochene tradition like a shadow. Antiochene theology easily suggested Paul of Samosata to Alexandrians, just as Alexandrian theology resembled Arianism or Apollinarianism in Antioch. The development of a universal, intercultural language for the Church's self-understanding was still not an accomplished task. Only conciliar theology would later accomplish it.

Paul, native of Samosata, became bishop of Antioch about 260. According to Leontius of Byzantium, Paul held an understanding of the Trinity that was a trinity in name only. He gave the name Father to the Creator, the name Son to one who was only human, and the name Spirit to the grace operative in the apostles. Jesus was greater than Moses, but still only human, different from us in degree only. Paul's name is often associated with heretical

Adoptionism. Three synods at Antioch rejected his teaching. In 268 he was deposed from the see. Yet his name continued to be associated with Antioch, and his followers, the Paulianists, continued.

Lucian of Antioch (d. 312), also a native of Samosata, was the founder of Antioch's theological school, which both complemented and rivaled Caesarea's. It dedicated itself to the literal interpretation of Scripture. Lucian himself was a Hebrew scholar; he corrected the Greek version of the Hebrew Scriptures. Lucian's name itself has been clouded. Some have associated his teaching with Paul of Samosata, others with Arianism. We earlier saw divided opinion about the "Lucianist" and/or "Origenist" roots of Arianism. Arius had been a student of Lucian's at Antioch. So Alexandria had its reasons for holding Antioch suspect, and vice versa. In fact, we know little about the theological thought of Lucian. Both his association with Paul of Samosata and his relation to Arianism have been disputed as well.

Antioch, like Alexandria, was affected not only by a particular approach but also by distinct individuals. The theologies of John Chrysostom, Theodore of Mopsuestia, and Nestorius were not identical. Nor is it accurate to set up Antioch and Alexandria in complete opposition. Even if during the debates between Nestorius and Cyril animosity reached a peak, this hostility did not characterize the entire history of the two schools. Yet Alexandria's preoccupation and contribution had been a Logos theology, which was both its weakness and its strength. Antioch's preoccupation and contribution was its theology of the humanity of Jesus, also its weakness and its strength. Later, when the Council of Chalcedon arrived at a Christological language for a universal Church, Alexandria contributed its emphasis on the unity of Christ, Christ's oneness with the Logos, and Antioch contributed an insistence on a full human nature or *physis,* and thus the necessity of affirming two *physeis* (natures) in Christ.[33]

The Christological framework associated therefore with the Antiochenes is often called a Logos-anthropos framework, in contrast with the Alexandrian Logos-sarx framework. *Anthrōpos* makes clear that Jesus was a complete human being, not lacking

---

[33]Cf. R. V. Sellers, *The Council of Chalcedon: A Historical and Doctrinal Survey* (London: S.P.C.K., 1953/1962).

anything essentially human, whereas *sarx,* as we have seen, can easily imply a human body without a human soul, a defective humanity. Yet *anthrōpos* carries with it the risk of an Adoptionism of sorts, that there is a complete human person in Jesus apart from his union with the divine Word, and thus that one has not only two natures in Christ but two persons or two beings. We will begin our effort to appreciate and understand the Antiochene tradition with Eustathius of Antioch, an early fourth-century representative of the tradition; then John Chrysostom, Antioch's greatest theologian; and finally Theodore of Mopsuestia and Nestorius, who bring us to the heart of Antiochene Christology.

Eustathius of Antioch. Bishop of Antioch from about 324 until 330, Eustathius attended the Council of Nicea and was among the prominent anti-Arian supporters of the Nicene doctrine, along with Marcellus of Ancyra and Athanasius.[34] His opposition to Arianism ended in his own deposition and exile in 330, once the pro-Arian party grew strong. He was accused of Sabellianism (see below). Both Marcellus and Eustathius, in their refutation of Arianism, interpreted the Nicene *homoousios* (the same substance) as an affirmation of the divinity of the Logos so strongly that they appeared to deny any real distinction between the Father and the Son.[35] Only Athanasius was able to maintain the middle ground of the eternity and equality of the Son with the Father but at the same time clearly distinct from the Father. Yet Eustathius was still a victim of Arian opponents, such as Eusebius of Nicomedia. Eustathius died in all probability by 337. Chronologically he came after Paul of Samosata who had become bishop of Antioch about 260, and before the later Antiochenes, Diodore, Theodore, and Nestorius. Opinion is divided as to whether Eustathius stands in the theological tradition of Paul of Samosata.[36]

Opinion is likewise divided over whether Eustathius was Sabellian in his Trinitarian theology or not.[37] Sabellius had taught a

[34]Cf. R. V. Sellers, *Eustathius of Antioch, and His Place in the Early History of Christian Doctrine* (Cambridge: Cambridge University Press, 1928).

[35]See M. D. Chenu, "Marcel d'Ancyre," *Dictionnaire de Théologie Catholique* 9:1993–1998, for his understanding of *homoousios.*

[36]Sellers, *Eustathius of Antioch,* sees Eustathius' Christology as akin to that of Paul's, 96–97, 114–115. Quasten, *Patrology,* vol. 3, 302–306, repudiates such a similarity. So does Grillmeier, *Christ in Christian Tradition,* 296.

[37]See Sellers, *Eustathius of Antioch,* 82–99.

form of Monarchianism, a monotheism that did not do justice to the distinctiveness of the Son. *Monarchia* implies God's oneness of power. Adoptionism was one form of Monarchianism: Jesus was God only in the sense that he was an adopted son, and there is no real distinction in the Godhead itself. Modalism was another form of Monarchianism, which maintained that the distinction in the Godhead was simply successive modes or ways of operating. Such was Sabellianism. It is tempting to trace a continuity from Paul of Samosata's type of Adoptionism to the moderated but modalist type of Monarchianism to Eustathius. Each seems to be removed from the heterodoxy of the former. Yet it is not clear that the thought of the later Antiochene can be rooted in the thought of Paul of Samosata.

R. V. Sellers argues that for Eustathius the *Logos* was only an attribute of one God, which when put forth is the divine *energeia* (operation, action, power), and it is this *energeia* that dwells in the human Jesus. The most frequent expression for Eustathius for the humanity of Jesus was *ho anthrōpos*. Two other terms are *naos* and *skēnē (temple* and *tent)*. God dwells in Jesus as in a temple; Jesus is a specific instance of the divine indwelling. Eustathius placed much weight on the doctrine of the divine omnipresence. The indwelling of the *energeia* can be elsewhere at the same time. In his argument against the Arians, Eustathius insisted on the complete humanity of Jesus. It is in this milieu rather than Adoptionism that one ought see the origins of the Logos-anthropos framework. It arose as the needed alternative to the Logos-sarx framework which diminished the humanity of Jesus. The Alexandrians themselves had not criticized the Arians on this point; for them it was the Arian theology of the Logos that was an issue. In Antioch, however, it was the Arian defective humanity that was equally at issue. *Anthrōpos* preserves that humanity fully. Eustathius wrote against the Arians, "Not in appearance of supposition, but in every reality God was clothed with a whole man, assuming him perfectly."[38] Thus Jesus truly experienced human development.

Eustathius did not regard Jesus as a person distinct from the Logos; his perspective was not that of Adoptionism. Jesus was the temple in which the Logos continuously dwelled. The rela-

[38]Ibid., 104–105.

tionship between the Logos and the human soul of Jesus is described by Sellers as one of reciprocal presence.

Eustathius used the word *prosōpon* (*persona,* person) and referred it to Christ. The "person of Christ" implied both the divine and the human natures. "The devil gazing into the person of Christ saw within God in fact and operations, and true Son of God by nature, beholding Him clothed without with a man, holy, undefiled and spotless, even a most beautiful temple, consecrated, inviolate" (*De engastrimytho,* 40, 2).[39] One can only speculate about what kind of union existed here. The union was the *prosōpon* of Christ, which appeared to be more a conjunction *(synatheia)* of the two natures, effected because the human soul always willed what was in harmony with the divine will, more of a moral union of wills.

In Eustathius, then, we already find those elements that will be associated with Antiochene Christology—a concern for the full humanity of Jesus, a clear distinction of two natures in Christ, a Logos-anthropos framework, the language of indwelling, the word *prosōpon* to describe the union in Christ, a union that is more of a moral union of wills.

Grillmeier distinguishes between the early Eustathius and the later Eustathius,[40] the dividing line being the struggle against Arianism. In the early Eustathius, Grillmeier does not see all the marks of the Antiochene Christology to which we have referred. Grillmeier notes that the early Eustathius used the *theotokos* title of Mary without hesitation. The distinctively Antiochene Christology in Eustathius developed as a result of the Arian controversy. Eustathius seems to have been the first to have recognized in Arianism a Christological heresy as well, its Logos-sarx dismissal of the human soul of Christ. For Athanasius, as we saw, Arianism had been a false theology of the Trinity or Logos. Eustathius gave theological significance to the human soul of Christ. The soul of Christ was the genuine subject of his sufferings. This affirmation of the soul of Christ is what led Eustathius, as we have suggested, to the new Logos-anthropos framework. In stressing the distinction and completeness of the two natures, however, the tradition following Eustathius had to face the challenge of whether

[39]Ibid., 110.

[40]Grillmeier, *Christ in Christian Tradition,* 296–301.

it could maintain a union of the two natures that did justice to Christ's being one person. Antiochene Christology developed over against the Arian and later Apollinarian Logos-sarx pattern. And to preserve the humanity of Jesus, it stressed the distinction of the two natures.

If we could study the legacy of Eustathius in greater detail, we would next consider Diodore of Tarsus, a native of Antioch who became bishop of Tarsus in 378 and followed in the Antiochene tradition as an opponent of Apollinarianism. John Chrysostom and Theodore of Mopsuestia were both his pupils. Instead we will move directly to these two great theologians of the Antiochene school.

John Chrysostom (ca. 347–407). Born at Antioch of a Christian family, John Chrysostom studied theology at the school in Antioch under Diodore of Tarsus. He lived an ascetical and eremetical life for four years according to the Pachomian Rule, was ordained a deacon in 381 and priest in 386, and was given the special task by his bishop to devote himself to preaching, for which he became famous and which gave him the name Chrysostom (golden-mouthed). During these twelve years of preaching, from 386 to 398, he delivered his expository homilies on many of the books of the Bible. In 398, against his wish, he was consecrated as Patriarch of Constantinople and the Antioch years came to an end.

The Constantinople years were filled with trouble. His efforts toward reform met with resistance; clergy, fellow bishops, Empress Eudoxia, and Theophilus, the Patriarch of Alexandria, were among the opposition. The Synod at the Oak (403), packed by Theophilus with twenty-nine Egyptian bishops out of a total of thirty-six, deposed the Patriarch of Constantinople, who was exiled but recalled the next day. The following year, 404, despite the opposition of the people of Constantinople and the Western Church, including Pope Innocent I, John was exiled again. After three years his exile ended in his death.

Chrysostom was not so much a theologian as he was a preacher, pastor, and reformer. Like Athanasius, his inclination was not speculative. Yet he came to be considered one of the four greatest Fathers of the ancient Greek Church (the other three being Basil, Gregory Nazianzen, and Athanasius). He left the Church more writings than any of the Greek Fathers, including his well-known

On the Priesthood; 236 letters from the period of exile and an extensive collection of sermons—exegetical homilies on books of both the Old and New Testaments, mainly from the Antiochene period; a series of homilies on the nature of God directed against post-Nicene radical Arians, the Anomoeans; and eight homilies against the Jews who were still a significant group in late fourth-century Antioch. Chrysostom's ninety homilies on Matthew are the oldest complete commentary on Matthew to survive.

We do not include Chrysostom here because he typified "Antiochene Christology" but because he was a great Antiochene theologian. Yet there are respects in which Chrysostom was "Antiochene" in his Christology. He distinguished words for nature *(ousia* or *physis)* from words for person *(hypostasis* or *prosōpon).* He used the Nicene *homoousios* for the relation between Father and Son, although other expressions such as "equal to the Father" are more frequent. He acknowledged the divinity of Christ against the Arians and the complete humanity of Christ against the Apollinarians. He affirmed two natures in Christ, the Antiochene Dyophysitism. Yet there was one Christ. He did not speculate about the nature of this union: "By a union and conjoining, God, the Word, and the flesh are one, not by any confusion or obliteration of substances but by a certain union ineffable and past understanding. Ask not how" (Homily 11, on John 1:14). This quotation reflects as well a certain "Alexandrian" way of speaking in its use of Logos-sarx terminology. Chrysostom was Antiochene, however, in his literal, in contrast to allegorical, interpretation of Scripture.

Theodore of Mopsuestia (352–428). Born in Antioch, Theodore was converted to Christianity in 368, studied in the school of Diodore of Tarsus, was ordained a priest about 383, and became bishop of Mopsuestia in Cilicia in 392. Johannes Quasten writes, "Theodore is the most typical representative of the Antiochene school of exegesis and by far its most famous author."[41] Theodore commented on almost all the books of the Bible, rejected the allegorical method of interpretation, and became known in the Syrian Church as the Interpreter. There has been a greatly renewed interest in Theodorian studies today, partly stimulated by the recent discoveries of his *Catechetical Homilies* in 1932 and

[41]Quasten, *Patrology,* vol. 3, 402.

his *Commentary on John,* published in 1940.[42] Theodore's significant *De incarnatione* was discovered in 1905 but was lost again during World War I before it could be published. Among other works, Theodore also wrote *Against the Allegorists,* directed against Origen.

The exegesis of Antioch, of which Theodore was a supreme exemplification, rejected the Alexandrian and Origenist methods. At times the Antiochenes and Theodore have been called Aristotelian in contrast to the Middle Platonism and Neoplatonism of the Alexandrians. This is only partially true. Even though Antioch was not a center of Neoplatonic thought, there was still Neoplatonic influence there. Theodore was not Aristotelian in the sense of being explicitly opposed to Platonism, nor in the sense of the philosophical content of his thought, but rather in the sense of methodology or method of exegesis. He was realistic and philological.

Theodore's reputation in his lifetime was that of a learned and orthodox theologian. Unfortunately that reputation suffered a severe setback a century after his death. After the condemnation of Nestorius in 431 (Council of Ephesus) and even during Cyril's attack on Nestorius, some began to read Nestorianism into Theodore. At the Council of Chalcedon (451) Theodore was still considered a theologian in good standing, but he gradually gained the false reputation of being a Nestorian before Nestorius. Nestorius had been a student of Theodore's. At the Second Council of Constantinople, the fifth general council of the Church, in 553, over a century after his death, Theodore was condemned as a Nestorian. A contributing factor was Theodore's opposition to Origenism. Some followers of Origen blamed the Antiochenes for

[42]The *Catechetical Homilies* were discovered and published with an English translation by A. Mingana. *Commentary of Theodore of Mopsuestia on the Nicene Creed* (Cambridge: W. Heffer and Sons, 1932) Woodbrooke Studies 5; and *Commentary of Theodore of Mopsuestia on the Lord's Prayer and on the Sacraments of Baptism and the Eucharist* (Cambridge: W. Heffer and Sons, 1933) Woodbrooke Studies 6. The commentary on John was published with a Latin translation by J. M. Vosté, *Theodori Mopsuesteni Commentarius in evangelium Johannis Apostoli,* Corpus Scriptorum Christianorum Orientalium 115-116 (Louvain, 1940). Also see J. M. Vosté, O.P., "Le Commentaire de Théodore de Mopsueste sur Saint Jean, d'après la version syriaque," *Revue biblique* 32 (1923) 522-551; and "La Chronologie de l'activité litteraire de Théodore de Mopsueste," *Revue biblique* 34 (1925) 54-81. Also J. L. McKenzie, "The Commentary of Theodore of Mopsuestia on John 1:46-51," *Theological Studies* 14 (1953) 73-84.

the condemnation of some of Origen's opinions in 543. The condemnation of Theodore was practically a political quid pro quo manifesting the continuing tension between Alexandria and Antioch into the sixth century. Today, however, with the recently discovered works of Theodore, interest has been renewed and his orthodoxy defended, although the debate over Theodore continues. We consider him here as an aid to understanding "Antiochene Christology."

As we begin a discussion of Theodore's Christology, it is helpful to consider his theological anthropology as well, since the two are closely linked.[43] Theodore's doctrine on the nature of the soul was more Neoplatonic than Aristotelian. Yet, unlike the Platonist, he did not view reason as a contemplative faculty. Reason was rather associated with the practical realm and moral conduct. Rationality is essentially related to the capacity for choice. There was a practical and ethical cast to Theodore's concerns, in which the will played a central role.

In his understanding of the human person as the image of God, this practicality and realism manifested itself. Theodore did not develop any doctrine of divinization. The soul is a creature far removed in its nature from God. The human person is only like the Creator, a resemblance or reminder of the Creator. And this resemblance is most evident when one's will is in harmony with God's will. There the union between God and the human person is not a result of the soul's participation in the divine nature (Neoplatonic) but rather a moral union effected through obedience to God. The human person as the image of God is the human per-

---

[43] Cf. R. A. Norris, *Manhood and Christ: A Study in the Christology of Theodore of Mopsuestia* (Oxford: Clarendon, 1963). Also, Joanne Dewart, *The Theology of Grace of Theodore of Mopsuestia* (Washington: The Catholic University of America Press, 1971). Also see Milton V. Anastos, "The Immutability of Christ and Justinian's Condemnation of Theodore of Mopsuestia," *Dumbarton Oaks Papers* 6 (Cambridge: Harvard University Press, 1951) 125-160; P. Galtier, "Théodore de Mopsueste: sa vraie pensée sur l'Incarnation," *Recherches de Science Religieuse* 45 (1957) 161-186; John L. McKenzie, "A New Study of Theodore of Mopsuestia," *Theological Studies* 10 (1949) 394-408, and "Annotations on the Christology of Theodore of Mopsuestia," *Theological Studies* 19 (1958) 345-373; Kevin McNamara, "The Problem of Theodore of Mopsuestia," *Irish Theological Quarterly* 24 (1957) 175-184; Alphonse Mingana, "Synopsis of Christian Doctrine in the Fourth Century According to Theodore of Mopsuestia," *Bulletin of the John Rylands Library* 5 (1919) 296-316; and John S. Romanides, "Highlights in the Debate Over Theodore of Mopsuestia's Christology and Some Suggestions for a Fresh Approach," *Greek Orthodox Theological Review* 5 (1959/1960) 140-185.

son at one with the will of God. This oneness is a moral union or union of the wills, which is the highest kind of union between creature and Creator. Even Theodore's understanding of sin makes this point clear: Sin is the consequence of a rebellious will, not the Augustinian inherited and defective nature but voluntary disobedience.

One of Theodore's major contributions to the history of Christology was his insistence on the full humanity of Christ, a hallmark and strength of the Antiochene tradition. In this he was a critic of Logos-sarx Christology and its most exaggerated representatives, Arius and Apollinaris. Theodore insisted on the reality of Christ's human soul; to deny a human soul to Christ is to deny his full human nature.

> It is, therefore, great madness not to believe that Christ assumed the soul; and he would even be madder who would say that [Christ] did not assume human mind, because such a one would imply that He either did not assume the soul or that He did assume the soul not of man but an irrational one akin to that of animals and beasts. . . .
>
> Because of all this our blessed Fathers warned us and said: "He was incarnate and became a man," so that we should believe that the one who was assumed and in whom God the Word dwelt was a complete man, perfect in everything that belongs to human nature, and composed of a mortal body and a rational soul, because it is for man and for his salvation that He came down from heaven.[44]

Theodore not only affirmed with clarity the reality of Christ's human soul, he clearly recognized the theological significance of it, something that had not been accomplished by the Alexandrians, not even by Athanasius or the pre-Ephesene Cyril. The human soul is the life-giving principle for the body of Christ. Also, the human soul with its inclination to sin must have been assumed in order for it to have been redeemed. Here we see not only Theodore's anthropology with its emphasis upon the human will and its role in sin but also the patristic principle that what is not assumed is not saved. Redemption then involves in some sense or to some degree Christ's human decision, obedience, and will.

[44]A. Mingana, ed., *On the Nicene Creed,* Woodbrooke Studies 5, pp. 58–59.

Theodore's theology of the humanity of Christ and his theological anthropology, which insisted that the soul of Christ actually functioned, along with his opposition to both Arianism and Apollinarianism, provided the basis for the Antiochene insistence on two natures in Christ. Against the Arians and particularly Eunomius, Theodore affirmed the full divinity of the Logos and of Jesus Christ; against the Apollinarians he affirmed the complete humanity of Christ. Thus anything other than a two-nature, dyophysite way of speaking would seem heretical for the Antiochenes.

> He is not God alone nor man alone, but He is truly both by nature, that is to say God and man: God the Word who assumed, and man who was assumed. It is the one who was in the form of God that took upon Him the form of a servant, and it is not the form of a servant that took upon it the form of God. The one who is in the form of God is God by nature, who assumed the form of a servant, while the one who is in the form of a servant is the one who is man by nature and who was assumed for our salvation.[45]

An implication of this duality in Christ manifested itself in Theodore's exegesis of the sayings of Christ and in a way of speaking that was a contrast to the Alexandrian based *communicatio idiomatum*. For Theodore, certain sayings of Christ or about him pertained to his humanity and others to his divinity. Did this loosen the bond between the two natures too much? Would the appreciation of the duality that Christ is create a problem for appreciating the unity that Christ also is? Has the Christological duality become a Christological dualism? Did the twofold attribution of the sayings of Christ indicate two subjects (or persons) in Christ? All of these were sensitive issues for the Alexandrians. And Theodore's way of speaking justified asking the questions: Some of Christ's sayings in the Scriptures were the human Jesus speaking and others the divine Jesus. The saying, "I cannot do anything of myself," is not fittingly applied to the divine nature; it is rather to be attributed to the human nature.[46] Today exege-

---

[45]Ibid., 82.

[46]Vosté, ed., *Commentary on the Gospel of John,* pp. 85–87 of Latin translation, comment on John 5:30.

sis tends to make the distinction between the pre-Easter or earthly Jesus and the post-Easter Jesus or Church, but this interpretative approach proceeds from a modern historical consciousness that was not Theodore's milieu. This Theodorian way of speaking made sense of the text, but did it do justice to the reality that Christ is one person? Does it deny the *communicatio idiomatum?*

Another characteristic way of speaking that aggravated the dilemma was a distinction Theodore made between the Son or Word and "the assumed man," a way of speaking almost equivalent for Theodore to the language of two natures, but it almost suggested that the two natures are two persons or subjects. Each nature had already become a distinguishable subject of attribution with respect to the sayings. Theodore wrote in his commentary on the Psalms, "How is it not plain that the divine Scripture clearly teaches us that God the Word is one thing, and the man another, and that it shows us the great difference between them?"[47] Theodore seems not to have been aware of a distinction between the abstract and the concrete, between the nature and the person. Do two natures imply two persons? We cannot expect a Chalcedonian way of speaking from Theodore any more than we can expect a Nicene theology in the pre-Nicene Church. Yet the question about Theodore's understanding of the unity in Christ is important. Of his insistence on the duality there is no question.

The strength of the Antiochene Logos-anthropos framework (two natures) also became its weakness (two persons?), just as the strength of the Alexandrian Logos-sarx framework (the unity of one person) had been its weakness (a less than complete humanity). A final resolution had not yet been achieved in the first half of the fifth century. Certainly among the Alexandrians, Theodore's language would sound like the theology of Paul of Samosata; yet Theodore was far from Paul. His language, different from that of the Alexandrians, spoke in terms of indwelling and *prosōpon* (person).

For Theodore, the coming together of the two natures in Christ was not a mixture *(krasis),* as if two substances are mixed to form a *tertium quid* (a third reality, intermediate, neither divine nor

---

[47]Robert Devreesse, ed., Theodore of Mopsuestia, *Le Commentaire sur les psaumes* (Cittá del Vaticano, 1939) on Ps 8, p. 46. Translation from Norris, *Manhood and Christ,* 199.

human), but a union *(henōsis)*. But this union was conceived along the lines of an indwelling or inhabitation. The Word for Theodore not only became flesh (John 1:14) but "dwelt among us." Thus the evangelist himself interpreted himself: the Word came to dwell on earth within a human being. The relationship between the Word and the humanity of Jesus was one of indwelling.

Divine indwelling is also the more general or ordinary way in which human beings are united to God. God's nearness affects the disposition of our wills. It facilitates a union, a moral union, a union of wills between us and God. Yet the indwelling that Christ is cannot be seen as simply one instance among others. The divine indwelling in Christ is unique.

> When, then, he is said to dwell in either the apostles or just men generally, he makes his indwelling as taking pleasure in men who are just. . . . But we do not say that the indwelling took place in this manner in him [Christ]—for never would we so rave—but so as in a son. For it is in this way that he took pleasure [in him] and indwelt [him]. But what is meant by "as in a son"? It means that in coming to indwell, he united the assumed [Man] as a whole to himself, and made him to share with him in all the dignity in which he who indwells, being Son by nature, participates: so as to be counted one prosopon according to the union with him, and to share with him all his dominion; and thus to work everything in him. . . ."[48]

One must distinguish between what constitutes the union and the consequences of that union. That which constitutes the union is the Word or Son's assumption of the one assumed to itself, and the assumed one's sharing in the divine life. The consequence of this union is *one prosōpon*. R. A. Norris comments on the above passage.

> Theodore simply asserts that in the case of Christ, the indwelling is a *union* of the Word and the Man. *He does not allude to the idea of "co-operation" as in any sense constitutive of this union.* What is to the fore here is not any mutual or recipro-

"H. B. Swete, ed., *Theodore of Mopsuestia, In Epistolas B. Pauli Commentarii,* The Latin Version with the Greek Fragments (Cambridge: University Press, 1882) 2:295-296. Translation from Norris, *Manhood and Christ,* 221.

cal action of God and the Man, but simply the action of the divine Son, who himself, by the disposition of his will, unites the human nature to himself. It is this fact which, as Theodore sees it, distinguishes the divine indwelling in Christ from other instances of his indwelling. The union is logically prior both to the prosopic unity which it effects, and to the sort of co-operation to which, as we have seen, Theodore alludes in other passages.[49]

From the perspective of the Word, the union is a freely chosen "condescension"; from the perspective of the one assumed, it is an elevating grace. The Word is the active agent in the union, the human nature the recipient of all the dignity. The union is the voluntary indwelling of the Son, who takes the human nature to himself. This union takes place at the beginning of Jesus' life. "For he had straightway from the beginning, in his formation in the womb, union with him."[50] Norris comments, "His [Theodore's] contention is not that the union itself is progressively realized; but rather that the fact of the union is necessarily manifested in different ways and to different degrees as the assumed Man grows from childhood, to manhood, to a new and immortal life."[51]

> . . . God the Word came to be in him when he had been formed. For he was not only in him as he ascended into heaven, but also as he rose from the dead. . . . Nor was he in him only as he rose from the dead, but also as he was crucified and baptized, and as he was living the evangelical life after his baptism: and also even before his baptism, as he was fulfilling the requirement of the law. . . . Moreover he was in him even as he was being born, and when he was in his mother's womb, straightway from his first formation. For he imposed an order on the things which concerned him, bringing him to perfection step by step.[52]

[49]Norris, *Manhood and Christ*, 222.

[50]Swete, *Theodore of Mopsuestia*, 2:296. Translation from Norris, *Manhood and Christ*, 224.

[51]Norris, *Manhood and Christ*, 224.

[52]Swete, *Theodore of Mopsuestia*, 2:314. Translation from Norris, *Manhood and Christ*, 225.

From what has been said, we can see that the union in Christ of the two natures was *not* for Theodore a merely moral union of wills, a concern so central to his anthropology and something of which he has been falsely accused. The divine condescension took the initiative from the start and dwelled in this human being. This is incarnational, not Adoptionist. The activity of the Word constitutes the union; the moral union of wills is a consequence or effect of the union. The union is not merely moral. The moral union is an effect of the incarnation, not the cause of it. The "grace of union" makes the perfect moral union of wills possible as Christ lives perfect obedience throughout his life.[53]

To speak of a moral union is necessary for Theodore; it is an aspect of the full humanity of Jesus, the union of the human will with the divine will. But this effect cannot be confused with the cause. "Theodore distinguishes between the union once for all effected, and the cooperation of the Word with the Man: they are two distinct phases of the relationship between the natures."[54] The grace of union, the divine condescension, is both the presupposition of and prior to the moral cooperation of the human being and God. Whether or not there are two "subjects" in Christ, there is but one cause of the union. This union is a divine indwelling similar to but surpassing any other creature's union with God, for it is the action of the Word assuming this one human being to itself from the beginning of his coming-to-be. This union resulted in both a moral perfection and in a common *prosōpon*. More must now be said about this "prosopal unity." Although the word *prosōpon* was the common Antiochene word for "person," it is better to come to its meaning without translating it, as is true of the expression "hypostatic union" as well. *Prosōpon* for Theodore did not mean the same thing as *hypostasis* did for Cyril, nor does either mean what we moderns mean by "person."

Whatever else may be said of Theodore's Christology, it must be said that he intended to teach the unity of Christ as clearly as he did the duality of natures.

> In their profession of faith our blessed Fathers (at Nicea) wrote
> . . . they followed the Sacred Books which speak differently

[53]Dewart, *The Theology of Grace of Theodore of Mopsuestia*, 77-86.

[54]Norris, *Manhood and Christ*, 226.

of natures while referring (them) to one *prosōpon* on account of the close union that took place between them, so that they might not be believed that they were separating the perfect union between the one who was assumed and the one who assumed. If this union were destroyed the one who was assumed would not be seen more than a mere man like ourselves.[55]

And also:

We should also be mindful of that inseparable union through which that form of man can never and under no circumstances be separated from the Divine nature which put it on. The distinction between the natures does not annul the close union nor does the close union destroy the distinction between the natures, but the natures remain in their respective existence while separated, and the union remains intact, because the one who was assumed is united in honor and glory with the one who assumed according to the will of the one who assumed him.

From the fact that we say two natures we are not constrained to say two Lords nor two sons; this would be extreme folly. All things that in one respect are two and in another respect one, their union through which they are one does not annul the distinction between the natures, and the distinction between the natures impedes them from being one.[56]

The word *prosōpon* here ought not be seen as an ontological equivalent of what *hypostasis* will mean for Chalcedon; it is not, strictly speaking, an ontological meaning of the word but rather speaks of the countenance or appearance or mask. This *prosōpon,* which is a result of the union, is not a mixture, as we have seen, not a third thing in addition to the two natures, but rather simply an effect of the union, not a kind of union in itself (as hypostatic union will later imply) but rather the outward manifestation of the underlying unity already there. There is only one *prosōpon* for Theodore. In the genuine works of Theodore there is no teaching about two *prosōpa* and a third common one. Such references come only from doubtful fragments.[57] The one *prosōpon* is not

[55]Mingana, ed., *On the Nicene Creed,* 63–64.

[56]Ibid., 89–90.

[57]Cf. Grillmeier, *Christ in Christian Tradition,* 432.

the metaphysical union but its outward presentation. The one *prosōpon* is a result of the Logos' one divine *prosōpon* permeating and shaping Jesus. The union that gives rise to the one *prosōpon* is achieved through the subordination of the humanity of Jesus to the Word and the predominance of the Word in and through the humanity. The one *prosōpon* is the expression or manifestation of the union, not the union itself. Thus prosopal unity is not the same as the hypostatic union, but neither does the former deny the latter. Theodore is expressing a unity of appearance, a united front, in his terminology; the underlying substantial unity is the Word's indwelling.

We do not yet have the distinction between *physis* and *hypostasis,* which will follow upon Chalcedon. At Alexandria both words were still closely related, thus one *hypostasis* implied one *physis.* In Antioch both words were also closely related but in reverse, two *physeis* implied two *hypostaseis.* Theodore used the word *hypostasis,* but it was not his way of expressing the union or the unity. The word *hypostasis* was ultimately derived from Apollinaris, who introduced it into Christological discussion. Yet Theodore used it in his own way. And ordinarily, with one possible exception,[58] it was related to *physis.* Thus *physis* and *hypostasis* are two in Theodore, *prosōpon* one, and *prosōpon* does not mean a substantial union, which (in contrast to an accidental union) Theodore accepted but expressed through the language of indwelling.

Theodore did not deny the title *theotokos* to Mary—a step which Nestorius took and which went one step too far for the Alexandrians. Theodore asked: "Is Mary the mother of God or the mother of man?" His answer: both. "She is the mother of man by nature, since what was in the womb of Mary was a man. . . . But she is the mother of God, since God was in the man who was born, not confined within him by nature, but in him by the disposition of the will."[59]

---

[58]Grillmeier, *Christ in Christian Tradition,* 438–449. There is a text from Theodore's *De incarnatione* that says that "both the natures are a single *prosōpon* and *hypostasis."* Yet there are doubts about the authenticity of the expression, since elsewhere he distinguishes *prosōpon* and *hypostasis* and relates *hypostasis* to *physis.*

[59]Swete, *Theodore of Mopsuestia,* 2:310. Translation from Norris, *Manhood and Christ,* 215.

In Christ, then, we have both the profound union, in which the Word united the assumed man to itself by indwelling it, and a moral union, which is an effect of this. Christ was unique for Theodore in both ways—in the grace of the union, and in the abundance of graces during his lifetime, which were a consequence of that union and the perfection of a moral union. The moral union is not to be dismissed. Given Theodore's anthropology, however, it is important to note that he did not try to explain Christ in terms of moral union alone, an approach that would have flowed easily from his morally directed anthropology. Yet there was a source for his Christology in addition to his anthropology, and there was a union in Christ other than the moral union.

Theodore's understanding of the sinlessness of Christ was distinctive. Christ was sinless for Theodore, but his sinlessness was not an *impeccabilitas* (inability to sin) but an *impeccantia* (the reality of not having sinned). It was possible for Christ to sin, although he did not. This is to be expected in one who was careful not to diminish the full humanity of Jesus, who saw a theological significance in Christ's soul, and who emphasized moral freedom as a central element in human nature. Christ had a human will of his own and his struggle was real.

It is difficult to assess Theodore's Christology. We cannot expect his language to be that of Chalcedon. We cannot expect in him the distinction between *physis* and *hypostasis* still to come. He saw Christ as one in two natures. The oneness was more profound than a moral union and antecedent to it. The oneness manifested itself in one *prosōpon*. He was not Nestorian and in that sense was wrongly judged, whatever inadequacy may be found in his Christology. He did not perceive the deeply ontological character of the union, but he was primarily an exegete and not a philosophical theologian. Yet his Logos-anthropos framework provided a needed alternative to the deficiencies of the Logos-sarx framework. There could have been no Chalcedon without his theology. More than any other, he saw theological significance in the soul of Christ and appreciated more thoroughly the full humanity of Christ.

Nestorius (d. ca. 451). Having studied theology at Antioch, probably under Theodore of Mopsuestia, Nestorius later became famous for preaching. In 428, the emperor, Theodosius II, chose him to be Patriarch of Constantinople, a position that John Chrysostom had earlier filled. As Patriarch of Constantinople, he became the political rival of Cyril, who had become Patriarch of Alexandria in 412. The ensuing conflict ended with Nestorius' deposition by the Council of Ephesus in 431. More will be said of the conflict when we discuss that council in the next chapter.

Nestorius wrote many works but little remains. In 435 Theodosius II ordered his writings burned. The *Bazaar of Heraclides,* written after the Council of Ephesus, discovered in 1895, is the only work extant in its entirety, and it has led to a revival of Nestorian studies. After the Council of Ephesus there gradually emerged a Nestorian Church which has existed until the present day; its liturgical language is Syriac.

A major issue in Nestorian studies today is whether Nestorius was a "Nestorian."[60] Nestorianism, as a heresy, as it has come to be classically defined, was the result of conflict, polemic, and politics as well as doctrine. Was Nestorius himself and his theology rightly understood? Did he truly teach what we have come to identify as Nestorianism, or was the latter a false product of the Antiochene and Constantinopolitan conflict with Alexandria? What did Nestorius himself hold? R. V. Sellers writes, "From all this it seems clear that Nestorius is hardly deserving of the title 'Nestorian'; and that this is a legitimate conclusion is borne out by statements of his which show that for him Jesus Christ is very God incarnate."[61]

The conflict was precipitated over the use of the title *theotokos* (the Godbearer, mother of God) with reference to Mary. When Nestorius became bishop, the title was already being disputed; Nestorius got himself drawn into the conflict. He attempted a middle position between those who called Mary *theotokos* and those who called her *anthrōpotokos.* He suggested the expression *christotokos* (mother of Christ) since it implied both God and humanity. To the Antiochenes, who were consciously protective of the humanity of Christ, the title *theotokos* could imply Apollinari-

---

[60]See Grillmeier, *Christ in Christian Tradition,* 447–472; F. Loofs, *Nestorius and His Place in the History of Christian Doctrine* (Cambridge: University Press, 1914); G. L. Prestige, *Fathers and Heretics* (London: S.P.C.K., 1977) 120–149; R. V. Sellers, *Two Ancient Christologies* (London: S.P.C.K., 1954).

[61]Sellers, *Two Ancient Christologies,* 164.

anism. The Apollinarians remained an enemy of Nestorius as well, and Nestorius even saw the early Cyril as Apollinarian in his theology. Throughout the conflict Nestorius felt that he was defending orthodoxy and opposing Apollinarianism. To deny the title *theotokos* of Mary, however, would imply for the Alexandrians either a denial of the divinity of Christ or a denial of the unity of his person, which was in fact the basis for the *communicatio idiomatum* and proper worship of Christ. Unresolved issues and different theological concerns surfaced around the title *theotokos,* which is a proper description of Mary according to the unity of person in Christ and the *communicatio idiomatum.* To reject or call into question the *communicatio* was to question the whole way of speaking about Christ that had developed in the tradition of the Church.

Nestorius' theology, as Antiochene theology in general, was less a theology of the Logos than it was a theology of the humanity of Christ and the two natures. Alexandrian Logos theology rightly perceived the unity of Christ on the basis of its "preoccupation" with the Logos. Antiochene *anthrōpos* theology rightly perceived the duality of Christ on the basis of its concern for his humanity. The problem was still not resolved as to how Christ could be both *one* and *two.*

Nestorius spoke less frequently of the Logos, and preferred to speak of Christ, Son, or Lord; these seemed to do more justice to the two natures. Referring to the Nicene creed, Nestorius wrote, "Notice how by putting 'Christ,' the indication of the two natures, (the Nicene Fathers) did not first of all say, 'We believe in the one God-Logos,' but chose a name which describes the two."[62] Nestorius preferred the word "Christ." Yet the use of the word "Christ" was a way of avoiding the problem; it was a superficial solution. What or whom does the word "Christ" represent? For Nestorius it was the two natures. "Christ" was simply "the common name of the two natures."[63]

Yet Nestorius did recognize one subject in the incarnation, even though his concerns and language drew one in the direction of duality. Nestorius did not teach a doctrine of two persons in

[62]F. Loofs, ed., *Nestoriana, Die Fragmente des Nestorius* (Halle: Max Niemeyer, 1905) 295; translation from Grillmeier, *Christ in Christian Tradition,* 454.

[63]Ibid., 175; Grillmeier, 454.

Christ; in that sense he was not Nestorian as the Nestorian heresy came to be understood. Nestorius, in a sermon preached in 430, said, "I did not say that the Son was one [person] and God the Word another; I said God the Word was by nature one and the temple by nature another, one Son by conjunction."[64] Note the Antiochene language of indwelling as in a temple and the concern with the two natures. Yet Nestorius proclaimed the unity of Christ: one Son. And elsewhere: "Even before the incarnation the God-Logos was Son and God and together with the Father, but in the last times he took the form of a servant; but as already previously he was a Son both in name and in nature, he cannot be called a separate Son after taking this form, otherwise we would be decreeing two sons."[65]

Nestorius, like Theodore, used *hypostasis* in connection with *physis:* they were not yet distinguished. *Hypostasis* connoted the concreteness and reality of the nature. One can thus speak about the hypostasis of the human nature. And, as in Theodore, there was also a unity of *prosōpon,* which must be understood more in the Theodorean than in the Chalcedonian sense of personal unity. Unlike Theodore, however, Nestorius rarely used *henōsis* to describe the union of the natures; he preferred *synapheia* (*coniunctio* or conjunction). Perhaps the latter expression loosened the bond to an even greater extent. Although Nestorius saw only one Christ and not two persons, he was not able to explicate the unity adequately. It was not clear whether *synapheia* was a truly substantial union or only an accidental one. The word *prosōpon* did not solve this dilemma, for this was not the basis of the union but its effect. It signified the oneness of appearance, the collective characteristics, all the properties, the manifestation rather than actualization of the unity. Each nature had its *prosōpon,* and there was also the *prosōpon* of the union, but this did not mean that there was more than one subject in Christ. Neither the moral union nor the prosopal unity was the ultimate basis of the oneness in Christ for Nestorius.

Nestorius' Christology was pre-Chalcedonian at this point, but so was Cyril's. Nestorius' intent was orthodox, his enemies were the Arians and Apollinarians, his framework was Antiochene, and

---

[64]Ibid., 308; Grillmeier, 455.
[65]Ibid., 275; Grillmeier, 455.

his problem was the willingness to question the appropriateness of the *theotokos* title. His questioning it, however, did not imply what his opponents interpreted it to mean—two persons in Christ, only a moral union, or a denial of Christ's full divinity. But we will leave the rest of the story until we come to Cyril and the Council of Ephesus in the next chapter.

A Concluding Theological Reflection

What can be said by way of conclusion about the development of Christology from the second to the fifth centuries, especially as it developed along the lines of different emphases *(Logos-sarx* and *Logos-anthrōpos)* and in different centers (Alexandria and Antioch)?

Both the Alexandrian and Antiochene theological traditions were balanced efforts to articulate the mystery of Jesus Christ. At their best neither represented the extreme to which they were sometimes forced. The vulnerable point for the Alexandrians was whether they could sustain the unity of the two natures in Christ without confusing or impairing them, and for the Antiochenes whether they could distinguish the two natures without dividing the person of Christ into two. Yet, as R. V. Sellers has argued, it seems that among their ablest representatives (Athanasius, Cyril, Theodore, Nestorius) basic orthodoxy prevailed—an awareness that Christ was one person in two natures—although their frameworks were not yet nor could not have been Chalcedonian. In other words, the theologies and emphases of the two schools were complementary, not antagonistic, and they simply needed to be joined to form a more theologically satisfying Christology. There could have been no Chalcedon without both the Antiochene duality and the Alexandrian unity. Sellers may be overstating the case when he concludes "that there is no fundamental difference between the Christological teaching of the Alexandrines and that of the Antiochenes,"[66] but he has moved us in a correct direction. The theological tension between the two was not that of two contradictory positions but rather of an unresolved complementarity.

66Sellers, *Two Ancient Christologies,* 202.

These two complementary theological traditions of the Greek East manifested the three principles that we have observed in the history of Christology: diversification, individualization, and consolidation. Egypt, Palestine, Syria, and Asia Minor: one Jesus Christ, diverse cultural settings; one faith, diverse Christologies. And not only diversity, but also individuality: The late Cyril cannot be reduced to Athanasius, nor Apollinaris to Arius, nor Origen to Clement; nor can Theodore be equated with Nestorius, nor either of them with Chrysostom, nor any of them with Paul of Samosata. But at work within the stream that led to diversity and individuality was also the drive toward the reconciliation of tensions, the joining of that which complements, the emergence of catholicity, the consolidation of a theology that had been pushed to a deeper level of insight. This consolidating tendency to save diverse and individual theologies for the church catholic was most operative in the great councils: Nicea, Constantinople, Ephesus, Chalcedon, to which we will turn in chapter four. Each council, however, was not simply a leap forward in consolidation but was also a new beginning for ongoing diversification. Councils do not arrest theology; they give theology new starting points.

In our brief survey of Alexandria and Antioch, we have learned several things about God and our salvation. Both traditions denied a theology of the transcendence of God that removed God completely from presence in the world. Transcendence does not mean an unbridgeable gulf between God and world. God is not *totally* other; God is manifestly present or near. Also, although both traditions gave witness to God-in-Christ, and both saw Christ as the incarnation of the Logos of God or the intensification of the Logos' activity in history, neither reduced the activity of the Logos or confined it to the earthly activity of Jesus Christ. In other words, there was more to the history of the Logos than its "earthly Jesus phase," and this was true even during the earthly phase of Jesus' life. While incarnate, the Logos was not confined or limited to the locus of the incarnation. The Logos remained omnipresent even during its incarnational presence.

Sellers derived two foundational principles on which both Alexandria and Antioch would agree. These two principles and these two schools thus provided the foundational work on which Chalcedon would build. First, "In Jesus Christ, the Logos, while remaining what He was, has, for our salvation, united manhood to Himself, thereby making it His own; He is not, therefore, two Persons, but one Person, the Logos Himself in His incarnate state."[67] Second, "In Jesus Christ, the two elements, each with its properties, are to be recognized; therefore, since these remain in their union in His Person, any idea of confusion or of change in respect of these elements must be eliminated."[68]

In our discussion of these two traditions, we have concerned ourselves primarily with their theological content rather than with their socio-political and personal contexts. If we were to take more time to survey the latter, we would see therein the basis for the antagonism between the two centers. Although their theologies were complementary and not antagonistic, theology cannot be abstracted from its historical setting. The personalities of Cyril and Nestorius as well as the politics of power between Alexandria and Constantinople account for much of the direction of history. Neither the Cyrillians nor the Nestorians wanted to understand the other's position. There were other agenda at work as well. They thus misinterpreted each other's language.

It must be admitted that the prestige of the ancient sees and their patriarchs was at stake as well as fidelity to the Catholic tradition. At the Council of Nicea, the Church had passed from a pre-Constantinian, persecuted Church to a Constantinian Church and imperial theology. Theology was now clearly a political concern as well. It had ramifications for the Empire. It was an emperor's concern. At Nicea, the canons of the council had indicated a ranking of the Christian sees with the order of Rome, Alexandria, and Antioch. Alexandria manifested a supremacy in the East. At the Council of Constantinople in 381, however, there was a twofold blow for Alexandria. First, Apollinaris had been condemned, although bishop of Laodicea, an Alexandrian in his theology. And second, not to be discounted, Constantinople was ranked among the sees after Rome and before Alexandria, since it had become the new Rome with Constantine's move of the capital from Rome to Constantinople. Constantinople had become a new kind of rival to Alexandria in the East. To a great degree, the next great council, at Ephesus in 431, was Alexandria's strike back, for it felled Antiochene theology and the bishop of Con-

⁶⁷Ibid., 243.
⁶⁸Ibid., 253.

stantinople. There was much at stake in Cyril's dispute with Nestorius, and Cyril was determined to maintain the ancient see associated with St. Mark as supreme.

Let us look back briefly at this history of pre-Chalcedonian Christology and take note of some of its insights.

Christology responds to the need for intellectual clarity as well as pastoral applicability. Sometimes it is pulled in a more learned, philosophical, or speculative direction, sometimes in a more mystical or spiritual direction, and sometimes in a practical pastoral direction, or some combination thereof.

God is transcendent and incomprehensible, and known only through the Word (or Logos). Thus, theology (the theology of God) is a theology of the Word/Logos. The theology of Jesus Christ came to be situated quite naturally in the context of this Logos theology. The Alexandrians in particular developed this theology of the Logos. It was one of their primary contributions to the history of Christian thought. For Clement, the Word became Son and also increasingly incarnate through creation, the prophets, and finally Jesus Christ.

In Origen the Logos was clearly eternal and divine but not yet equal to the Father. With Nicea and Athanasius, subordinationism came to an end and a Trinitarian orthodoxy emerged. The major contribution of Arius to theology was that the Church had been pushed to articulate more clearly its understanding of the Trinity—which it did through the Council of Nicea.

Apollinaris made explicit what had been unresolved in much of Alexandrian Christology, whether Jesus had a human soul and what purpose if any it served. Apollinaris denied Jesus a human soul and thus a fully human psyche, and thus made clear a weakness in those (Logos-sarx) Christologies that were predominantly theologies of the Logos. Antiochene Christology was more prominently a theology of the humanity of Jesus and a theological anthropology, but these (Logos-anthropos) Christologies also proved to be vulnerable. Their Achilles' heel was their less-satisfying theology of the union that Jesus Christ is—what the Alexandrians feared about Antioch and sensed in Nestorius' rejection of the title *theotokos* for Mary. The overarching orthodox model for interpreting the two-nature Christology of the Antiochenes was that of the divine indwelling. But could that satisfy the Alexandrian concern?

The persistent Alexandrian emphasis on the unity of *Jesus Christ as one* came to be expressed insightfully by Athanasius as "The Word was made human and did not come into a human." It was repeated by Cyril. To state it otherwise would imply a human being prior to the incarnation, which would exacerbate the problem of the unity and divinity of Jesus Christ. But is the nature of the unity of Christ something about which we ought to speculate anyway? Is it expressible? However one answers such a question, Christological language must still be confessionally responsible.

The development of Christology is inseparable from the development of theological language, and the capacity of language to articulate mystery. Christological language was not ready-made and there from the beginning. Origen used the word *homoousios* to express the relationship between the Son and the Father, and this same word was later used to express the Christian faith at Nicea. For Christology, the technical theological words which had their own cultural and historical meanings but which would eventuate as the language for expressing the historically developing Christian faith were *physis* and *hypostasis*. Apollinaris had already used both words, and much of Alexandrian and Antiochene theological history would be wrapped up with their development.

The difficulty of expressing the faith and mystery of Jesus Christ in human language is particularly evident in what is called the *communicatio idiomatum,* or communication of attributes or properties, which is a way of talking about Jesus Christ that shows the close relationship between faith and language. How can we talk about Jesus Christ in a way that does justice to our faith in him? To their credit, the Alexandrian tradition recognized the necessity of affirming one *hypostasis* (or *physis,* since these were practically synonymous for Alexandrians) in Christ; and to their credit, the Antiochene tradition recognized the necessity of affirming two *physeis* (or *hypostaseis,* since these were also practically synonymous even if understood differently from the Alexandrians) in Christ.

Human language never does full justice to the mystery of Jesus Christ. Yet, in looking back, we must admit that any articulation of that mystery ought to remain within the limits of Adoptionism and Docetism, or "Nestorianism" and Apollinarianism.

SUGGESTED READINGS

Bigg, C. *The Christian Platonists of Alexandria.* Oxford: Clarendon, 1913.

Crouzel, Henri. "The Literature on Origen, 1970–1988." *Theological Studies* 49 (1988) 499–516.

Daniélou, Jean. *Origen.* New York: Sheed and Ward, 1955.

——————. *Gospel Message and Hellenistic Culture.* Trans. John Austin Baker. Philadelphia: Westminster Press, 1973.

Dewart, Joanne. *The Theology of Grace of Theodore of Mopsuestia.* Washington: The Catholic University of America Press, 1971.

Greer, Rowan A. *Theodore of Mopsuestia, Exegete and Theologian.* London: The Faith Press, 1961.

Grillmeier, Aloys. *Christ in Christian Tradition: From the Apostolic Age to Chalcedon (AD 451).* Trans. John Bowden. Rev. ed. London: Mowbrays, 1975. The best history of Christology during the first five centuries.

Kannengiesser, C. "Arius and the Arians." *Theological Studies* 44 (1983) 456–475.

Kelly, J. N. D. *Early Christian Doctrines.* 2nd ed. New York: Harper & Row, 1960.

Lienhard, J. T. "Marcellus of Ancyra in Modern Research." *Theological Studies* 43 (1982) 486–503.

Lilla, S. R. C. *Clement of Alexandria: A Study in Christian Platonism and Gnosticism.* London: Oxford University Press, 1971.

Loofs, F. *Nestorius and His Place in the History of Christian Doctrine.* Cambridge: University Press, 1914.

Mingana, Alphonse. "Synopsis of Christian Doctrine in the Fourth Century According to Theodore of Mopsuestia." *Bulletin of the John Rylands Library* 5 (1919) 296–316.

Norris, R. A. *Manhood and Christ: A Study in the Christology of Theodore of Mopsuestia.* Oxford, Clarendon, 1963.

Prestige, G. L. *Fathers and Heretics.* London: S.P.C.K., 1977.

Richard, M. "L'introduction du mot 'hypostase' dans la théologie de l'incarnation." *Mélanges de Science Religieuse* 2 (1945) 5–32, 243–270.

Romanides, John S. "Highlights in the Debate Over Theodore of Mopsuestia's Christology and Some Suggestions for a Fresh Approach." *The Greek Orthodox Theological Review* 5 (1959/60) 140–185.

Sellers, R. V. *Eustathius of Antioch, and His Place in the Early History of Christian Doctrine.* Cambridge: University Press, 1928.

_____. *Two Ancient Christologies.* London: S.P.C.K., 1954.
Young, Frances. *From Nicaea to Chalcedon: A Guide to the Literature and Its Background.* Philadelphia: Fortress, 1983.

4

West, East, and the Great Councils

In the three previous chapters we looked at the emergence of
the distinctive Johannine Christology, varied biblical, pastoral,
and philosophical developments in the theology of the second century and after, and the contrasting and even conflictual approaches and emphases of Alexandria and Antioch. Most of this,
especially after the earlier forms of Judeo-Christianity, was the
story of the encounter between the gospel and Greek culture. But
just as the gospel was being enculturated in the Greek-speaking
world, so it would become enculturated in an increasingly Latin-
speaking West, another testimony to the tendency of theology toward diversification. We will now look briefly at other movements
in these first centuries of the Christian Church—the Latinization
of theology and liturgy, the ecclesial and imperial need for general councils, and the two early primary ecclesial and theological
traditions, East and West.

The Latin West

The development of Christology in the first centuries of the
Christian Era was heavily influenced by the culture, language,
politics, and theology of the East. Apart from Irenaeus, our focus in the earlier chapters has been primarily on Alexandria, Antioch, and Constantinople. Yet the West had a brilliant theological
history as well, with names like Tertullian, Cyprian, Hilary, Am-

brose, Jerome, Augustine, Leo, and Gregory coming quickly to mind.

North Africa was the original center for Latin-speaking Christianity and the Africans gave Latin Christianity their first great theologians, namely, Tertullian and Cyprian. Unlike Antioch and Alexandria in the East, however, Carthage and Rome did not become theological rivals. Carthage saw itself as closely related to the Roman Church. Tertullian and Cyprian manifested in still another way the tendency in Christian theology to diversify. Jean Daniélou's three-volume history of pre-Nicene theology reflects the three major cultural variations that Christian thought had pursued: Judean, Hellenistic, and Latin. With Tertullian in North Africa and Novatian in Rome, the Western Church went through a transition and began to express theology in its vernacular language, Latin. Tertullian still knew Greek well, and four of his works were first published in Greek.

Although Hippolytus (ca. 170–236) in Rome and Tertullian (ca. 155–220) in North Africa were witnesses to a "Greek" Church in the West still in the third century, Christine Mohrmann's research has shown that the transition to Latin had begun about the middle of the second century.[1] Prior to the original theological works of Tertullian and Novatian in Latin in the third century, there were Latin translations of works originally written in Greek. Preeminent among these translations was that of the Bible. A biblical Latin, the basis for much Christian Latin, was being formed by these early translations.

The Latin of the translations was no longer classical Latin but was based on the vernacular or popular Latin of the people. The translations were intended primarily for popular use. Greek continued to be the official liturgical language in Rome until the fourth century. In North Africa the Greek gave way to the vernacular Latin earlier. But prior to the liturgical changes in the third and fourth centuries and prior to the theological Latin of Tertullian and Novatian in the third century, Latin was the language of the people in Rome and Carthage, and the Bible was being translated for their sake. Latin translations of the New

[1]Cf. Christine Mohrmann, "Les origines de la latinité chrétienne à Rome," *Vigiliae Christianae* 3 (1949) 67–106, 163–183; "Le Latin langue de la chrétienté occidentale," *Aevum* 24 (1950) 133ff.; "Quelques observations sur l'originalité de la littérature chrétienne," *Revista di Storia della Chiesa in Italia* 4 (1950) 153ff.

Testament, or at least parts of it, existed in Africa by 180 and in Rome by the late second century as well. It appears that by 250 there was a widely recognized Latin translation of the whole of the Scriptures that Cyprian had quoted. The Old Latin manuscripts and variant translations provided the motive for Jerome's *Vulgate* in the late fourth century.

The transition to a "Latin Church" took place in stages. By the middle of the second century, the language of the ordinary Christian in Rome was becoming Latin. This linguistic shift necessitated the translation of the Bible into a vernacular Latin. By the end of the second century there were such translations in both Rome and Africa. Then in the early third century, with Tertullian in Africa and Novatian in Rome, original theological works and no longer just translations were being written in Latin. With Tertullian, "Latin theology" found its first truly creative voice. In mid-third century the "official language" of the Western Church changed to Latin, as demonstrated by papal letters of the time. Finally, in the fourth century, during the papacy of Damasus (366–384), Latin replaced Greek as the liturgical language of the Roman Church. It is Damasus who commissioned Jerome in 382 to produce his revision of the Latin text of the Bible.

Tertullian, born of non-Christian parents, a native of Carthage, the first great Church Father of the West, converted to Christianity before 197. Whether he was a practicing lawyer or not is uncertain. He later joined the Montanists, an ascetical movement of the late second century that was based upon a belief in the outpouring of the Spirit as manifested in prophets of that age, Montanus being one of them. As stated above, we find in Tertullian the transition from Greek as the theological language to Latin. Hans von Campenhausen has written, "In Tertullian's writings, we come across the living language of the Christians of that time, the Latin of the growing Latin church. . . . It observes and adopts at the same time even in grammatical details the language actually spoken by the society of Carthage."[2]

Tertullian is a contrast to the Alexandrian tradition in his evaluation of philosophy. Unlike his contemporaries, Clement and Origen, he did not seek to bridge the gap between philosophy and the Christian faith. He made this clear in his often quoted ques-

---

[2]Hans von Campenhausen, *The Fathers of the Latin Church,* trans. Manfred Hoffman (Stanford, Calif.: Stanford University Press, 1969) 8.

tion: "What indeed has Athens to do with Jerusalem? What concord is there between the Academy and the Church?" He did not reject rationality and intelligibility, however, and saw paradox as a way of understanding. In his refutation of Gnosticism, Tertullian did not remain open to a Christian gnosis as did Clement of Alexandria. For Tertullian, the Gnostics were disciples of Plato, and Platonism was not a path to truth. Tertullian was influenced by philosophy but it was the philosophy of Stoicism, particularly Seneca.

One of Tertullian's major contributions to Christian theology was his theology and language with respect to the Trinity. Especially important here was his work *Against Praxeas*. Tertullian was the first of the Latin authors to use the Latin word *trinitas* (*Against Praxeas,* 2). Tertullian's challenge was to defend the Christian conception of God over against Roman polytheism and Marcionism (against which he emphasized the oneness of God), as well as Christian heretical Monarchianism (against which he emphasized the real distinction among the persons of the *trinitas*). In this debate Tertullian contributed the words *substantia* (substance) and *persona* (person) to Trinitarian vocabulary.

Tertullian made it clear that the Christian conception of God is that God is one. The concept *monarchia,* God's oneness or singleness of power, was introduced into Christian theology by the apologists, derived from Alexandrian Judaism. The word "monarchian" can be used in a completely orthodox sense to refer to one who is monotheist and believes in the unity of God. Tertullian began to apply the term to heretical Monarchians as well (*Against Praxeas,* 3 and 9), the modalist Monarchians who affirmed the unity but failed to see the distinctiveness of the three *personae*. For Tertullian the concept *monarchia* did not imply that the Father can have no Son. He worked out the unity and distinctions in God with the help of the concepts *substantia* and *persona*.

God is *una substantia* (one substance). It is disputed whether the word *substantia,* found in Tertullian's writings more than three hundred times, should be understood in a philosophical sense as a rendering of a Greek concept,[3] or in a legal or juridical sense,[4]

[3]So Ernest Evans, "Tertullian's Theological Terminology," *Church Quarterly Review* 139 (1944-1945) 56-77.

[4]So Justo Gonazlez, *A History of Christian Thought* (Nashville: Abingdon Press, 1970) 1:183.

or simply as derived from ordinary language and everyday speech.[5] Daniélou seems to favor the last.[6] Tertullian's language in general did not derive from technical terminology. *Substantia* meant the underlying, persistent reality of a thing. It denoted material substances, or the distinction between matter and spirit as different substances, or the distinction between the human, spiritual soul and the Spirit which is given to humankind as distinct substances. In his Trinitarian teaching, God—Father, Son, and Spirit—are of one substance (*Against Praxeas*, 2, 4).

The task then was to explain the distinction among the three in the *trinitas.* Tertullian protected the divine monarchy with his notion of *una substantia,* which Father, Son, and Spirit all have in common. The three persons are distinct, however, and here the words *gradus* and *persona* are used. *Gradus* points to a series or degrees in a hierarchy or stages of progress. It does not imply a scale of values but rather an order of succession. Thus the word *gradus* can indicate the order of succession of the three persons, which does not imply a difference in *substantia*. There is an order in their origin. The Father is *tota substantia;* the Son is of the substance of the Father *(de substantia Patris);* and the Spirit is from the Father through the Son *(a Patre per Filium).* Yet they are all of one substance *(tres unius substantiae et unius status et unius potestatis) (On Modesty,* 2-4).

Tertullian was the first author to use the word *persona* in the theology of the Trinity. The Logos is distinct from the Father in the sense of person, not in the sense of substance. The Son is a second person. So with the Spirit whom Tertullian called the third person (*Against Praxeas,* 12).

Tertullian clearly affirmed the unity of God (the *monarchia, una substantia*) and equally clearly affirmed the distinction of the three, whom he called three persons (against modalist Monarchians), who are, however, of one divine substance. This *trinitas* does not destroy the unity of God, for it is the one God. At least in terms of vocabulary, Tertullian made his impact on Western Trinitarian theology: one God, three divine persons—and all this before Nicea and the controversies in the East. Yet there remained

[5]René Braun, *"Deus Christianorum,"* recherches sur le vocabulaire doctrinal de Tertullien (Paris: Presses Universitaires de France, 1962) 167-199.

[6]Jean Daniélou, *The Origins of Latin Christianity,* trans. David Smith and John Austin Baker (Philadelphia: Westminster Press, 1977) 345-348.

an inadequacy with respect to later orthodoxy. Tertullian's theology of the Trinity did not escape pre-Nicene subordinationism. The origin of the Son and Spirit are related to the economy of salvation, and the origin of the Son is linked to creation.

Both Tertullian's *Against Praxeas* and *On the Flesh of Christ* contributed to his Christology, the latter being clearly anti-Docetic. The flesh of Christ is real human flesh. Tertullian also rejected the common Judeo-Christian apocalyptic interpretations of Christ as an angel.

Not only is Christ's flesh real, so is his soul. It is amazing how Tertullian so early in the West avoided those controversies that plagued the East in the fourth and fifth centuries. Tertullian did not question whether Christ had a real human soul. He had early developed a doctrine on the human soul in *The Testimony of the Soul,* written in 197. It is a topic about which he wrote again later in *On the Soul* (ca. 210–213), and he was prepared to emphasize Christ's soul as central to his human existence. His anthropology enabled him to maintain a clear distinction between soul and body or flesh (*On the Flesh of Christ,* 10).

Thus, early in the West, with Tertullian, we have an awareness of the two complete natures in Christ, although Tertullian did not use the Greek language of *physis* but his own Latin concept of *substantia.* Just as *substantia* was valuable in his Trinitarian theology where God was *una substantia,* so it was valuable in his Christology: In Christ there are two substances, *duae substantiae* (*On the Flesh of Christ,* 5 and 18). Christ partakes of both the divine *substantia* and the human *substantia.*

Nor is there a confusion of the two substances. There is a twofold *status,* condition or way of being, in Christ (*Against Praxeas,* 27). Tertullian wrote, "We see a twofold state, which is not confused but is joined together in one person, Jesus, both God and a human being" [*Videmus duplicem statum non confusum sed coniunctum in una persona, Deum et hominem Jesum*]; and continued, "and so the property of each substance is preserved [*et adeo salva est utriusque proprietas substantiae*], so that the Spirit did its own things in Jesus, such as miracles and deeds and signs, and the flesh exhibited its own passions." The flesh was hungry, thirsty, wept, troubled, and died.

There was a distinction of the two states or substances in Christ, as so insisted upon by the Antiochenes; and there was also but one person, as insisted upon by the Alexandrians. And all this before the heightened tensions between them. Tertullian affirmed the unity of Christ and denied the possibility of distinguishing between Jesus and Christ, an error he attributed to the Valentinian Gnostics (*Against Praxeas,* 27). Tertullian's theology of the Trinity was an asset to his Christology. He had already shown that the Logos (Tertullian's term was the Latin *sermo*)[7] was a distinct *persona* even if one in *substantia* with the Father. The divine *persona,* the *sermo,* really clothed itself with flesh *(caro).* Tertullian rejected the word "transfigure" in describing how the Word became flesh (*Against Praxeas,* 27), for that would imply a *tertium quid,* an intermediate being neither divine nor human. Rather, there are two distinguishable *substantiae* and the one *persona* in Jesus Christ.

In his dispute with Praxeas and his heretical Monarchianism, Tertullian came close to affirming what would later be considered orthodox in the East. For Praxeas, the divine element in Christ was the Father; Son referred to the human Jesus. The divine element was named Christ and the humanity Jesus. But for Tertullian Jesus could not be divided like this. Nor was the Son simply the flesh. The Son was the second *persona* of the *trinitas.*

Although in Tertullian we practically have the formula of Chalcedon, more than two centuries away in the East, we cannot attribute to Tertullian's use of *persona* Cyril's understanding of *hypostasis,* nor the Antiochene meaning of *prosōpon.* Tertullian's understanding was not that of Greek philosophy.[8]

The Latin word *persona* had in its background the Roman theater and the meaning "mask" or "theater role," a character in a play. It also then came to express the notion of a human person or individual. Cicero used it in various senses. For Tertullian, the word seldom meant mask or theater role, but rather most often meant "person," a human individual. The Latin *persona* came to imply more than the Greek *prosōpon,* more than countenance or appearance; it implied individuality, although *prosōpon* and *persona* mutually affected the meaning or use of the other. They were not always far apart, but neither were they the same.

[7]Cf. Mohrmann, "Les origines de la latinité chrétienne à Rome," 166-167.

[8]Cf. Raniero Cantalamessa, "Tertullien et la formule christologique de Chalcédoine," *Studia Patristica* 9 (1966) 141-142.

Tertullian had the popular idea of a person as one who speaks and acts. He could apply it to the Trinity because the Father and Son each speak or act individually. They are the same substance but they are distinct *voces* (voices). In God's *una substantia* there are three *gradus* or *personae*. In Christological language, *in una persona* does not describe the mode or kind of union as Cyril's hypostatic union would. Tertullian was not primarily concerned with explaining the unity. He was more concerned, against the Monarchians, of distinguishing the Son from the Father (as two persons, one substance), and that is as the Son, the second *persona*, who took on flesh. Thus, although there is one *persona* in Christ (and *duae substantiae*), it was not yet with the understanding that would be brought to Chalcedon. Yet with Tertullian we did have an affirmation of both the "unity" and the "duality" with which the Greeks struggled.

Cyprian (d. 258), the second great African theologian, considered Tertullian his master. He was born in Carthage, was converted to Christianity, became a priest, and about 248 was elected bishop of Carthage, holding that office during the Decian persecution (250–251). He died as a martyr during the Valerian persecution. All his writings were pastoral and practical. He made no original contribution to Christology.

Hilary of Poitiers (ca. 315–367), however, did make a contribution to Christology. He was one of the major Latin theologians of the fourth century, a married man who was elected bishop of Poitiers (ca. 350). The major opponent of Arianism in the West, he has been called the Athanasius of the West.[9] He was the West's first major exegete, and his works included a commentary on Matthew and on some of the psalms. His principal work, however, was the *De Trinitate,* a defense of the divinity of the Son written during the period of exile in the East. He defended the *homoousios* (of the same substance) of Nicea but also showed how *homoiousios* (of similar substance) could be understood in an or-

---

[9]Cf. Paul C. Burns, *The Christology in Hilary of Poitiers' Commentary on Matthew* (Rome: Institutum Patristicum Augustinianum, 1981). Burns emphasizes the need for a historical approach to Hilary's theology that recognizes the significance of his exile (356–360), during which "a Latin speaking bishop from western Gaul came into prolonged contact with the Greek speaking church in Phrygia" (p. 9). Hilary's major theological contribution came after he had been sent East, but Burns argues that the Latin tradition and his earlier writings also enabled Hilary to deal with the issues he later encountered. Hilary's theology is genuinely Latin, not Greek (contra Emile Mersch).

thodox fashion, which later helped the reconciliation between the Niceans and the homoiousians. Hilary was also the first of the Western theologians to compose hymns, and hymnody in general was important in the history of Christology in the West.

In contrast to the struggles in the East to resolve Christological differences, Hilary presented an orthodox theology of Christ fairly early (*De Trinitate,* 10, 19 and 61–62). He clearly distinguished the two natures in Christ, clearly recognized a human soul in Christ (which was not even found in Athanasius), and recognized the unity in Christ and the consubstantiality of the Son or Logos with the Father. Hilary's explicit acknowledgment of the soul in Christ preceded the Apollinarian controversy.

Hilary made a contribution by distinguishing between the "ontological elements" in Christ, the unity and duality within the incarnation, and the "historical elements": the pre-existence, kenosis (self-emptying) or incarnation, and exaltation of Christ. He recognized both what we would later call a two-nature Christology and a three-stage Christology. The kenosis was strongly described (*De Trinitate,* 8, 45); it consisted in the renunciation of the *forma Dei*. Christ refrained from showing himself in his identity with God. Yet the divine nature remained the ontological subject even in the kenosis. The kenosis meant that the Logos on earth surrendered the glory due him as God, although that glory still shined through his humanity.

For Hilary, the divinity or divine glory permeated Jesus' humanity so strongly that the natural condition of Christ's body even before the resurrection was the glorified one. Hence the miracles and transfiguration were a mode of acting and being that were natural to Christ. The "miracles" were that Christ got hungry, thirsty, and suffered. These all involved the conscious choice of the Logos. The manifestations of human weaknesses needed each time a freely chosen self-limitation on the part of the Logos (*De Trinitate,* 10, 24ff.). Philippians 2:7 does not imply a "depotentiation" of the Logos, but rather repeated voluntary acts (*De Trinitate,* 9, 14; 11, 14). The "natural" condition of Christ's body and soul was that manifested in the state of transfiguration. Both the divinity and the humanity of Christ were manifest, and the natural state of Christ's humanity was its divinized state, although this divinized human state was suspended when Christ suffered and died. Christ's divinity was most clearly manifest, however, in his exaltation, when the divinity influenced the humanity completely. Grillmeier writes, "So Hilary has a Christology of divinization and union within the context of the 'Word-man' framework and in this respect comes close to Gregory of Nyssa."[10] Hilary gives us a well-worked-out Christology, orthodox in its main elements, a kenotic Christology in three stages: *ante hominem Deus* (God before being human, Christ is only God, the preexistent Logos); *homo et Deus* (the incarnation, and the kenosis *in forma servi*); post hominem et Deum, totus homo, totus Deus (the exalted state of being still fully human and also fully God) (*De Trinitate,* 9, 6). He understood the kenosis as having one subject, the Son or Logos, as well as the two substances or natures. The kenosis also permitted a divinization of Christ's humanity. Many of the concepts are ingredients for a modern Christology. They were already present in the fourth-century West with an orthodoxy not even found in the Logos-sarx theology of Athanasius and without the turbulence that accompanied Antiochene debates.

Ambrose (339–397) was one of the great Fathers of the Latin Church and ranks with Jerome and Augustine as formative of Western Christian thought. Born in Trier of a noble Roman family, he himself later held an official position based in Milan. While still a catechumen there, he was elected bishop of Milan by both the Arian party and the Catholic, becoming bishop in 374, eight days after his baptism. He later baptized Augustine. His literary output was extensive, but he was not inclined toward speculative thought. He was the most significant champion of the Nicene faith and opponent of the Arians in the West after Hilary. Also like Hilary, he was a composer as well. He was even more successful than Hilary in introducing congregational singing and is known as the creator of Latin hymnody.

Jerome (331–419/420) was born in Dalmatia of Catholic parents but received his education in Rome.[11] Around 373 he made a pilgrimage to Jerusalem but, because of illness, stopped in Antioch. There he attended lectures of Apollinaris and learned or improved his Greek. He also learned Hebrew while living as a

---

[10]Aloys Grillmeier, *Christ in Christian Tradition: From the Apostolic Age to Chalcedon (AD 451),* trans. John Bowden (London: Mowbrays, 1975) 399.

[11]Cf. J. N. D. Kelly, *Jerome, His Life, Writings, and Controversies* (New York: Harper & Row, 1975).

hermit nearby in the Syrian desert. In 379 he was ordained and left Antioch for Constantinople, where he heard lectures of Gregory Nazianzus and came to admire Origen. Pope Damasus invited him to attend a Roman synod in 382 and later commissioned him to revise the Latin texts of the Scriptures. The rest of his life was devoted to the study of Scripture. In 385 he left Rome to go a second time to Jerusalem and eventually settled in Bethlehem, where he lived a monastic life and spent up to thirty-four years in literary activity. At the time of Gregory the Great (d. 604) Jerome's text of the Bible was considered the equal of the ancient Latin texts, and later it surpassed them in being the recognized Latin text. The term "Vulgate" *(vulgata editio)* has been common since the thirteenth century. Jerome also translated many of the works of Origen. Although Jerome did not treat Christology with the detail that Hilary had, he emphasized strongly the humanity of Christ. In spite of having heard Apollinaris, Jerome stressed that the soul of Christ truly suffered. This idea may reflect Origen's influence, since Origen alone among the Alexandrians assigned a function to Christ's human soul. Jerome also stated that Jesus' body had human feelings like our own.

Augustine (354–430) was the most influential of all the Latin theologians.[12] He was born at Thagaste (in modern Algeria) in Numidia and studied rhetoric at Carthage. He later had a concubine for more than twelve years, and a son, Adeodatus. He lived as a Manichean "hearer" for nine years, and later as a Neoplatonist and professor of rhetoric in Milan, where he heard the sermons of Ambrose. After his conversion and baptism by Ambrose in 387, he returned to Thagaste to live a monastic type of life. He was called to be ordained in 391 by the bishop of Hippo, whom he succeeded as bishop four years later. His theological struggles against the Manicheans and then the Donatists and then the Pelagians, his over ninety writings not to mention his sermons and letters, his fame as a preacher, his death as the Vandals were conquering North Africa—these are well known.

His literary output was voluminous: his famous *Confessions,* written between 397 and 401, which represented a new literary genre; his major dogmatic work *De Trinitate,* from the middle

---

[12]For Augustine's own autobiography of the first thirty-three years of his life, see his *Confessions.* An excellent biography of Augustine is that by Peter Brown, *Augustine of Hippo* (Berkeley, Calif.: University of California Press, 1969).

of his life, on which he worked from 399 to 419; and the monumental work of his later years, *The City of God,* published in installments between 413 and 426, with its theology of history occasioned by Alaric's Gothic conquest of Rome in 410. Much of Augustine's theology and writings can be divided into three periods: his refutation of Manicheism (*On Free Will* as one among many); his struggle against Donatism (*On Baptism* as an example); and the conflict of his later years, for which Augustine became famous, against Pelagianism and in particular against Julian of Eclanum, within which conflict Augustine developed his theology of original sin, grace, and predestination (*About Nature and Grace, Against Julian, About Predestination of the Saints,* and *About the Gift of Perseverance*).

Although Augustine's primary contribution was not to Christology as much as to the theology of the Trinity, creation, original sin, and grace, among others, it is his Christology that is our primary concern. In this he was clearly orthodox, even if not yet as clear as Chalcedon would be. Like the other theologians of the West, he manifested an awareness of the unity of Christ, the duality (often expressed as *duae substantiae* rather than two natures as such), and the reality of Christ's human soul.

In one of his sermons, Augustine states, "The whole human being was taken up by the Word, that is, a rational soul and body, that the one Christ, the one God, the Son of God, should not only be Word, but Word and a human being."[13] It is clear that Christ's humanity was both soul and body. And the oneness in Christ resulted from a pre-existent Word taking to itself a human nature. For Augustine, Christ is one person from two substances, one person in both natures, although *persona* for Augustine did not imply the same metaphysical level that the later hypostatic union would convey.[14]

We find in Augustine a succinct Christological statement and also a famous analogy for understanding the unity in Christ: the body-soul analogy. This analogy was not intended to convey the

[13]Augustine, Sermon 214, 6. In Migne, *Patrologia Latina* 38:1069. Also see Grillmeier, *Christ in Christian Tradition,* 407.

[14]"Propter quam personam unam ex duabus substantiis divina humanaque constantem, aliquando secundum id quod Deus est loquitur . . . aliquando secundum id quod homo est. . . . " *In Johannis Evangelium* 99:1. In Corpus Christianorum Series Latina 36:582, 42–46. Also see Grillmeier, *Christ in Christian Tradition,* 409.

absence of a human soul in Christ replaced by the Logos as so often seemed the case in the Alexandrian Logos-sarx Christologies, for we have seen Augustine's emphasis on Christ's humanity involving both body and soul. The Alexandrian Logos-sarx theology was never the framework for the Latin West. Rather the body-soul unity provided an analogy. Augustine saw both duality *(duae substantiae)* and unity, which was akin to the unity in one human person of a body and a soul (which in a Neoplatonic framework would also be two substances); thus that union provided an analogy for the incarnation. Augustine wrote:

> Some insist upon being furnished with an explanation of the manner in which the Godhead was so united with a human soul and body as to constitute the one person of Christ, when it was necessary that this should be done once in the world's history with as much boldness as if they were themselves able to furnish an explanation of the manner in which the soul is so united with the body as to constitute one human person, an event which is occurring every day. For just as the soul is united to the body in one person so as to constitute a human being, in the same way is God united to the human in one person so as to constitute Christ. In the former person there is a combination of soul and body; in the latter there is a combination of the Godhead and the human. Let my reader, however, guard against borrowing his idea of the combination from the properties of material bodies, by which two fluids when combined are so mixed that neither preserves its original character; although even among material bodies there are exceptions, such as light, which sustains no change when combined with the atmosphere. In the human person, therefore, there is a combination of soul and body; in the person of Christ there is a combination of the Godhead with the human; for when the Word of God was united to a soul having a body, he took into union with himself both the soul and the body. The former event takes place daily in the beginning of life in individuals of the human race; the latter took place once for the liberation of humankind.[15]

With Augustine we can see the flowering of another strand of Christian theology. As we saw, the earliest Christian authors in

[15]Augustine, Letter 137, 11. In Migne, *Patrologia Latina* 33:520. Also see Grillmeier, *Christ in Christian Tradition*, 410.

the West wrote in Greek. During the second century, however, a popular Christian Latin began to appear. Then Latin Christian literature began to replace Greek literature in the West. Tertullian was the leading figure in the creation of this Latin Christianity. By the time of Augustine, the greatest of the Latin theologians, we have someone who did not know Greek. Alexandria and Antioch were the major centers of Eastern Christianity, but they were culturally and theologically distinct. Rome, Carthage, and Milan became the centers in the West, but they were culturally one. The struggles of the Churches, East and West, varied, and the particular cultures, languages, and struggles were formative of their theologies. The great Trinitarian and Christological struggles of the East were never as intense in the West, and Donatism and Pelagianism did not arouse much controversy in the East. Ecclesiology, sin, and grace were the areas within which the Western Church developed theologically.

Leo I, or Leo the Great, was bishop of Rome (440–461) at the crucial period in Roman history when the West was being subjected to foreign invasions. Given this period of history in the life of the Church as well as the Empire, Leo's activities on behalf of orthodoxy and order come as no surprise. These necessarily became his pastoral concerns. Leo was concerned with the unity of faith and the communion of the Churches. His pastoral and theological concerns were Christological and ecclesiological. His extant writings include 143 letters and 97 sermons, his most famous work and theological contribution being the *Tome of Leo to Flavian,* the letter to the bishop of Constantinople. Leo also developed the teaching on the primacy of Rome.

Leo's concern for the unity of faith brought him into the history of the Council of Chalcedon. In 448 Eutyches had appealed to Rome. Leo did not pronounce on the matter until being better informed. There followed a series of letters including the famous letter to Flavian. Theodosius convoked a council to meet at Ephesus in 449. Leo sent legates, although with some reservations, since he considered the matter resolved in his earlier letter to Flavian. This council Leo later described as a robbery, and it was a disaster for Leo and Flavian. As we will see, the events thus led to the Council of Chalcedon in 451 which agreed with Leo, who thereafter continually defended the faith of Chalcedon as the middle way between Nestorius and Eutyches.

The dual consubstantiality of Christ is the core of Leo's Christology. On the basis of the dual birth of Christ, two natures are to be distinguished, each with its properties and activities although united in one single subject (letter 28). In later letters, Leo adopts the Eastern formula, "consubstantial with the Father—consubstantial with the mother," but even earlier sees Christ as both born of God and born of Mary—an affirmation for Leo that is significantly soteriological as well.

We can now move from the Christologies of Alexandria, Antioch, Carthage, and Rome to the conciliar, or ecumenical, or imperial Christology formed under pressure at critical points in the Church's and Empire's history. We will note the tendency toward consolidation, which we have seen in Ignatius and Irenaeus, as well as the inseparability of Christology from culture and politics, which we have seen in the Antiochene-Alexandrian struggles. The theology of the councils shows both the relationship between theology and its social world and the tendency of theology at certain points to consolidate and move on. Each council represents a new beginning, a metamorphosis. Theology is in some ways the same and in some ways different after a great council. Nicea reflects the Church's interaction with Arianism, Constantinople with Apollinarianism, Ephesus with Nestorianism, and Chalcedon with Monophysitism.

The Council of Nicea, 325

Pre-Nicene (third-century) Trinitarian thought tended toward subordinationism. The tradition of the Christian Church was expressed in the baptismal formula that was grounded in the post-resurrection biblical injunction of the Lord: to baptize in the name of the Father and of the Son and of the Holy Spirit. Thus, every Christian was initiated into the faith with an awareness of a certain divine triad. The historical Christian faith cannot be separated from its Trinitarian language for the one God. Yet it took the Church almost three centuries to clarify its understanding.

The issue first at stake was the relationship between the Logos or Son and the Godhead. Was the Logos really and fully divine or not? The preaching and teaching of Arius forced the question into the open. Arius was carrying an accepted but unclarified subordinationism to a natural but unacceptable conclusion: The

Word is the first among creatures, not truly God in the strict sense, for there was a time when the Word was not. Thus the background for Nicea was the conflict between Arius and his bishop, Alexander of Alexandria, with other bishops such as Eusebius of Nicomedia and Eusebius of Caesarea taking the side of Arius. Nicea was set within the context of both the theological and the political implications of the Arian controversy.

The council was called by the emperor Constantine and met in the summer palace at Nicea, not far from Constantinople. Over three hundred bishops attended, the majority from the Greek-speaking East. The bishop of Rome was unable to attend but was represented by two of his priests. For many of these bishops, persecution was still a vivid memory. This assembly must have struck them as nothing short of a miracle. The most historic decision of the council was its condemnation of Arianism.

We cannot easily interpret the faith of Nicea, for the understanding of what had been done would vary, as the aftermath of the council shows. Yet a step was taken which moved Christian theology toward a new starting point for theology itself, the Nicene Creed. We quote here the Christological clause of the Creed.

> (We believe) in one Lord Jesus Christ, the son of God, begotten from the Father, uniquely [monogene], that is, from the substance of the Father, God from God, Light from Light, true God from true God, begotten not made, consubstantial with the Father, through whom all things were made, both those in heaven and those on earth, who for us and for our salvation came down and was made flesh, became one of us, suffered and rose again on the third day, ascended to the heavens, and will come to judge the living and the dead.[16]

A few comments must suffice. Jesus Christ, the one Lord, is the Son of God. The preexistent Son (the Creed does not use the expression "Logos") is begotten from the Father. Thus a distinction is made between the Father who is unbegotten *(agennētos)* and the Son who is begotten *(gennētos)*. The Son is "uniquely

---

[16] I use here the translation of T. E. Pollard, *Johannine Christology and the Early Church* (Cambridge: University Press, 1970) 176–177. Also see J. N. D. Kelly, *Early Christian Doctrines*, 2nd ed. (New York: Harper & Row, 1960) 232.

begotten"; I prefer this translation of *monogenēs* (E. R. Hardy)[17] to the more common "only begotten." The Son is uniquely begotten in that he is "from the substance of the Father" *(ek tēs ousias tou patros).* The Son and the Father share the same divine *ousia.* Thus, against the Arians, the Son is not subordinate to the Father, nor is he derived from the Father by an act of will. The Son is true God, truly divine, and not created. The Son is distinct from the Father in being begotten, but distinct from creatures in being uncreated. The Son is begotten but not made *(gennēthenta ou poiēthenta):* another "no" to Arianism. The Son is nothing other than *homoousios* with the Father, consubstantial, of the same substance or nature *(homoousion tō patri).*

The word, *homoousios,* so identified with the Nicene faith, was challenged as a nonscriptural expression. Yet such terminology was needed to clarify the traditional faith of the Church. Apparently, the term *homoousios* was proposed by Constantine himself at the suggestion of his theological adviser, Hosius of Cordova.[18] The Latin equivalent, *consubstantialis,* was by this time already in use in Latin theology.

The Nicene Fathers did not see themselves as Hellenizing the faith. They were not imposing a technical philosophical concept. Much about the word was still imprecise. But the Nicene Fathers did want a term that would make the Scriptures clear. For them it was a nonscriptural word expressing the theology of the Scriptures. They needed a new expression in order to prevent the Scriptures from being falsely interpreted. The precise meaning of the expression would only be developed and articulated in the period after the council. *Homoousios* ended the period of pre-Nicene subordinationism.

The Son was made flesh. The Creed attempts to remain faithful to Johannine theology while clarifying it in accord with the needs of the time and in accord with the traditional understanding of the Church. The Son, now Jesus Christ, was one of us. The Nicene statement is a theology of the Son, an affirmation of his true divinity, over against the Arians. The Creed did not

---

[17] Cf. Edward R. Hardy, ed., *Christology of the Later Fathers,* Library of Christian Classics (Philadelphia: Westminster Press, 1954) 338. Also Pollard, *Johannine Christianity and the Early Church,* 179.

[18] Cf. Henry Chadwick, "Ossius of Cordova and the Presidency of the Council of Antioch, 325," *Journal of Theological Studies* 9 (1958) 292-304.

resolve the problem created concerning the unity of God; therefore, it was not a theology of the Trinity. Such would be developed on the basis of the Creed by Athanasius and the Cappadocians. Rather the Creed was a resolution of a particular concrete issue facing the Church. After Nicea, Christology became more and more Christology "from above."

The Nicene Creed was also supposedly the resolution of a concrete problem for the empire (or so Constantine thought).[19] A divided Church meant to Constantine a divided empire. One creed was to help hold the empire together as well as the Church. Constantine was at first the ruler of only the Western half of the empire. Licinius, his brother-in-law, ruled in the East. When in 324 Constantine invaded Licinius' territory and defeated him, the whole empire was Constantine's. With it he inherited the Arian controversy, which had affected the Eastern half of his empire, from Nicomedia to Antioch to Caesarea to Alexandria. Whose idea it was to summon a general council of the empire is unknown, but Constantine convoked it early in 325, for political rather than religious reasons.

The problems for both Church and state, however, did not come to an end. Only the Council of Constantinople in 381 closed the Arian controversy. Bitter struggles followed before the Nicene doctrine became accepted. Eusebius of Nicomedia spearheaded an anti-Nicene coalition. This coalition was to depose its opponents, Athanasius, Eustathius of Antioch, Marcellus of Ancyra. Constantine was not baptized until he was dying, and by none other than Eusebius of Nicomedia, an Arian.

After 337 Constantine's empire was divided among his three sons. Constantius in the East was pro-Arian; Constans and Constantine II in the West were pro-Nicea. From 350 to 361 Constantius became the sole emperor—a blow to the Nicene party. After 361, however, Arianism was gradually defeated, and at the Council of Constantinople the Nicene faith was reaffirmed.

In the aftermath of Nicea, we can detect at least four parties, four theologies, the fortunes of which were partly intertwined with imperial and ecclesiastical politics. The *homoousians,* or the Nicene party itself, found their greatest champion in Athanasius in

[19]Cf. G. H. Williams, "Christology and Church—State Relations in the Fourth Century," *Church History* 20 (1951) no. 3, pp. 3-33; no. 4, pp. 3-26.

the East and Hilary in the West. The *homoiousians* reacted against the Nicene formula. They maintained that the Son was not of the same substance but of similar substance. The Son was not a creature; they were not semi-Arian. But the similarity between Son and Father is not an identity of *ousia*. Rather, the Son is like the Father but not identical in *ousia* to the Father. The *homoiousians* were more in the middle, neither pro-Nicea nor pro-Arian. They were later reconciled to the *homoousians* and the Nicene faith.

The radical anti-Nicene and pro-Arian party were the *anomoeans*. Their catchword and name came from their stance that the Son is not like *(anomoios)* the Father. The Son is neither of the same *ousia* (not *homoousios*) nor of like *ousia* (not *homoiousios* either) as the Father. The final party, the *homoeans* (Greek *homoios,* or similar), affirm that the relationship of Son to Father is one of similarity, but they are deliberately ambiguous about the meaning of that similarity. Thus, unlike the *homoiousians,* they did not clearly reject Arianism. In fact, they were pro-Arian, or "political Arians," maintaining that the controversial term should be avoided, neither insisted upon nor blatantly repudiated.

Thus Nicea did not fully resolve the Arian controversy. It made a contribution toward a theological language and provided a basis on which the theology of the Trinity would eventually be formulated. It also created the pro-Nicene and pro-Arian disputes, which would dominate theology and theological politics during a major portion of the fourth century.

The Council of Constantinople, 381

The background for the Council of Constantinople was the aftermath of the Council of Nicea, which had provided a creed for the Church and affirmed the full divinity of the Son but had not resolved the Arian problem. In 361 Constantius died and was succeeded by Julian the Apostate, who systematically opposed Christianity. He was followed by Jovian, a Catholic, then by Valentinian in the West, who was Catholic, and Valens in the East, who was Arian. When Valens was killed in 378, Theodosius became emperor. As Constantine had convened the general Council of

Nicea, so Theodosius now convoked a council to convene in Constantinople.

Unlike the council at Nicea, the West was not involved, not even represented. Neither the bishop of Rome nor his representatives were there. Thus it was not strictly speaking a general or ecumenical council. It later came to be recognized as such, however, first in the East by the time of the Council of Chalcedon in 451, and later in the West. Pope Gregory the Great, following some of his predecessors, recognized it with respect to its dogmatic declarations.

The major dogmatic contribution of the Theodosian council was its reaffirmation of Nicea as representing the faith of the Church. It did not draw up a new creed. The well-known Nicene-Constantinopolitan Creed cannot be attributed to the council of Constantinople as such.[20] The council itself enacted four canons. The first reaffirmed the Nicene Creed. It condemned Arianism in its varied post-Nicene forms, the anomoeans and homoeans. It also condemned the pneumatomachi, the "enemies of the Holy Spirit," thus affirming the full divinity of the Spirit as well as of the Son. It also condemned the Apollinarians. The latter condemnation was new to the council at Constantinople and had explicit Christological implications. What Nicea had said of the Arians in their defective theology of the pre-existent Son, Constantinople said of the Apollinarians and their defective Logos-sarx theology of the humanity of Jesus. The way was being prepared for further clarification. The Son is both consubstantial with the Father (Nicea) and complete in his humanity (thus more or less consubstantial with us, although this would not be said as such until the Council of Chalcedon).

The third canon had historic consequences: "The bishop of Constantinople shall have the primacy of honor after the bishop of Rome, because the same is new Rome"—a canon with political consequences for the history of theology, which aggravated the rivalry between Alexandria (Cyril) and Constantinople (Nestorius). The canon was a consequence of Constantine's having moved his capital to Constantinople and partially the consequence of the West's as well as Egypt's lack of representation at

[20]Cf. J. N. D. Kelly, *Early Christian Creeds,* 2nd ed. (London: Longmans, Green and Co., 1960) 296-331.

the council, absences contributing to the dilemma as to whether it could be considered ecumenical or not. The claim of the see of Constantinople was ignored by Alexandria and later declared null by Pope Leo I. The primacy of Rome had been recognized in both East and West by the fourth century. Nicea had also acknowledged, after Rome, the preeminence of Alexandria and Antioch, in that order. It also gave special recognition to Jerusalem. According to canon three of Constantinople, the ranking of the sees would be Rome, Constantinople, Alexandria, Antioch, and Jerusalem. Political power is not, however, reshuffled so easily. The canon in question did not refer to ecclesiastical jurisdiction but to a primacy of honor. The issue would surface again in the twenty-eighth canon of the Council of Chalcedon.

With the First Council of Constantinople, a council controversial in its own way, Arianism was finally defeated, the basis for Trinitarian orthodoxy established, and Apollinarianism condemned. Now the arena would shift from Trinitarian conflicts to Christological ones. How can the Son, who is of the same substance as the Father, enter into a true union with the flesh? What would that mean?

The Council of Ephesus, 431

Alexandria watched closely and attempted to influence who occupied the see of Constantinople. Alexandria was sensitive about an Antiochene occupant of the see. In 397, Nectarius died. Theophilus, bishop of Alexandria, had a candidate of his own, but Eutropius, governing in the name of the emperor, selected instead for this prestigious position a saintly monk from Antioch, John Chrysostom, whom Theophilus was forced to consecrate in 398. The rivalry between the two sees, Alexandria and Constantinople, dating back to 381, was further exacerbated by the appointment of John Chrysostom. At the Synod of the Oak (403), which was stacked with Theophilus' bishops, Chrysostom was condemned and deposed. He died in 407. The Pope in the West refused to accept the action of the synod and even broke relations with both Alexandria and Antioch, who had recognized a new bishop as John's successor. Theophilus was still not in communion with Rome when he died in 412. His nephew, Cyril of Alexandria, was his successor. Antioch submitted to Rome by restoring John's name to the list of deceased bishops prayed for by the Church. The young Cyril, stubborn as his uncle, refused to do so at first. Eventually, however, around 417, he too restored John's name.

The already apparent and open conflict between Alexandria and Constantinople was made worse when Nestorius was consecrated bishop of Constantinople in 428. Nestorius, like John Chrysostom, was also an Antiochene. Cyril remained the bishop of Alexandria, and his concerted efforts against Nestorius matched and even surpassed Theophilus' earlier efforts against John. The watchword of the new controversy, as we have already seen, was *theotokos,* a title accepted in the Church's tradition, which was a simple expression of Alexandrian Christology, and which, with the support of the bishop of Constantinople, was being called into question. In the ensuing conflict Cyril carefully and wisely sought support from the bishop of Rome while Nestorius had the support of the bishop of Antioch.

Nestorius himself attempted to keep Rome informed, but Cyril did a more effective job. An envoy of Cyril's accompanied Cyril's dossier on Nestorius to Rome. The dossier contained the Cyril-Nestorius correspondence and a Latin translation of extracts (the errors) of Nestorius. In it, Pope Celestine I received the Cyrilline interpretation of Nestorius' teaching. In August of that same year (430) Celestine held a synod in Rome and pronounced against Nestorius. The Pope forwarded his judgment in the case first to Cyril, whom the Pope instructed to seek from Nestorius a recantation of his errors. Cyril, of all people, was charged with implementing Rome's decision! Nestorius was to be given ten days to make his retraction in writing. Besides informing Cyril of his decision, the Pope also wrote to Nestorius as well as to other bishops in the East.

The tension between Nestorius and Cyril was not only political, it was profoundly theological, and two "schools" of theology were being called into question. To Cyril's unsympathetic hearing, Nestorius was interpreted as another Paul of Samosata. To Nestorius, Cyril was an Apollinarian. As we saw, the early, pre-Ephesene Cyril was simply a successor of the Logos-sarx Christology, Athanasian, not Apollinarian, yet Logos-sarx Christology to an Antiochene always smelled of Apollinarianism. Cyril's Logos-sarx Christology, however, was orthodox, akin to Athanasius'; yet Apollinarian type formulae entered Cyril's theological language, namely, the *mia physis* and the *mia hypostasis* formulae, characteristic of Alexandria's Christology with emphasis on the unity of Christ.

We can see why Apollinaris spoke of one *physis* in Christ. There was in Christ no complete human *physis*. For the Antiochenes, one could affirm the complete humanity of Christ and avoid Apollinarianism only with two *physeis*. In the conflict with Nestorius, however, Cyril clearly recognized a human soul in Christ, which was the subject of Christ's human suffering, and thus Cyril went beyond Athanasius and his own earlier Christological way of speaking. Yet Cyril persisted in speaking about one *physis*. The Cyril of the Nestorian/Ephesene phase presented no typical Logos-sarx Christology; yet his language did not always make that clear. One *physis* sounded like Apollinarianism to Antiochenes, just as a denial of *theotokos* sounded like a denial of the oneness in Christ to Alexandrians. Of course, before Chalcedon, it had not been resolved how best to express both the unity and the duality of Christ. Despite its ambiguity, Cyril did not abandon the *mia physis* formula, because it preserved and expressed the unity in Christ, the Alexandrians' contribution to later orthodoxy. Two *physeis* for an Alexandrian was too close to two Christs. Christological language was still in process. For Cyril, *physis* and *hypostasis* were closely related though not synonymous. For Cyril, in Christ there could be only one *hypostasis,* the one *hypostasis* of the Word of God. The Logos was united at the level of "person" *(kath' hypostasin)* to the flesh that he had taken.

Theological emphases, ambiguous theological language, the personalities of Cyril and Nestorius, and the tension between Alexandria and Constantinople played their roles in the course of events. Cyril set about the task of implementing Pope Celestine's judgment, and in so doing went beyond what Celestine had requested. Before acting, he convoked a synod of Egyptian bishops who condemned Nestorius in a harsh manner. Then, in the famous third letter of Cyril to Nestorius, Cyril not only conveyed the decision of Rome, and in addition the judgment of the Alexandrian synod, but also attached twelve propositions or anathemas of his own. These twelve additions reflected the feared Cyrilline Christology, to which Nestorius was supposed to consent. Needless to say, Nestorius did not capitulate. Rather, he replied with twelve anathemas against Cyril.

Before Cyril's delegates arrived in Constantinople with Cyril's letter, Theodosius II had already decided to convene a general council at Ephesus on Pentecost of the following year (431). Invitations had been sent to Rome and Hippo. Augustine died shortly before (430). The bishop of Carthage designated a deacon to represent the African Church. Celestine was concerned to maintain Rome's authority in the question, and a Rome-Alexandria alliance seemed the effective way to do this. Constantinople's growing power was of concern to Rome as well as to Alexandria. Thus Celestine instructed his three delegates to align themselves with Cyril. The Antiochene bishops were also preparing for the council. Organized around John, bishop of Antioch, they were ready to have Cyril condemned as an Apollinarian. Both Nestorius and Cyril expected the condemnation of the other. Nestorius had support from John of Antioch and his party and from the emperor; Cyril had the support of Rome.

Cyril arrived in Ephesus a few days early. Nestorius had been there since Easter. Cyril had brought over forty Egyptian bishops. The bishop of Jerusalem arrived late with fifteen anti-Nestorius supporters. The delegates from Rome had not yet arrived and word came that because of travel difficulties, the over forty Antiochenes would be late as well.

Finally, two weeks after the date of June 7, set as the opening for the council, with the Romans and Antiochenes not yet there, Cyril announced on June 21, on his own authority, against the protest of the representative of the emperor as well as a group of sixty-eight bishops, that the council would convene on the next day, June 22. About a hundred fifty bishops attended the synod, which assembled around Cyril. Nestorius and a few bishops refused to attend until the Antiochenes arrived.

The procedure of those assembled was to evaluate Nestorius' teaching in terms of the Creed of Nicea. Nestorius' rejection of *theotokos* was seen not to be in accord with Nicea. The action of the synod consisted primarily in the reading of two letters: the second letter of Cyril to Nestorius and Nestorius' reply to Cyril. The former was accepted as being in accord with Nicea. The latter was condemned. The verdict of the synod (understandably) was the condemnation of Nestorius. Cyril's third letter to Nestorius was included in the *acta* of the synod, as was the Pope's letter to Nestorius, but there had been no vote on them. The

Fathers of Ephesus had considered the Nicene faith authoritative, and Cyril's second letter was considered to express officially the Nicene doctrine.

Although the Council of Ephesus was not over, the major work of the council was done in a single but long day. A couple of days later, John of Antioch and the Antiochene party arrived. After hearing what had happened, they formed a synod of their own and deposed Cyril and Memnon, bishop of Ephesus, and informed the emperor of their action. When the emperor heard the report of his own representative he declared the decisions of the Cyrilline synod void and instructed them to meet again. By the time the emperor's decision reached Ephesus, the Roman delegates had also arrived. According to their instruction, they would side with Cyril.

In early July a majority of the bishops met again. The Pope's letter to the council, which agreed with the denunciation of Nestorius, was read. The papal delegates confirmed the judgment of the earlier Cyrilline synod. But the conflict was not resolved, any more than Arianism had been by Nicea. For a couple of weeks, the Antiochene group had rejected the synod as a council and had deposed Cyril. Before the end of July the bishops, meeting in council, solemnly excommunicated the entire Antiochene group. The emperor rejected the council but accepted the deposition of all three—Nestorius, Cyril, and Memnon. The unity which the emperor had hoped to establish by a general council in Ephesus was hardly established. Protests came to the emperor. Alexandrian wealth also carried a voice. The emperor himself held a conference with representatives of both sides at Chalcedon in September. The effect was to withdraw the condemnation of Cyril and Memnon, to refuse to reconsider the question of Nestorius, and to refuse to condemn John and the Antiochene party. The third general council had extended from June into September, but the net effect of it had been accomplished during the first day— the denunciation and deposition of Nestorius. But just as it had really taken two councils to settle the Arian crisis, so it would take another council to settle this one.

The Council of Chalcedon, 451

Other than the condemnation of Nestorius, which is being re-evaluated in modern times, the Council of Ephesus in 431 accomplished little. The divisions in Christendom had been even further aggravated. The hoped-for reconciliation was accomplished two years later, though for only a short time. The challenge was to reconcile John of Antioch and Cyril of Alexandria. In the year after the council (432) the emperor, Theodosius II, attempted to heal the schism. His representative, Aristolaus, went first to Antioch, then to Alexandria, and there was also an exchange of letters between John and Cyril. The result was that John explicitly declared Nestorius to be heretical, which enabled him to accept the *fait accompli* of the Council of Ephesus. But he was not asked to accept Cyril's twelve anathemas, which had not been submitted to a vote as such at the Council of Ephesus. Cyril was not asked to withdraw his anathemas either. He did, however, agree to accept the formula, or Symbol of Union, drawn up by the Antiochenes. This Symbol of Union of 433 was the temporary reconciliation of the two parties. In effect, John agreed to denounce Nestorius, and Cyril agreed to the formula of union.

The Symbol of Union of 433 had its origin in an Antiochene creed drawn up at Ephesus by the council or synod which had gathered around John of Antioch. Thus John, in 433, accepted the major conclusions of Cyril's earlier council or synod, the deposition of Nestorius, and Cyril accepted the major declaration of John's council or synod, the Antiochene creed, although in a redaction worked out in 432 for the purpose of reconciliation. The text of the Symbol of Union ran:

> We confess, then, our Lord Jesus Christ, the only-begotten Son of God, perfect God and perfect man, consisting of a rational soul and body, begotten of the Father before the ages as to his Godhead, and in the last days the Same; for us and for our salvation, of Mary the Virgin as to his manhood; the Same *homoousios* with the Father as to his Godhead, and *homoousios* with us as to his manhood. For there has been a union of two natures; wherefore we confess one Christ, one Son, one Lord.
>
> In accordance with this thought of the unconfused union, we confess the holy Virgin to be "Theotokos," because the divine Logos was incarnate and made man, and from the very conception united to himself the temple that was taken of her.
>
> And with regard to the sayings concerning the Lord in the Gospels and Apostolic [writings], we know that theologians take

some as common, as relating to one person, and others they divide as relating to two natures explaining those God-befitting in reference to the Godhead of Christ and those lowly in reference to his manhood.[21]

We can see in this statement, upon which both parties could agree, a contribution toward the statement eventually to be endorsed at Chalcedon. We see expressed in it the Antiochene concerns: an explicit exclusion of any Apollinarianism, an affirmation of the two natures in Christ (a twofold *homoousios*), a union without a confusion of the natures. We also see expressed the Alexandrian concerns: an acceptance of the title *theotokos,* (and thus an appreciation of the unity of Christ as a basis for the *communicatio idiomatum*), and a statement of Christological unity based on Jesus and the Logos as being one and the same, not two persons, but the divine Logos incarnate. The statement itself was based on the Nicene faith and almost anticipated the formula of Chalcedon.

John of Antioch died in 440 and Cyril in 444. Both parties and their contrasting schools of theological thought made a lasting contribution toward an eventual solution. The Cyril of the Symbol of Union of 433 was not exactly the same as the Cyril of the twelve anathemas, nor as the Cyril of the pre-Nestorian controversy. Likewise for Nestorius. He survived the Council of Chalcedon, though in exile, and the Nestorius of the *Liber Heraclides,* written after the Council of Ephesus while he was in exile, showed a Nestorius still trying to show his orthodoxy.

The reconciliation accomplished in 433 was significant but brief. Controversy again broke out. This time it was centered on the monk Eutyches (ca. 378–454), the superior of a large monastery in Constantinople, thus in the sphere of influence of Antiochene theology. Yet Eutyches was Alexandrian in his thinking, a disciple of Cyril, and anti-Nestorian. All this made for a conflict, which was precipitated in 448. The cast of characters in this phase of the drama were Eutyches; Flavian, the bishop of Constantinople; Eusebius, bishop of Dorylaeum; the accuser, Dioscoros, the bishop of Alexandria; as well as Leo, Pope in Rome from 440 to 461.

---

[21]According to the translation of R. V. Sellers, *The Council of Chalcedon: A Historical and Doctrinal Survey* (London: S.P.C.K., 1953) 17–18.

Eutyches claimed to be a strict adherent of Cyril's Christology. In this regard he took over Cyril's *mia physis* or one *physis* (nature) formula. For Cyril, however, one *physis* was practically synonymous or closely related to one *hypostasis*. Eutyches used the formula without all the necessary accompanying theological clarification to reject the two *physeis* in Christ of the Symbol of Union of 433, an almost nonnegotiable affirmation of Antiochene Christology. Eutyches rejected the "*homoousios* with us" and the "two natures" after the union of the Symbol of Union. In this he was the founder of Monophysitism, or Eutychianism. Eutyches' Monophysitism was not Cyril's, who was able to accept two natures in Christ. Since the clarification of theological language had not yet been established, the old dispute broke out. The more *physis* was seen as indistinguishable from *hypostasis,* the more likely the possibility of speaking of one *physis* (an Alexandrian characteristic). The more *physis* was distinguished from the one underlying subject of the incarnation, the Logos, the more persuasive was the argument for two *physeis,* or two natures (an Antiochene characteristic), and the aptness of *prosōpon* as an expression for the unity of Christ. Eutyches was Monophysite in a sensitively Dyophysite part of the world. Thus, several years after Cyril's death, we find an influential monk claiming to be loyal to Cyril but not adhering to the Symbol of Union of 433. Next to the bishop of Constantinople, Eutyches, as the head of a large monastery, was a significant religious figure. Eutyches saw himself as fighting Nestorianism while his opponents saw him as reviving Apollinarianism. In 448, at a local synod of bishops gathered in Constantinople, Eusebius of Dorylaeum denounced Eutyches, and the conflict broke out again. The synod pronounced him a heretic and deposed him from his post in the monastery.

After 431 (the synod or council at Ephesus), and 433 (the formula of the Symbol of Union), and 448 (the condemnation of Eutyches by the synod in Constantinople), the next important date was 449, when a second synod met at Ephesus. It was to become known as the Robbers' Council. The bishop of Alexandria did not allow the condemnation of Eutyches. Rather, Dioscoros called his own synod and annulled the condemnation. But when Flavian's report of the Constantinople proceedings reached Rome, Leo I judged against Eutyches. Emperor Theodosius summoned another council to meet at Ephesus in 449. Pope Leo sent three representatives, as Celestine had done in 431. Leo also sent Flavian a letter in which he stated that Eutyches had been justly condemned and he included a statement of what "the catholic church universally believes and teaches." This *"Tomus ad Flavianum,"* or the Tome of Leo as it has come to be known, is as significant to the history of doctrine as was the formula of 433.

The council, intended by the emperor to be a general council, opened in August of 449 with about a hundred thirty bishops present and with Dioscoros of Alexandria presiding, according to the emperor's command. Dioscoros was, of course, pro-Eutyches. Both Flavian and Leo considered him heretical.

The papal representatives called for a reading of the Pope's letter to the council, but Dioscoros omitted it. Eutyches made his appeal. The papal legates were again denied permission to speak. The emperor forbade those who had previously participated in the condemnation of Eutyches to vote. The new vote was thus almost unanimously favorable to Eutyches. Dioscoros then, amid much chaos, proposed to depose the condemners of Eutyches, namely, Flavian and Eusebius. Hilarius, one of the papal legates, protested. The tone of the synod became riotous. Philip Hughes describes the scene:

> Dioscoros cried out that his life was in danger, and on his appeal the imperial officials threw open the doors of the church, and a mob of soldiers, seamen, monks, and the general rabble poured in. Flavian took refuge in the sanctuary, and clung to the pillars of the altar. In the end he was dragged away, and taken to prison. The bishops then voted his condemnation, 135 of them signing the decree, many of them through sheer fear, and unable to escape.
>
> Flavian was exiled, and after three days on the road he died, apparently from shock or from injuries received in the dreadful scene. But he managed to draft an appeal to the pope, and to get this into the hands of the all but helpless legates.[22]

The synod at Ephesus in 449, a would-be council, ended with a situation worse than that which had preceded it. It was not accepted as a general council and, in the words of Leo, was branded

---

[22]Philip Hughes, *The Church in Crisis: A History of the General Councils, 325-1870* (Garden City, N.Y.: Doubleday Image, 1964) 83.

as *"non iudicium sed latrocinium"* (not a council but highway robbery).

In the aftermath of the Nestorian affair, which had been a blow to Constantinople and Antioch, a constructive theological contribution was forthcoming in the Symbol of Union of 433. So in the Eutychean affair, which was a blow to Alexandria, a constructive theological contribution came forth in the *Tome* of Leo. In the resolution of Eutyches' Monophysitism (and it took the general Council of Chalcedon to restore some unity), the three great theological traditions of Alexandria, Antioch, and the West found themselves all contributing toward a solution.

Leo's *Tome* was a monument to Western Christology, which had never known Christological conflict as had the East. Leo's Christology affirmed two natures, each complete; the coexistence of the two natures in the one Christ; redemption as already rooted in the being of Christ and not only in his acts; that Christ is one in person *(persona)* while two in nature *(natura),* hence neither Nestorianism nor Eutychianism; and the *communicatio idiomatum.*

In February of 450, Valentinian III, emperor in the West; Galla Placidia, his mother (the daughter of Theodosius I, a strong supporter of Leo I); and Eudoxia, Valentinian's wife and daughter of Theodosius II, all left Ravenna to reside in Rome. In July of 450 the emperor Theodosius II died suddenly, and his sister Pulcheria became empress. She was also a supporter of Leo I. She married Marcian and in August proclaimed him emperor. Leo had expressed his desire for another council and his wish was to come true. Conditions in East and West were favorable for Leo. Pulcheria and Marcian arranged for another council, although Leo now saw it as less necessary. It was to meet on September 1 at Nicea. The bishops assembled at Nicea but the emperor then decided that it would be more convenient for him to meet closer to Constantinople. Therefore it was located at Chalcedon. About five hundred bishops attended. Dioscoros was not allowed to sit among the bishops.

The council itself resisted drawing up another symbol of faith or creed. It did not wish to add to what had been done at Nicea (325) and Constantinople (381). Under pressure from Marcian, however, the bishops finally gave way and established a committee of twenty-three bishops to work out a new formula.

Thus Chalcedon, the setting for the Church's fourth general council, provided the Church with a formulation of faith concerning Christology and a Christological language for future discussion. Today many see Chalcedon's formulation as too historically relative and limited. We can also see, however, its lengthy pre-history and the significant step that it was for both Church and empire. We quote the Chalcedonian definition here:

> Following therefore the holy Fathers we unanimously teach that the Son, our Lord Jesus Christ, is one and the same, the same perfect in divinity, the same perfect in humanity, true God and true man, consisting of a rational soul and a body, consubstantial [*homoousios*] with the Father in divinity and consubstantial with us in humanity, "in all things like as we are, without sin" (Heb 4:15), born of the Father before all time as to his divinity, born in recent times for us and for our salvation from the Virgin Mary, Mother of God, as to his humanity. We confess one and the same Christ, the Son, the Lord, the Only-Begotten, in two natures unconfused, unchangeable, undivided and inseparable. The difference of natures will never be abolished by their being united, but rather the properties of each remain unimpaired, both coming together in one person [*prosōpon*] and substance [*hypostasis*], not parted or divided among two persons, but in one and the same only-begotten Son, the divine Word, the Lord Jesus Christ, as previously the prophets and Jesus Christ himself taught us and the Creed of the Fathers handed down to us.[23]

The contents of the definition are not new. They came from the second letter of Cyril to Nestorius, the Symbol of Union of 433, and the *Tome* of Leo. In this statement Rome, Alexandria, and Antioch spoke with one voice, an accomplishment not to be underestimated. Eutychean Monophysitism was rejected, Antiochene Dyophysitism confirmed as orthodox faith, and Cyril's hypostatic union was accepted as the way of preserving the unity of Christ. *Hypostasis* and *physis* were clearly distinguished. The first was able to serve the Alexandrian concern for the substantial unity that is Christ. The second was able to serve the An-

---

[23]See Denziger, 301–302. This translation comes from Josef Neuner and Heinrich Roos, *The Teaching of the Catholic Church* (New York: Alba, 1967) 153–154.

tiochene concern for the duality of natures that Christ is. The council explicitly recognized that the *mysterium Christi* was not a question of either unity or duality but a question of both/and. Christ was both one *(hypostasis)* and two *(physeis)*.

Although the Chalcedonian statement brought a resolution to centuries of Christological tensions, it effected unity no more than previous councils. One of the unfortunate effects of the "Christological councils" of Ephesus and Chalcedon was a split in the Church with the emergence of the Nestorian as well as the non-Chalcedonian Churches.

The Second Council of Constantinople, 553

The next two councils were simply a part of the aftermath of Chalcedon. In one sense Docetism and Adoptionism represented the two extremes to which Christian theology would not go. In another way, Nestorianism and Monophysitism were the concrete historical parameters between which orthodox Catholic thought would eventually steer its course. In this, the Church showed its fidelity to Ephesus and Chalcedon, and in turn to Nicea. But the Church's fidelity to those two councils cost a great price, the loss of the Nestorian Church and the Monophysite Churches to Catholic Christianity. The century after Chalcedon reflected the Monophysite crisis.

The Second Council of Constantinople was convoked by the emperor Justinian (527–565) to resolve the controversy over the Three Chapters, that is, over the names and writings of three theologians long dead—Theodore of Mopsuestia, Theodoret of Cyrus, and Ibas of Edessa. A Monophysite backlash after Chalcedon saw these three as tainted with Nestorianism and sought their repudiation and, through their condemnation, something of a repudiation of Chalcedon as well. Justinian's interest in the condemnation lay with his sincere desire to reconcile Monophysites to the Church. Yet the attack on the three was an attack on Antiochene theology, the *Tome* of Leo, and the Chalcedonian definition, all of which reflected the orthodox two-nature doctrine. The condemnation of the three did not in fact effect a reconciliation of the Monophysites but did effect a further estrangement of the West from the East.

The Pope, Vigilius, refused to be present at the council. His decision reflected the increased tension between pope and emperor, Church and empire, Vigilius and Justinian. It was Justinian who forced the condemnation. Vigilius was unconvinced of it and in no way wanted to repudiate the work of Chalcedon. Almost all the bishops at the council were from the East. The Pope issued a separate judgment, refusing to condemn any of the three by name and accepting only twelve of the seventy-one extracts from the writings of Theodore provided by the emperor as heretical. The council went much further: a condemnation of Theodore of Mopsuestia, a repudiation of Theodoret's writings against Cyril, and a repudiation of the letter of Ibas of Edessa to Maris. The Latins resisted the decisions; the Pope himself had resisted. But by late 553, the Pope accepted the council's condemnation of the Three Chapters.

The Third Council of Constantinople, 680–681

In the fifth century a solution to the Christological dilemma was effected with the Council of Chalcedon, but in both the sixth and seventh centuries the struggle was with the strength that lay within Monophysitism. In the seventh century it surfaced in a new form, as Monothelitism, which was the object of condemnation by the sixth general council of the Church, the third to convene in Constantinople.

Monothelitism was an outcome of the desire to bring Monophysites back into unity with the Church and restore unity within the empire as well. The emperor Heraclius (610–641); Sergius, the Patriarch of Constantinople; and Cyrus, the patriarch of Alexandria, were involved in the origination of the new theory. In fact, in 633 Cyrus was able to effect a reunion of Catholics and Monophysites in Egypt on the basis of Monothelitism. It was only a question of time, however, before Monothelitism stirred the fires of another controversy.

Monothelitism affirmed that there were two natures in Christ, in accord with Chalcedon, but only a single will. It began by saying that in Christ there was but a single operation *(energeia)* or a single source of Christ's actions. In correspondence between Sergius of Constantinople and Pope Honorius I (625–638), a second expression came into use; it was also a question of whether there were one or two wills in Christ (*thelēmata,* wills).

There was an orthodox sense in which one could talk about one will in Christ: the sense of the moral union of the divine will and human will. In fact, orthodox teaching affirmed such a union of wills in Christ. There was no question but that the two wills in Christ were united. But Monothelitism affirmed not a union of wills, but that Christ lacked a human will and a human source for his activities. It was Apollinarianism and Monophysitism and a denial of the complete human nature in Christ. Discussion over Monothelitism persisted for fifty years before it was rejected at the Third Council of Constantinople. At its seventeenth session the council decreed, "We teach that in our Lord, Jesus Christ, there are two natural wills, and two natural operations, indivisible, inconvertible, inseparable, without any fusion, as the holy fathers have taught, and that these two natural wills are not contrary as wicked heretics have said" (Denziger, 291).

Much more happened to Church and empire in the seventh century than the controversy over Monothelitism, however. The seventh century witnessed the birth of Islam. Muhammed died in 632. In 634 Damascus fell, in 637 Jerusalem, in 638 Antioch, in 639 Caesarea, and in 642 Alexandria. The face of the empire and of Christianity changed. Perhaps no change had been so great since the transition from the persecuted Church to the post-persecution Constantinian Church and empire, which had given birth to the new institution of a general council. Much Christian and Roman history had passed since that first council called by Constantine in 325. And Egypt, Syria, and Palestine, cradles of the Christian faith and of ecclesiastical power, had been lost to Monophysitism and then to Islam. The Church was moving into another period of its history.

Byzantine Christology

If we look back at the first centuries of Christianity through which we have so quickly moved, we can take note once again of the diversification, the individualization, the efforts at consolidation, the crises faced, the ongoing challenges, the accomplishments effected. We have seen Christianity define itself over against Judaism, Hellenism, and heresy. It worked through and lived through its initial identity within Judaism, came to grips with classical culture and the truth contained within philosophy, was forced into a process of self-clarification, and met and repudiated the challenge of Docetism. We have seen an emerging Catholic tradition in a movement from kerygma to doctrine and the coming-to-be of an apostolic, biblical canon. We looked at the effort on behalf of continuity with an apostolic past and tradition as well as at the evolution of creeds. "So it was that 'apostolic,' 'Catholic,' 'traditional,' and 'orthodox' became synonymous terms."[24] A Church, catholic and apostolic, had endured both heresy and schism, developing typological and allegorical methods of exegesis as well as a theology of history. Its doctrine of God became imbued with the Greek doctrine of divine impassibility. Faith encountered reason and theology encountered culture and language. Finally, the typically Christian form of monotheism came to be articulated in the widespread struggle against Arianism, leaving subordinationism behind: God is Father, Son, and Spirit.

Nicea became normative of what would be the orthodox expression of the faith. The doctrine of the Trinity had been established as well as a state Church. Scripture appeared in the vernacular. Christology was expressed in liturgical hymns and Christian theology came to terms with liturgy. Unity and diversity in the theologies of Jesus Christ, present in the New Testament, continued into the patristic age. The two most prominent approaches to Christology were what is often called Alexandrian and Antiochene, what Grillmeier has called the Logos-sarx and Logos-anthropos frameworks, what Pelikan prefers to call the doctrine of the hypostatic union and the doctrine of the indwelling Logos, and what I at times have simply called a Logos-theology and a theology of the humanity of Christ. We have seen theology as inseparable from politics. In 457, the Patriarch of Alexandria was hanged during Holy Week for his Christological position. And in Egypt, Palestine, Syria, Asia Minor, North Africa, Italy, and Gaul, we recall the names and achievements of Ignatius and Irenaeus, Origen and Athanasius, Chrysostom and

---

[24]Jaroslav Pelikan, *The Emergence of the Catholic Tradition (100–600)*, The Christian Tradition, A History of the Development of Doctrine 1 (Chicago: University of Chicago Press, 1971) 120.

Theodore, Basil and the two Gregorys, Tertullian and Augustine, Ambrose and Jerome.

The major divisions within Christendom developed gradually but in three stages, at approximate intervals of five hundred years. The first of these came in the fifth and sixth centuries with the separation of the Nestorians and Monophysites from Eastern Christianity, which became restricted to the Greek-speaking world. The second major break was that between East and West, by convention dated as 1054. There were then two main bodies of Christians, the Roman Catholic Church and the Orthodox Church. The third break that split the Church was in the West with the Reformation of the sixteenth century.

To this day there still exist Nestorian Christians who did not and still do not accept the decisions of Ephesus. Their history lay outside that of the Byzantine Empire, in the direction of Persia. The five Monophysite Churches of Armenia, Syria (known as the Syrian Jacobites), Egypt (the Coptic Church), Ethiopia, and India are non-Chalcedonian Christians. The Monophysites of Syria and Egypt in particular played a continuing role in Byzantine history. In fact, the history of the sixth and seventh centuries was to a great degree the story of trying to win them back into the increasingly Byzantine Church in order to restore unity in the empire. The degree of theological difference between the Monophysite and Chalcedonian Churches is today an open question, with the weight being more on the side of there being little significant theological difference between them.[25] Such, however, was not the mood of the sixth and seventh centuries.

Although Chalcedon had seemingly taken the "middle way" between Alexandrian and Antiochene Christologies, with a genuine contribution from the West in the *Tome* of Pope Leo, Chalcedon nevertheless did not effect unity in Christendom. "Alexandrian" and "Antiochene" interpretations of Chalcedon emerged. Some saw Chalcedon as Cyrillian and others as Nestorian, or at least leaning more in one direction or the other. Just as the Nestorian Church would remain faithful to Nestorius, so

[25]John Meyendorff, *Christ in Eastern Christian Thought* (New York: St. Vladimir's Seminary Press, 1975) 29–46. Also see *The Greek Orthodox Theological Review* 10, 2 (1964–1965); and 13, 1 (1968). For an interpretation of Leontius of Byzantium's Christology different from that of Meyendorff, see J. J. Lynch, "Leontius of Byzantium, A Cyrillian Christology," *Theological Studies* 36 (1975) 455–471.

the Monophysites would choose the authority of Cyril over Chalcedon if they were forced to choose.

John Meyendorff[26] classifies the post-Chalcedonian theologians into four groups: (1) Antiochene Dyophysites who rejected Nestorius but interpreted Chalcedon as a victory for Antioch and for Theodore, and partially as a disavowal of Cyril; (2) strict Monophysites who rejected the Council of Chalcedon as Nestorian, following Dioscoros and Timothy Aelurus; (3) those today termed neo-Chalcedonians who interpreted the council neither as an Antiochene victory nor as a disavowal of Cyril but only as condemnation of Eutyches, a moderate interpretation between that of the two previous groups and one that did not require a rejection of Chalcedon; (4) a creative and Origenist interpretation of the council, exemplified in Leontius of Byzantium.

Since the post-Chalcedonians were dominated by the Antiochene interpretation (group one), it is no wonder that Chalcedon was unable to effect a reconciliation. Just as the "Antiochenes" had earlier gone the route of the Nestorian split from Christianity after Ephesus, so the "Alexandrians" would take the route of Monophysitism after Chalcedon. The differences between Antioch and Alexandria were thus never fully resolved. For the Monophysite theologians (Timothy Aelurus, Severus of Antioch), the words *hypostasis* and *physis* were synonymous, as they had more or less been for Cyril and also Athanasius, and Chalcedon was not justified in innovating a distinction between them. For strict Cyrillians, two *physeis* or natures still meant two distinct beings.

From the sixth through the ninth centuries the three major Eastern groups—the Nestorians, the Monophysites, and the Chalcedonians—articulated distinctive Christological positions that would perdure for centuries.[27] The leading Nestorian theologian of the seventh century was Babai the Great. The Nestorians' enemies were Cyril, Justinian with his condemnation of the

[26]Meyendorff, *Christ in Eastern Christian Thought*, 29–30. For a thorough and immensely helpful history of post-Chalcedonian Christology, also see Aloys Grillmeier, *Christ in Christian Tradition: From Chalcedon to Justinian I*, trans. Pauline Allen and John Cowte (Atlanta: John Knox, 1987) esp. pp. 238–317.

[27]Jaroslav Pelikan, *The Spirit of Eastern Christendom (600–1700)*, The Christian Tradition, A History of the Development of Doctrine 2 (Chicago: University of Chicago Press, 1974) 37–90. Also Grillmeier, n. 26 above.

Three Chapters, and the expanded Trisagion of the "Theopaschites," who held that God suffered.

The Monophysite Christology was the primary rival to Chalcedon and obstacle to unity in the empire. With Severus of Antioch as one of their founding theologians, their definition of Christ in contrast to the Chalcedonian one was the phrase from Cyril: "One incarnate nature of God the Logos." The incarnation did not exist "in two natures," although Monophysites were ready to admit that it was "from two natures." Chalcedon had rejected "from" and said "in." For Monophysites, after the incarnation there was only "the one incarnate nature." Severus cautioned: Do not use the word "two" after the union.

Thus the Monophysites taught one hypostasis and one nature; the Chalcedonians (Melchites) taught one hypostasis and two natures; the Nestorians taught two hypostases and two natures in the one *prosōpon*. Unfortunately, the Chalcedonians lacked any great theologians immediately after the council, such as Athanasius after Nicea.

Chalcedonian or Byzantine theology has an apostolic, conciliar, orthodox, traditional flavor. The Chalcedonian churches of the East are referred to as Orthodoxy. Their life can be practically summed up in the word "tradition." They are the Church of Seven Councils.

The first of the councils, Nicea, has primacy in authority as well as in time. It is the council to which all the others referred. In a similar vein, the first four councils are granted a special prestige: Nicea, I Constantinople, Ephesus, and Chalcedon. Later, however, the East came to be seen as the Church defined in the first seven councils, with II and III Constantinople and II Nicea joining the above four in comprising the seven great councils. In the eighth century Nicephorus wrote, "I honor the seven holy and ecumenical councils."[28] In the eleventh century the metropolitan of Russia wrote, "All profess that there are seven holy and ecumenical councils, and these are the seven pillars of the faith of the Divine Word on which He erected His holy mansion, The Catholic and Ecumenical Church."[29] The seven councils are seen as having articulated the core of the Christian faith in the doc-

---

[28]Pelikan, *The Spirit of Eastern Christendom*, 25.

[29]Timothy Ware, *The Orthodox Church* (New York: Penguin Books, 1976) 27.

trines of the Trinity and the incarnation, and in their defense of the two words associated with them, *homoousios* and *theotokos*. The seventh and last of these great councils recognized by the East was held in 787 at Nicea and defended the veneration of icons. Timothy Ware has written, "Orthodoxy has always attached great importance to the place of councils in the life of the Church. It believes that the council is the chief organ whereby God has chosen to guide His people and it regards the Catholic Church as essentially a *conciliar* Church."[30]

Orthodoxy has a strong sense of a living tradition, which does not contrast with Scripture as controversies in the West later did. Tradition is both a conservative and a creative principle and manifests itself in the Scriptures as well as in the seven councils, the creeds, the liturgy, and holy art or the icons.

Sacred art, liturgy, and the theology of beauty are closely woven together in Byzantine theology, which is particularly a liturgical theology. Christology and theology are fundamentally doxology. Liturgy, art, and doctrine cannot be separated. A distinctive feature of Orthodoxy is the role of the icon, which is not an idol but a symbol, not adored but venerated.

The icon is a supreme form of religious art, for in iconography art and theology come together. The iconoclastic controversy of the eighth and ninth centuries was one area in which art history, political history, and the history of theology could not be separated from one another. The role of the icon is based on a theology, and a theology of art, which is the core of the Byzantine spirit.

The controversy over the use of icons began in the early eighth century with the emperor (first Leo III, then his son Constantine V) ordering their destruction. In the course of the controversy, the East had to work out for itself the relationship between Church and empire. The seventh general council, meeting at Nicea in 787, restored the veneration of icons and decreed the destruction of iconoclastic literature. Nevertheless, the decrees of the council did not put an end to the controversy. It broke out again in the ninth century under the emperors Leo V, Michael II, and Theophilus but was resolved with Theophilus' death in 842. The restoration of the icons in 842 came to be celebrated as a great feast in the East, the feast of Orthodoxy, on the first Sunday in Lent.

[30]Ibid., 23.

The theology disputed in the controversies involved the charge of idolatry as well as the Christological issues of the earlier centuries. The iconoclast argued that images of Christ pictured him only in his humanity (which was false representation and heresy) or tried to picture him in both his divine and human natures (which was not possible because the divine nature could not be circumscribed). In contrast, the iconodule argued that the incarnation itself made the portrayal of Christ possible. To the iconoclast the icon manifested a dividing of Christ, behind which lay the entire Nestorian-Monophysite history. John of Damascus, Theodore of Studios, and Nicephorus provided the theological defense of icons. Christology was only one of the issues, but an important one. Iconoclasm was considered a form of Docetism and a denial of the full reality of the incarnation. The icons did not circumscribe God or Christ but depicted the Word incarnate. The gospel could be depicted pictorially as well as verbally. Art as well as Scripture could give witness to Christ.

In addition to Antiochene Dyophysite, Severian Monophysite, and neo-Chalcedonian interpretations of Chalcedon, Meyendorff refers to another, creative and distinctive interpretation, influenced by Origenist thought and the Origenism of Evagrius Ponticus (346–399). The chief representative of this fourth approach to Chalcedon was Leontius of Byzantium, an anti-Monophysite theologian of the sixth century influenced by Origenist/Evagrian philosophy. His Christological definition of the unity in Christ was in terms of an "essential union." He used the expressions "union according to *hypostasis,*" and "hypostatic" rarely. In Evagrian Christology, "essential knowledge" was the state of the pure intellect united to the Logos. The intellect of Christ remained in this state while others fell from it, a theory reminiscent of Origen. Leontius did not speak of this "essential knowledge" but rather of an "essential union," being careful at the same time to avoid the condemnations that Origenism underwent in the sixth century. Leontius did not designate the subject of the union as the Logos, but rather as Christ, who was the non-fallen intellect in an essential union with the Logos and who willingly took on flesh in order to save it.

The word *hypostasis* for Leontius meant a particular individual, someone, someone by oneself. There is only one Christ and therefore one *hypostasis*. This *hypostasis* is not the pre-existent

Logos, but the Christ formed at the time of the incarnation in an "essential union" with the Logos and of two natures. Leontius' Christology escaped the condemnation of Origenism because it appeared to be in accord with Chalcedon (one *hypostasis,* two natures), but these terms were interpreted in his own particular way.

Leontius' lasting contribution to Christology was his use of the term *enhypostaton.* Both Nestorians and Monophysites maintained the notion that there is no *physis* without *hypostasis;* thus the former, the Dyophysites, held to two *hypostases* in Christ, and the latter to one *physis.* Leontius introduced the notion of something having its existence "in" something, which he calls *enhypostaton. Hypostasis* is not the same as *enhypostasis;* the former designates someone in particular, while the latter implies an essence that is not accidental but has real existence "in" another. Since the human nature in Christ is not a distinct *hypostasis* in relationship to the Logos, not a distinct "someone" over against the Logos, Christ's *human* nature is enhypostatic, not hypostatic.

If one takes Leontius' expression and uses it within a different Christology in which the *hypostasis* is the pre-existent Logos as the one subject of the incarnation, then Leontius of Byzantium can be seen as having made a contribution to Chalcedonian Christology.

This proper (Orthodox) setting for Chalcedonian Christology was actually effected by Leontius of Jerusalem, for a long time identified with Leontius of Byzantium. Leontius of Jerusalem's Christology is distinct, however. Writing approximately a century after Chalcedon, between 532 and 536, he was a Chalcedonian who formally identified the *hypostasis* of the union with the pre-existent *hypostasis* of the Logos, and he made it possible for Cyrillians to recognize a continuity between Cyril and Chalcedon. By now, however, it was getting too late to effect the reconciliation of the Monophysites. But Leontius of Jerusalem interpreted Chalcedonism as compatible with Cyrillism. He wrote, "The Word in the latter times, having himself clothed with flesh his *hypostasis* and his nature, which existed before his human nature, and which, before the worlds, were without flesh, hypostatized human nature into His own *hypostasis.* "[31] Christ's human

[31]Meyendorff, *Christ in Eastern Christian Thought,* 74.

nature thus possessed no *hypostasis* of its own. Its hypostasis was the pre-existent Word.

Leontius of Jerusalem was also able to understand the Theopaschite formula ("one of the Trinity was crucified or suffered in the flesh") in a Chalcedonian and orthodox sense. In his twelfth anathema against Nestorius, Cyril had said that "the Word had suffered in the flesh." Like *theotokos,* it was a key to understanding Cyril's theology. In explaining the formula, Leontius maintained the distinction introduced at Chalcedon between *hypostasis* and nature. It was a distinction, however, that had not been accepted by Antiochenes or Cyrillians. John Meyendorff writes, "The Word remains impassible in his divine nature but suffers in his human nature. Since, from the moment of the incarnation, the human nature had become as fully *his own* as the divine nature, one may (and one must) say that the 'Word suffered' hypostatically, in his own flesh, because his hypostasis is not a mere product of the divine nature but is an entity ontologically distinct from the nature. . . . "[32] The humanity assumed by the Logos is hypostatized in the Logos and deified by the Logos and becomes the source of divine life. The human nature is the Word's own flesh. Here we see the close relationship between the incarnation and the doctrine of deification so central to Byzantine theology.

The understanding of salvation as deification is characteristic of Eastern theology and spirituality: the human person is most fully human when participating in God's very own life. We were created for such participation, and it is our nature to be in union with God. The Byzantine doctrine of deification goes back to Athanasius: "God became human in order that we might become God in him" (*Ad Adelphium,* 4; *De Incarnatione,* 54) as well as to the patristic theological principle made so explicit by Gregory Nazianzen: "What is not assumed cannot be healed, and what was united to God is saved" (Epistle 101, *ad Cledonium*). The Eastern and Greek patristic doctrine of deification as the heart and soul of soteriology is based on the presupposition of an interpenetration of divine and human life, manifest in the hypostatic union or the deified human existence of the incarnate Word. This

[32]Ibid., 77.

union does not negate or diminish the specifically human but rather restores it to its natural state of union with God.

The Christological issues that confronted Eastern Christianity were not simply questions of semantics and politics, although language and culture were certainly involved. Yet the doctrine of the incarnation and its accompanying doctrine of deification and how they were conceptualized lay at the heart of the spiritual life of the Eastern Churches and its mysticism. Mysticism and theology were never separated in the East in the way that was true of the West. True theology was mystical. Otherwise it became "scholastic" or "academic" in the pejorative sense. And true mysticism must be rooted in theology and liturgy. Otherwise it becomes "subjective" or "private."

Western Theology

Christology per se was not the major issue for medieval theology in the West, nor the area in which medieval doctrinal development primarily took place. Ephesus and Chalcedon were accepted presuppositions of medieval Christology. Nevertheless, there were some conflicts and Christological contributions.

Adoptionism was one of the major Christological conflicts of the Middle Ages, arising during the Carolingian period. Since Adolf Harnack's history of dogma in the late nineteenth century, it has become common to use the term "Adoptionism," as I have also done, in reference to the earlier period of Christian history to describe the tendency associated with the Ebionites and with Paul of Samosata. The Spanish Adoptionism of the eighth century was of a different sort. It originated with Elipandus, archbishop of Toledo (ca. 718–802), and Felix, bishop of Urgel (d. 818). These theologians distinguished between Christ's divinity and humanity in such a way that Christ was considered to be Son of God by nature according to his divinity and son of God by adoption according to his humanity. They thus associated sonship with the natures rather than with the person and distinguished two kinds of filiation in Christ. These two filiations, however, were too reminiscent of a doctrine of two sons and they seemed to divide Christ into two. They seemed Nestorian.

The eighth century Adoptionists did not deny that Christ was divine. They were not saying that the divinity of Christ was of an adopted sort. As Logos, and in his divine nature, Christ was the natural Son of God. What was adopted was the humanity of Christ. As a human, they believed Christ was an adopted son of God. Christ was Son of God, both according to his divinity and according to his humanity, but in different ways. It was not that the Adoptionists opposed Nicea, Ephesus, or Chalcedon. But their language was dangerously close to a way of speaking that was unacceptable. Adoptionist language was too risky to be of service to the Church's understanding. Opponents maintained that the Adoptionists failed to distinguish between "adoption" and "assumption." The Word assumed a human nature but did not adopt it. To speak of Christ as an adopted son according to his humanity would also confuse the distinction between Christ and us, who are in fact adopted daughters and sons. Christ deserves to be worshiped. We do not. Another issue was whether sonship is a predicate that belongs to the nature or to the person. In Catholic tradition it had come to mean the person or *hypostasis*. Thus, two "sons" would be confusing.

The "Spanish heresy" was condemned at synods in Frankfurt (794) and in Rome (798) and was refuted by Alcuin among others. Modified variations of Adoptionism appeared in the twelfth and later centuries as well, but only to be rejected. Jesus as human is not a son of God by adoption but is the only begotten Son of the Father, enfleshed by assuming a human nature. He is Son of God by nature. We are children of God by adoption. This became orthodox Christological language.

The major Christological developments of the Middle Ages, however, were not Christological per se. They were soteriological. It was not so much the "person" of Christ as it was the "work" of Christ that was the object of discussion. During the tenth and eleventh centuries, the "monastic period" of Western theology, there developed more and more the "Western" approach to Christ. During this period we find names like Fulbert of Chartres (ca. 960–1028), under whose direction the cathedral school at Chartres flourished; Lanfranc (ca. 1010–1089), who joined the abbey at Bec, later became archbishop of Canterbury, and who is especially known for his criticism of the Eucharistic teaching of Berengar of Tours; and Peter Damian (1007–1072), who did much to develop Christocentric devotion in conjunction with Benedictine piety. And at the turn of the century, 1098, we have one of the most significant treatises of the Middle Ages, Anselm of Canterbury's *Cur Deus Homo* on the purpose of the incarnation.

With Anselm (ca. 1033–1109), another Benedictine monk, we enter into the twelfth century and the High Middle Ages. The twelfth century is the century of early Gothic, of romantic love, and of theologians like Peter Abelard (1079–1142), Bernard of Clairvaux (1090–1153), Hugh (d. 1142) and Richard (d. 1173) of St. Victor, and Peter Lombard (ca. 1100–1160). With the socioeconomic and commerical revolutions of the eleventh and twelfth centuries, theological learning moved from the great monastic centers to the urban cathedral schools and, eventually, to the great universities in the thirteenth century. A shift took place from the "monastic theology" of the tenth and eleventh centuries to the "scholastic theology" of the twelfth and thirteenth centuries.

In Anselm of Canterbury we see the close of the "monastic" or "Christocentric" period of theology, and with Abelard we see even more clearly the beginnings of the new theology, the "Scholastic" period. We shall turn to the two of them as great exponents of medieval Western soteriology. As we have seen, the doctrine of salvation in the East was primarily articulated in terms of deification. Such a theology of salvation was not completely absent in the West, though it was never dominant. In Irenaeus, early in the patristic period, salvation had been articulated in terms of "ransom" and as a "victory over the devil." This *christus victor* doctrine of atonement persisted even in the medieval period as development in the theology of atonement took place. The "work of Christ" as doing battle with the devil was not simply forsaken. But with Anselm another theology of atonement was articulated. It was associated with the notion of satisfaction in contrast to that of ransom.

Anselm was born in Piedmont. He later entered the monastic school at Bec in Normandy, where he succeeded Lanfranc as prior. In 1093 he was consecrated archbishop of Canterbury. Some of his most famous works, such as the *Monologion* and the *Proslogion,* in which he developed what was later called his "ontological argument" for the existence of God, were written at Bec. Anselm's theological method was to pose a theological problem and then respond to it through the use of reason, not as a rationalist or for any lack of faith, but in order to convince unbelievers on their own grounds of the reasonableness of what is believed. Perhaps better known than any other Anselmian doctrine is that in which he saw theology as faith seeking understanding (*Proslogion,* 1).

Anselm wrote his *Cur Deus Homo* during a three-year exile from the see of Canterbury, which had resulted from disputes with the king (1097–1100). In it both faith and reason came into play. His purpose was to show, apart from Christ and on rational grounds alone, that salvation required someone who was both truly God and truly human (*Cur Deus Homo,* prologue). Its setting was also the paradox of God's justice and God's mercy. The "work" of Christ, our salvation, must be seen to manifest both (*Cur Deus Homo,* 1, 12; 2, 20). God's mercy cannot leave God being unjust, and God's justice cannot leave God being unmerciful. Jaroslav Pelikan described the dilemma: "What was needed was a way of defining the grace of God that would not nullify the justice of God, a way of stating his "benignity" without impairing his 'dignity.' "[33]

Because of sin and its dishonor to God, humankind was in debt to God. God could not simply forgive humanity its sin without some satisfaction, for such would violate one's sense of justice (*Cur Deus Homo,* 1, 11–12). Another aspect of the dilemma is that humankind owed God this "satisfaction," and yet it was the kind that humanity itself was unable to pay. It was necessary and yet not possible for us by ourselves alone. It was only possible through Christ, through someone who was *both* God *and* one of us (*Cur Deus Homo,* 1, 25).

In the satisfaction theology of atonement, the metaphor of Christ as victor was changing to metaphors of Christ as victim and as sacrifice. These images reflected the close relationship between Christological and sacramental developments. The concept of satisfaction was itself related to developments in the practice of penance, and the theology of Christ as victim and sacrifice related to the developing theology of the Eucharist (Anselm, *On the Sacraments of the Church*).

The metaphors of satisfaction, victim, and sacrifice redirected the perspective within which the atonement was understood. In

<hr>

[33]Jaroslav Pelikan, *The Growth of Medieval Theology (600–1300),* The Christian Tradition, A History of the Development of Doctrine 3 (Chicago: University of Chicago Press, 1978) 110.

a ransom metaphor, the price or ransom was paid to the devil and we were freed from our bondage to him. In a satisfaction metaphor, the price of our redemption was paid to God. Christ's sacrifice was an offering to God, fulfilling the demands of justice. It was not a question of winning humankind back from the devil but of paying one's debt to God.

The framework of the Anselmian theory was juridical, a question of God's justice requiring either our punishment or our settling the debt, some reparation for our sin. "Without satisfaction, that is, without a spontaneous settlement of the debt, it is impossible for God to forgive a sin that has remained unpunished or for the sinner to attain to a beatitude such as the one he had before he sinned" (*Cur Deus Homo,* 1, 19).

Yet it was not only a question of God's justice. God also showed his infinite mercy in the sacrifice of Christ. Humankind was unable to pay the infinite debt owed God, for it was an infinite being whose honor had been violated. Proper atonement or satisfaction could be made only by God, by someone infinite. Yet the debt was ours. Thus proper satisfaction could only be made by one who was both God and one of us. This was the substance of Anselm's argument (*Cur Deus Homo,* 1, 23; 2, 6–7). God revealed his mercy by becoming one of us in order that we might be saved. Thus the Christology of two natures was put at the service of a soteriology of satisfaction, the requirement of which demanded a *Deus-homo,* a person who was both God and human. Anselm's theology of atonement has not only been called juridical but also objective, in that the price of our redemption was in fact paid. Neither of these labels is adequate, however. Anselm saw the "beauty" and the "rationality" in what God accomplished in Christ. In him God's justice was acknowledged and God's mercy revealed. In him we were saved by both God and a human being, by both God's grace and a work of Christ as human.

Peter Abelard (1079–1142) was the exponent of another medieval theology of atonement. In contrast to the metaphors of "satisfaction" and "victim," Abelard spoke about Christ as "example" and "teacher." Abelard's theology of atonement is often characterized as "subjective" in contrast to Anselm's. The two theologies were the two medieval approaches to salvation, distinguishable from patristic emphases on ransom and deification.

Of the two medieval views, Anselm's certainly became the prominent theology for later generations.

The text of John 15:13 ("Greater love than this no one has, than to lay down one's life for one's friends") was the biblical basis for Abelard's theology of the cross. The cross had revealed God's supreme love for us, and thus the passion of Christ both teaches us and sets an example. Abelard developed his view in his *Commentary on Romans* and in his sermons. "By the faith which we have concerning Christ, love is increased in us, through the conviction that God in Christ has united our nature to himself and that by suffering in that nature he has demonstrated to us the supreme love of which he speaks," (*Commentary on Romans* 1). Bernard of Clairvaux was one of the major opponents to Abelard's theology.

In 1121 at a council in Soissons, Abelard's teaching on the Trinity had been condemned, and in 1141 at a council in Sens, some of his other views were condemned.[34] Yet much in Abelard's theology of the atonement has an appeal even today. He rejected the traditional view that Christ had come to pay a ransom to the devil and the Anselmian view that the debt was paid to God. Abelard's perspective cannot be simply labeled "subjective," for Christ had in fact come, God had taken on flesh in history, and God's love had been "objectively" revealed. Yet there is a side of Christ's "work" that must be appropriated or imitated. Our own reconciliation follows upon our following the example that God-in-Christ has set (Luke 7:47).

Increasing emphasis on the passion and cross of Christ characterized medieval Christology and soteriology, and this new direction showed itself in spirituality, devotion, and art. The focus had shifted from Christology to soteriology. Anselm's perspective influenced theology and, as a result, spirituality in the West for centuries.

One of the giants of the twelfth-century West was Peter, the Lombard, the Master of the Sentences. Although not an original theologian, Peter was capable of summing up the theology of the previous period and passing it on to the thirteenth century. His four books of the *Sentences* were the basis for commentary by

---

[34]For some of the condemned views of Abelard, see Justo L. Gonzalez, *A History of Christian Thought*, vol. 2, From Augustine to the Eve of the Reformation (Nashville: Abingdon, 1971) 172.

beginning theologians during the next several centuries. He was most influential in fixing the number of sacraments at seven. He also bequeathed to future generations the so-called three opinions on the mode of union in the incarnation (the *assumptus, habitus,* and subsistence theories), to which we will return when we discuss Thomas' theology of the incarnation.

The major heretical movement of the twelfth century was that of the Cathari, called Albigensians in southern France, a revival of a form of Manicheism, whose doctrine and dualism led them to deny the real humanity of Jesus as well as the doctrine of the resurrection of the body. For the Albigensians, the visible world was evil, a creation of the evil god. The Son of God would not have partaken of creation for the physical body itself was evil.

The thirteenth century evokes special recognition among historians of Western theology, the century of the Gothic cathedral, the *Summa,* and the systematizations of the Catholic tradition. This century, which followed upon the footsteps of the spiritual leadership of Francis and Dominic and the mendicant movement, gave birth to the theologies of Alexander of Hales (ca. 1186–1245) and Bonaventure (ca. 1217–1274), the founders and greatest exponents of Franciscan theology, and to Albert the Great (ca. 1200–1280) and Thomas Aquinas (1224/5–1274), the founders and greatest exponents of Dominican theology. Certainly the syntheses of Bonaventure and Thomas stand with the giants of Christian thought, on whose shoulders many future generations have stood.

Bonaventure's synthesis manifested a masterly blend of "philosophical" theology and "mystical" theology. *Breviloquium,* a summary of his theology, presented a traditional Christology. His *Journey of the Mind to God,* a classic of medieval spirituality, along with *The Tree of Life,* his meditation on the life of Christ, presented a spirituality in which a primary focus was that of contemplating the humanity of Christ.

Thomas Aquinas' *Summa Theologiae,* in its threefold division, was a systematization of biblical, patristic, and speculative theology, ordered round the great theme of *exitus-reditus,* the origin of all from God and the return of all to God. The first part considers God, one, triune, and as Creator. The second part considers the human person, our final goal in our quest for beatitude, happiness, and life based on freedom, law, grace, and virtue. The third part considers the return to God through Christ, the mystery of salvation and incarnation. Thomas' *Summa* eventually replaced the *Sentences* of Peter Lombard as the starting point for beginners in theology. We will later give further consideration to his Christology, since it was both a summary of the Middle Ages and the foundation for Catholic Christology into modern times.

Theology in the Latin West during the medieval period could practically be summarized in one word: Augustinian. The Augustinian synthesis was the soul of Latin theology. Augustine was the primary influence on Gregory the Great (ca. 540–604), the Carolingian renaissance in the eighth and ninth centuries, and during the twelfth century and into the thirteenth century on the Franciscan theology of Alexander of Hales and Bonaventure. Such was the impact of one man. His theology played the central role in discussions on the theology of the Trinity as well as on the Christian praxis of faith, hope, and love (Augustine's *Enchiridion* originally bore the title *Faith, Hope, and Love*). Augustine's influence is found in the medieval controversies over grace, free will, and predestination as well as in the developing sacramental theology on the efficacy of the sacraments, with baptism as the key to sacramental reality. Thomas Aquinas himself cannot be understood apart from the Augustinian influence. But after Thomas, the Catholic tradition was no longer Augustinian in the same way. Augustine and Aquinas remained the chief exponents of Western theology.

It is difficult to characterize the spirit of any age or culture, and it is perhaps best to refrain from doing so. The Middle Ages have frequently been described as "the Age of Faith," and rightly so. But this period also deserves to be called "an Age of Reason." Perhaps this is not fully appreciated from a later or modern rationalist perspective, yet the Middle Ages witnessed to the importance of reason as well. This emphasis was central to the spirit and theology of the age. Only after a later generation had divided reason and revelation or reason and faith could the Middle Ages be characterized by faith alone. But it was in fact an age of balance, of synthesis, an age in which *virtus stat in medio* (virtue or courage stands in the middle). For we see due, and perhaps even undue, regard to reason being given by both Anselm and Abelard. And the claims of reason had been manifest in John Scotus Erigena and even in Augustine, not to mention the treatises of the thirteenth century.

Throughout the period, the authority of Scripture was recognized as supreme over that of reason. But it was not a period focused on Scripture alone. One of the underlying tensions as well as achievements of the Latin West in the medieval period was its respect for both reason and faith, an age of both philosophy and theology, a time characterized by a balance of revealed truth and rational inquiry. It was a period in the history of theology whose mode of thinking was truly both/and—perhaps a time such as would never be seen again, as either/or modes of thinking would later define reason over against faith rather than in their relationship to each other. Jaroslav Pelikan has written, "This combination of adherence to authority *(auctoritas)* with independent critical reflection *(ratio)*, in widely varying proportions, was to characterize Western theology throughout the Middle Ages."[35] Indeed, it was an era throughout which faith was in search of understanding. If anything, this was the medieval spirit in theology. This was perhaps captured best in the supreme genius and witness of the Middle Ages. For, as Dante's Virgil says, "As far as reason sees, I can reply. The rest you must ask Beatrice. The answer lies within faith's mysteries" (*Purgatorio* XVIII, 46–48, Ciardi translation).

A Concluding Theological Reflection

There is a sadness and a beauty in the history of Christology. Beauty is manifest in the diversity, individuality, continuity, profundity, pastoral sensitivity, and biblical fidelity to which the history of Christology gives witness. Sadness is felt when the diversity can no longer be held together within a communion of the Churches, when gifts given seem at times to serve egoism, socio-political concerns, or self-interests rather than the faith, when necessary consolidation is either rejected or abused by minds or temperaments unwilling to see beyond their own concerns or centers of power. The history of Christological doctrine and language is neither a smooth or progressive movement forward nor a complete mistake or regression from biblical simplicity. History is a revelation of God at work amid obstacles and amid complexi-

[35]Pelikan, *The Growth of Medieval Theology*, 11.

ties that we are always in danger of oversimplifying. We fail at times to grasp the reality that God's Word is incarnate.

We cannot unravel here the meaning of incarnation, but we can suggest one implication. We often welcome the revelation of an incarnate God, but lament the cultural, ecclesiastical, and political conflicts of theological history. But this is to forget that the only Word that comes to us is the incarnate Word, a Word enfleshed in history and thus a Word that cannot be separated out from the stuff of which history is made. To yearn for a "pure" history of doctrine disentangled from mundane concerns is to ask that somehow God or the Word or the gospel be disincarnate. One of the effects of God's decision to be an incarnate God is that God's self-revelation cannot be made ahistorical, or nonhistorical, or uncontaminated by humanness and human history. A Docetic or Monophysite theology of history or revelation of God's truth is impossible. God has joined self-revelation to human history, and the Spirit works in our midst amid the complexities, conflicts, and developments of history. That history may not always be beautiful, but nevertheless beauty it still reveals. The history of Christology itself is a paradox. No wonder it is so interwoven with questions about language! This will be even more apparent in the chapters that lie ahead. Theology and language are inseparable and interdependent.

SUGGESTED READINGS

Barrett, H. M. *Boethius: Some Aspects of His Times and Work*. Cambridge: University Press, 1940.

Brown, Peter. *Augustine of Hippo*. Berkeley, Calif.: University of California Press, 1969.

Burns, Paul C. *The Christology in Hilary of Poitiers' Commentary on Matthew*. Rome: Institutum Patristicum Augustinianum, 1981.

Daniélou, Jean. *The Origins of Latin Christianity*. Trans. David Smith and John Austin Baker. Philadelphia: Westminster Press, 1977. An excellent survey.

Davis, Leo Donald. *The First Seven Ecumenical Councils (325–787): Their History and Theology*. Wilmington, Del.: Michael Glazier, Inc., 1987.

Evans, D. *Leontius of Byzantium: An Origenist Christology*. Dumbarton Oaks Studies 13. Washington, 1969.

Fransen, Piet F. *Hermeneutics of the Councils and Other Studies*. Collected by H. E. Mertens and F. de Graeve. Leuven: Leuven University, 1985. See especially "Unity and Confessional Statements," pp. 247–86, which pertains to my discussion of the two tendencies toward diversification and consolidation. Also previously published in *Bijdragen* 33 (1972) 2–38.

Frend, W. H. C. *The Rise of the Monophysite Movement*. Cambridge: University Press, 1972.

Gregorios, Paulos, William H. Lazareth, and Nikos A. Nissiotis, eds. *Does Chalcedon Divide or Unite? Towards Convergence in Orthodox Christology*. Geneva: World Council of Churches, 1981. Excellent collection of ecumenical studies between the Eastern Orthodox and Oriental Orthodox Churches.

Grillmeier, Aloys. *Christ in Christian Tradition: From the Apostolic Age to Chalcedon (AD 451)*. Trans. John Bowden. Rev. ed. London: Mowbrays, 1975.

_____. *Christ in Christian Tradition*, vol. 2, pt. 1, *From Chalcedon to Justinian I*. Trans. Pauline Allen and John Cowte. Atlanta: John Knox, 1987. A significant substantive treatment of the history of post-Chalcedonian Christology.

Hughes, Philip. *The Church in Crisis: A History of the General Councils, 325–1870*. Garden City, N.Y.: Doubleday Image, 1964.

Jalland, T. G. *The Life and Times of St. Leo the Great*. London: S.P.C.K., 1941.

Kelly, J. N. D. *Jerome, His Life, Writings, and Controversies*. New York: Harper & Row, 1975.

Lebon, J. *Le monophysisme sévérien. Étude historique, littéraire et théologique sur la résistance monophysite au concile de Chalcédoine jusqu'à la constitution de l'Église jacobite*. Louvain, 1989.

Lonergan, Bernard. *The Way to Nicea*. Trans. Conn O'Donovan. Philadelphia: Westminster Press, 1976.

Lynch, J. J. "Leontius of Byzantium: A Cyrillian Christology." *Theological Studies* 36 (1975) 455–471.

McIntyre, J. *St. Anselm and His Critics: A Reinterpretation of the Cur Deus Homo*. Edinburgh: Oliver and Boyd, 1954.

Meyendorff, John. *Christ in Eastern Christian Thought*. Crestwood, N.Y.: St. Vladimir's Seminary Press, 1975.

Ommen, Thomas B. "The Hermeneutics of Dogma." *Theological Studies* 35 (1974) 605–631.

Pelikan, Jaroslav. *The Emergence of the Catholic Tradition (100–600)*. Vol. 1 of *The Christian Tradition: A History of the Development of Doctrine*. Chicago: University of Chicago Press, 1971.

_____. *The Spirit of Eastern Christendom (600–1700)*. Vol. 2 of *The Christian Tradition: A History of the Development of Doctrine.* Chicago: University of Chicago Press, 1974.

_____. *The Growth of Medieval Theology (600–1300)*. Vol. 3 of *The Christian Tradition: A History of the Development of Doctrine.* Chicago: University of Chicago Press, 1978.

Sellers, R. V. *The Council of Chalcedon: A Historical and Doctrinal Survey.* London: S.P.C.K., 1953/1961.

von Campenhausen, Hans. *The Fathers of the Latin Church.* Trans. Manfred Hoffman. Stanford, Calif.: Stanford University Press, 1969.

Ware, Timothy. *The Orthodox Church.* New York: Penguin Books, 1976.

Williams, G. H. "Christology and Church-State Relations in the Fourth Century." *Church History* 20 (1951) no. 3, pp. 3–33; no. 4, pp. 3–26.

Young, Frances. *From Nicaea to Chalcedon: A Guide to the Literature and Its Background.* Philadelphia: Fortress, 1983.

5

Symeon the New Theologian,
Catherine of Siena,
and the Language of Mysticism

We now leave behind the centuries that were most formative in the development of Christological doctrine and move into the theological pluralism of the medieval world. Continuity, consolidation, and orthodoxy had been woven together with development, diversity, and originality in the history of doctrine. Just as pluralism had characterized the first centuries of Christian thought, so it characterized theology in the Middle Ages as well. Yet Christology, however formulated, remained a theology of the Word, a Logos Christology rooted in the doctrine of the incarnation.

Theology as well as the language that expressed it manifested varied emphases and approaches. These ranged from more rational, philosophical, or speculative theology to more mystical or spiritual theology to more practical, pastoral, or existential theology. Philosophical theology has been influenced by Stoicism, Platonism, Aristotelianism, as well as other philosophies. Mystical theology was so influenced as well. Mysticism varied from East to West and from northern to southern Europe, but it was always influenced by religious experience. Pastoral theologies were most influenced by the needs of the people, the period of history, and the "signs of the times." Philosophical reflection, religious experience, and the signs of the times all contributed to the making of Catholic Christology and should not be seen as being mutually exclusive. A particular theologian may have been pastoral, spiritual, and speculative. Yet the language of a particular theologian in expressing the doctrine of the incarnation often seems to manifest a preference for one emphasis over another.

In this chapter we will look at Christology as it is expressed in the language of mysticism, in the East and in the West, in the late tenth- and early eleventh-century Symeon and the fourteenth-century Catherine.

Symeon the New Theologian

The name by which Symeon is commonly known indicates the respect he is given within Orthodoxy. It situates him with John the Evangelist and Gregory of Nazianzen, the only others in the Orthodox tradition to have been given the title "theologian." John the Theologian, Gregory the Theologian, and Symeon the New Theologian all exemplify what it truly means to be a theologian and how true theology is rooted in life and experience—life with God and the experience of God. The theologian is a mystic.

Symeon was born in 949 at Galatea in Asia Minor. At some time near or before the age of twenty, he met Symeon Eulabes (Simeon the Pious or Symeon the Studite), a lay monk at the monastery of Stoudios in Constantinople. Symeon the Studite became the spiritual father of the younger Symeon. Symeon the New Theologian had his first vision or experience of God as light in his early twenties before entering a monastery himself.[1] His second such vision came when he was a novice at Stoudios, which monastery he entered at the age of twenty-seven. There the *hegoumen* or abbot placed him under the direction of Symeon the Studite. In less than a year he was asked to leave the monastery and his spiritual father directed him to the monastery of St. Mamas, where he was able to remain under the spiritual direction of the elder Symeon. Within three years he was professed, ordained, and

[1]See Symeon the New Theologian, Catechetical Discourse 22 and the second thanksgiving, in *The Discourses,* trans. C. J. de Catanzaro, Classics of Western Spirituality (New York: Paulist, 1980) 243–253 and 368–378; and Hymn 25 in *Hymns of Divine Love,* trans. George Maloney (Denville, N.J.: Dimension Books, 1976) 135–138. Also Basil Krivocheine, *In the Light of Christ: Saint Symeon the New Theologian,* trans. Anthony P. Gythiel (New York: St. Vladimir's Seminary Press, 1986) 215–238.

elected abbot, which position he held for twenty-five years. In 986 or 987, Symeon the Studite died, a profound loss for the younger Symeon, who began a cult in honor of his spiritual father in his own monastery of St. Mamas.

Conflict between Symeon and ecclesiastical authority began in 1003. Some of the issues involved included his defense of the right to confess to one's spiritual father whether he was ordained or not (a longstanding monastic tradition),[2] Symeon's understanding of the baptism of the Spirit as a second baptism, and his emphasis on the conscious experience of the presence of the Spirit. His major adversary in the conflict was Stephen of Nicomedia, which may have been more a result of Stephen's own jealousy.

Within two years, in 1005, Symeon resigned as abbot of St. Mamas. In 1008 he was tried before the Holy Synod in Byzantium, or Constantinople. In January of 1009 he was exiled to a small town on the Asiatic shore of the Bosphorus, accompanied by some disciples who helped construct a small monastery. Support and admiration for Symeon continued. His exile was eventually lifted, and he was even offered episcopal consecration. He chose rather to continue living his life at the new monastery, where he died about twelve years later, in 1022, at the age of seventy-three.

His writings ensured his reputation as a mystic-theologian, and his spiritual theology later became a major influence on the rise and development of Hesychasm, the Eastern mystical tradition associated especially with the monks of Mt. Athos and Gregory Palamas, which focused on the continuous praying of the Jesus Prayer ("hesychasm" comes from the Greek word for "quietness"). Symeon's major writings include thirty-four *Catechetical Discourses,* fifty-eight *Hymns,* the *Theological and Ethical Discourses,* the *Theological and Practical Chapters,* as well as homilies, thanksgivings, and Eucharistic prayers. The catechetical discourses were directed toward his own monks. The hymns exemplify his passionate love of God. The three theological discourses are a defense of his theology of the Trinity. The fifteen ethical discourses expand his teaching on the mystical life. The

---

[2]See Krivocheine, *In the Light of Christ,* 125–140; George Maloney, *The Mystic of Fire and Light: St. Symeon the New Theologian* (Denville, N.J.: Dimension Books, 1975) 169–176; Joost Van Rossum, "Priesthood and Confession in St. Symeon the New Theologian," *St. Vladimir's Theological Quarterly* 20 (1976) 220–228.

theological and practical chapters are concise, monastic, and restrained.

Symeon's life and theology were dominated by a single desire: to love God completely. He knew well the sinfulness of his own early life. In his writing, three qualities stand out: how biblical, personal, and Trinitarian his spiritual theology is. These are closely related. He knows the Trinity as three persons, and his personal, experiential knowledge and love for the Father, Son, and Spirit are confirmed in the testimony of the Scriptures. For the biblical character of his theology, one need only read from his *Catechetical Discourses,* selecting any of them. Symeon weaves together texts from Scripture as he moves with artistry toward making a point. These discourses, designed for his monks at St. Mamas, contain the essential ingredients of his mysticism. For the very personal character of his theology and the experiential character of his mysticism, one can select several of his hymns, but also very revealing passages from the catechetical discourses.[3]

The individual Christian's conscious, personal experience of God, a second baptism with the Spirit, was foundational for Symeon. There can be no substitute for it. "If a man cannot feel intuitively that he has put on the image of our heavenly Lord Jesus Christ, man and God, over his rational and intellectual nature, then he remains but flesh and blood. He cannot gain an experience of spiritual glory by means of his reason, just as men who are blind from birth cannot know sunlight by reason alone."[4] It is imperative not only that we believe in the presence of God and the gift of the Spirit, but also that we are conscious of the gift.

> What a terrible misfortune that takers of a heavenly calling (Heb 3:1), who are "heirs of God and fellow-heirs with Christ" (Rom 8:17) and have become citizens of heaven (Phil 3:20), have not yet come to the realization of so great blessings! We are, so to speak, without feeling, like iron that is thrown into fire, or like a lifeless hide that cannot feel it when it is dipped in scarlet dye. This is still our attitude though we find ourselves in the

---

[3]Cf. *The Discourses,* discourses 22, 34, also the two thanksgivings, 243–253, 347–358, 359–378.

[4]Symeon the New Theologian, *The Practical and Theological Chapters, and the Three Theological Discourses,* trans. Paul McGurkin (Kalamazoo, Mich.: Cistercian Publications, 1982) ch. 1:53, p. 46.

midst of such great blessings of God and admit that we have no feeling of it in ourselves![5]

Symeon did not hold back from sharing his consciousness, experience, and feelings with the other monks, even though these were personal, intimate, and at times upsetting to the monks. But he defends himself: "We have not written these things for the sake of exhibitionism. . . . I cannot endure to be silent about the things I have seen, about the wonders of God I have known by fact and experience."[6]

Thus the personal character of his writing, the poetic outpouring it necessitated, and the boldness it exhibits. It is the Spirit who speaks through him.[7]

Symeon's mysticism is apophatic, so aware of the mystery of God that our knowledge of God is more knowledge of what God is not rather than of what God really is.

> No man has ever known anything about God, indeed,
> neither His name nor His nature nor His image
>   nor His form nor His substance;
> to be able to say it or to write about it or
>   to share it with others;
> but, as the radiant sun which penetrates into the clouds
> and no longer lets itself be seen nor its light appear,
> but sheds on the inhabitants of the earth a pale glimmer,
> so, believe me, my God is hidden from us
> and a vast and profound darkness envelops us all.[8]

Yet the Trinity shines through the darkness. God is light. The Trinity is in a living relationship with us. Symeon uses the metaphor of a key, door, and house. The door is the Son, the key to the door the Holy Spirit, and the house is the Father.[9]

In the three theological discourses, Symeon defends his Trinitarian orthodoxy. He opposes those who ascribe an anteriority to the Father.

[5]*The Discourses*, discourse 8:3, p. 145.
[6]Ibid., discourse 34:1-3, pp. 347, 349.
[7]See *Hymns of Divine Love,* hymn 32, pp. 179-182.
[8]Ibid., hymn 12, p. 40. Also see hymns 23 and 31, pp. 113-125, 173-178.
[9]*The Discourses,* discourse 33:4, pp. 341-142.

If you do not imagine that the Father existed before the Son, you will not be led to say that he is prior to, or greater than, the Son. A being which pre-exists can be said to be prior to that which it has engendered, produced, or created, but how can he be spoken of as prior to the co-eternal? The Son is himself eternal and without beginning, just as the Father is. The Father, then, does not pre-exist, and never has been and never will be prior to the Son. On the contrary, he is complete in the complete and equally glorious Son, just as the Son is in the complete and consubstantial Father.[10]

The incarnation reveals the Word of God as God's Son.

Tell us then why the Theologian who rested on the breast of Christ did not say: "In the beginning was the Father," but "In the beginning was the Word"; and why did he say "Word" and not "Son," except to teach us that no one knew there was a Son, or that God was a Father, until God the Word descended and became incarnate? This is not to say that the three-personed Godhead, source of all that is, did not yet exist, but only that the mystery of the incarnation was as yet unknown. For it is only after the incarnation of God the Word that God the Father was also known by us believers as a Father, and that God the Word, who became incarnate for our sake, was known as the Son of God, in accordance with that word which the Father spoke from heaven: 'This is my beloved Son, listen to him.'"[11]

Symeon's theology is utterly triune, and his theology of the divine persons is grounded in his experience of the triune God who speaks to him through the Spirit.[12]

Symeon's most frequent reference to God is as light, which is how Symeon most profoundly experienced God.

As I ascended I was given other ascents, at the end of the ascent I was given light, and by the light an even clearer light. In the midst thereof a sun shone brightly and from it a ray shone

---

[10]*The Three Theological Discourses,* first discourse, 109, but the entire discourse as well.

[11]Ibid., first discourse, 110–111.

[12]Ibid. See the second theological discourse, 123–133.

> forth that filled all things. The object of my thought remained
> beyond understanding, and in this state I remained while I wept
> most sweetly and marveled at the ineffable.[13]

God is light.

> Yet God does not show Himself in a particular pattern or like-
> ness, but in simplicity, and takes the form of an incomprehen-
> sible, inaccessible, and formless light. We cannot say or express
> more than this; still, He appears clearly and is consciously
> known and clearly seen, though He is invisible.[14]

Christ is also light.

> Be not deceived (1 Cor 6:9), brethren! He who lives in the dark-
> ness is outside the door. He who thinks that he has come in,
> but has not entered through the light, is himself outside the
> sheepfold. If Christ is the Light of the world (John 8:12) and
> the door (John 10:7, 9), then surely the door is luminous, and
> not simply a door, and he who finds himself in it is in the Light
> of the world.[15]

Both the Godhead and each of the hypostases is light.[16]

Symeon's orthodoxy can hardly be questioned, yet his theology was somehow "new," a strange description within Orthodoxy, and it carries with it a nuance that can be construed either
positively or pejoratively. As Basil Krivocheine suggests, perhaps
the title "New Theologian" was first given to Symeon by his opponents and then taken up with respect by his disciples.[17] As stated
earlier, Symeon was a theologian in the best sense of that word
within the Greek tradition—a mystic who had reached the heights
of contemplation and vision of God. What was "new" is that
this theologian was a true theologian in a time when Christian

---

[13]*The Discourses*, discourse 17:1, p. 205; also see discourse 22, pp. 243–253. Also see
Krivocheine, *In the Light of Christ*, 215–238.

[14]*The Discourses*, first thanksgiving, p. 365. Also see discourses 15, 16, 28, pp. 193–197,
198–203, 295–307.

[15]Ibid., discourse 28:10, p. 303.

[16]See *Hymns of Divine Love*, hymns 11 and 33, pp. 36–38, 183–186; *The Discourses*, discourse 33, pp. 339–346; *The Three Theological Discourses*, third discourse, esp. pp. 138–139.

[17]Krivocheine, *In the Light of Christ*, 61–63. Also see 391–394.

life and monastic life had fallen into decline in Constantinople—
here was a true theologian who renewed the sense of life with
Christ. There was a newness here in this age, but it was not new
in the best sense of tradition.

We cannot dismiss the new emphases in Symeon's theology.
Yet these new emphases had their foundation in the tradition of
the Church. Symeon made boldly explicit his belief in the importance of our conscious experience of God. A true theologian is
one who truly possesses the Holy Spirit, and such seemed rare
in Symeon's day. Theology is not an intellectual understanding
of Scripture but a knowledge of God that follows upon a conscious, personal experience—and it is possible to experience and
see God in the present life. In fact, this mystical experience is at
the center of ordinary Christian life. We ought not speak of God
before we have experienced God and been born of God and the
Holy Spirit. As Symeon says, "It is not the one who does not
introduce new teachings into God's Church who is orthodox, but
the one whose life is in accordance with the true Word."[18] So
whether the New Theologian acquired his name from those ecclesiastical opponents who saw his charismatic mysticism as threat
or from his proponents who recognized in him the Spirit who
makes all things new, his orthodoxy was not to be questioned
within the terms that he and tradition most basically understood it.

Basil Krivocheine states: "To write a separate chapter on Christ
in the spirituality and theology of Symeon is a difficult task. For
Symeon, Christ is everything, and one would have to read his entire work in order to form an adequate picture of this."[19] And
also, "The Incarnation . . . is undoubtedly the cornerstone of
Symeon's theological vision."[20] Symeon himself writes, "Christ
is the beginning, the middle, and the end."[21]

Symeon's Christology and theology of the Trinity are inseparable. It is because of Jesus Christ that we come to know God
and have access to the Spirit. We would not know God were it
not for the incarnation, and we would not have the life of the
Holy Spirit were it not for Jesus Christ, and we would not reach

[18]From a letter of St. Symeon. Cf. Krivocheine, *In the Light of Christ*, 135.

[19]Krivocheine, *In the Light of Christ*, 239.

[20]Ibid., 393.

[21]*The Practical and Theological Chapters*, 3:1, p. 72.

our destiny as gods were it not for that selfsame Spirit. Thus, one can see the crucial role of Christ in the deifying process of salvation.

The incarnation is not so much something to be explained, as it often becomes in Western theology, as it is a fact to be contemplated, relished, and revered. One can praise the incarnation in poetry and prayer, but one does not as such explain the how of it.

> I who being God by nature became flesh
> and became two in My energies and in My wills
> as well as in My natures,
> being undivided without mixture,
> God-Man, as well as Man-God.[22]

The New Theologian's theology of Jesus Christ is fairly simple, since it is not particularly philosophical. One simply hears over and over again the fact of Jesus' having become one of us and one with us. The staggering implications of this are more important than the rational explanations. Similar to the theology of Irenaeus, Jesus Christ's full humanity sanctifies every stage of human development: "But God came down and was incarnate and became man like us, 'but without sin' [Heb 4:15], and destroyed sin. He hallowed conception and birth and, as He grew up, bit by bit blessed every age."[23] "The incarnation of the Son of God is intimately related to the deification of humankind. "It is heresy when someone turns aside in any way from the dogmas that have been defined concerning the right faith. But to deny that at this present time there are some who love God, and that they have been granted the Holy Spirit and to be baptized by Him as sons of God, that they have become gods by knowledge and experience and contemplation, that wholly subverts the Incarnation of our God and Savior Jesus Christ (Titus 2:13)!"[24]

Here St. Symeon reveals his fidelity to the Greek Fathers who preceded him. He writes: "The Son of God became the Son of

---

[22]*Hymns of Divine Love,* hymn 58, p. 289.

[23]*The Discourses,* discourse 5:10, p. 101.

[24]Ibid., discourse 32:2, p. 336.

Man in order to make us men the sons of God. By grace he lifts up our race to what he is by nature."[25]

For Symeon we are in the form of God, gods, gods by adoption, gods by grace, divinized, like to God, sons of God, children of God, immortals, gods united with God in the Holy Spirit, coheirs with Christ, partakers of the gift of the Holy Spirit, Christs, partakers and sharers of God's divinity and glory, friends of God.[26] Symeon's doctrine of deification is rooted for him in the Scriptures. He refers to Genesis 1:26; Psalm 82:6; Romans 8:17; Galatians 3:27; Titus 2:13; John 1:12; 3:3; 3:8; 10:33; 1 Peter 1:16; and 2 Peter 1:4. Although we too are sons and daughters of God, like the Son of the Most High, Symeon clearly distinguishes between our divinity and that of Jesus Christ: "But the union of the Son with the Father is by nature and has no beginning; our union with the Son is by adoption and grace. Nevertheless we are all united together in God, and inseparable. . . . "[27]

There is no comparison between the Creator and creature.

> "There is no creature
> who is equal in power to the Creator,
> for such a thought is unfitting.
> But, having seen a small ray of light,
> they receive a revelation that I really exist
> and they know that I am God
> and that I brought them into existence.
> And in wonderment and fear,
> they celebrate Me in song."
> For it is impossible that there be created another
> who is God by nature,
> equal in power with the Creator,
> having the same nature as He.
> It is indeed completely impossible
> that any creature be
> of the same essence as the Creator.

[25]*The Practical and Theological Chapters*, 3:88, p. 99. Also see *Hymns of Divine Love*, hymn 6, p. 27.

[26]*Hymns of Divine Love*, 15, 26, 27, 29, 30, 34, 45, 53–55, 192, 204, 228, 230, 254, 260, 264, 277; *The Discourses*, 146–148, 154, 162, 195, 217, 236, 263, 291, 336–338, 350, 353; *The Practical and Theological Chapters*, 34, 50, 56, 89, 95, 99, 136.

[27]*The Discourses*, discourse 34:4, p. 350.

> For how could the created
> ever become equal to the Uncreated?
> Created beings are inferior
> to Him who is always equally
> both eternal and uncreated.
> And indeed you bear witness
> that this is so
> and that there is as much difference
> as between a plow or a scythe
> and the one who made them.[28]

The foundation of our sharing in the divinity of Christ is the divine indwelling, which makes of us gods. This is effected through the Holy Spirit, through whom we are born again from above.[29] This union with the Holy Spirit through baptism is so intimate and intense that it makes us God-conscious. Our divinity is not only something we affirm in faith, it is something we experience and of which we are conscious. Here we come close to Symeon's defense of himself as a true theologian.

> And how is it that one made god by grace and by adoption
> will not be god in awareness and knowledge and contemplation,
> he who has put on the Son of God?
> If the God Logos became man unconsciously,
> then it is permissible that I also may become god in ignorance
> of the fact as is natural to suppose.
> But it is in knowledge, in fact and in conscious experience,
> that God has assumed a whole human nature.
> I am entirely god by sharing in God in a conscious awareness
> and by knowledge, not by essence
> but by participation, as is absolutely necessary to believe to be
> orthodox.[30]

Just as this God-man was conscious of his divinity, so, too, are we human gods capable of such consciousness. In fact, this is what it means to be thoroughly divinized.

---

[28]*Hymns of Divine Love,* hymn 35, pp. 192–193.

[29]Ibid., hymns 51–52, pp. 260, 264.

[30]Ibid., hymn 50, p. 254.

One can see that Symeon's theology of the incarnation and deification are inseparably connected to his theology of the Holy Spirit, that Christology and pneumatology are so joined that one is incomplete by itself alone. The doctrine of Christ and the Spirit bring together salvation, deification, resurrection, and regeneration.

In addition to the resurrection of Christ and the resurrection of the body at the end times, Symeon speaks of a spiritual or mystical resurrection. This resurrection of the soul precedes the resurrection of the body. It is a resurrection that takes place already now in this life and is truly a resurrection from death to life, a resurrection of the dead that takes place daily through the power of the Spirit, through which we ascend and are assumed even now into heaven with Christ. This resurrection is as important as the resurrection at the end.[31] This doctrine of Christ is inseparable from the doctrine of the Holy Spirit.

> Then the Creator,
> be attentive to what I am about to explain to you!
> will send the Divine Spirit.
> I am not speaking of another soul such as you have;
> but of the Spirit, I mean, who comes from God,
> who breathes where He abides,
> who will take His abode substantially in you
> and will illumine and cast His light and recreate you completely
> who will make incorruptible,
> you who are corruptible.
> He will make new again the antiquated house,
> the house of your soul, I mean.
> And with it He will render totally incorruptible your complete
>   body.
> He will make you god by grace, similar to your Model.[32]

Intimately and also inseparably connected are Symeon's theology of the Trinity, Christology, and pneumatology, just as the Father, Son, and Spirit are one. Life in the Spirit and life in Christ are one and the same. The Spirit is the key, Christ the door, and

[31] *The Discourses*, 129, 142, 181; *The Practical and Theological Chapters,* 82.

[32] *Hymns of Divine Love,* hymn 44, p. 228.

the Father the house. The Holy Spirit opens our minds and teaches us the things concerning the Father and the Son.

The Son is also light, and so is the Holy Spirit light, the source of our light and illumination. This illumination, which comes from the Spirit, is the fulfillment of all desire and the goal of every virtue. This illumination is the seal and the mark of Christ. It is the only seal, although its energies and virtues are numerous.

Symeon inquires into blasphemy against the Holy Spirit (Thess 12:10; Matt 12:22), which is attributing the Spirit's operations or gifts to the opposite spirit.[33] Compunction, tears, humility, divine knowledge, all come from the Spirit. To attribute these to the deceit of the devil is blasphemy against the Holy Spirit. Secondly, it is also blasphemy to maintain that one does not become a partaker of the Spirit or a child of God in the present generation. This latter blasphemy introduces a new heresy into the Church and is against the Holy Spirit, who continues works of regeneration even today.[34] To blaspheme against the Spirit is not to believe in the works of the Spirit and not to believe that those works are still taking place today. Deification is not something only for the days of old.

For Symeon there is another baptism besides the first, a "second baptism," which is the gift of the Spirit. In our first baptism we are indeed sanctified, although without knowing it, being infants, but with a sanctity we lose by repeated transgressions in our youth. Baptism regenerates us and refashions us and sets us free; even our first baptism is a being born again with the Holy Spirit. Yet there is a grace of the Holy Spirit that still awaits us, for many who are baptized do not keep the commandments. "They did not exhibit a life worthy of 'the vocation wherewith we are called' [Eph 4:1], nor did they become children of God but instead remained flesh and blood [1 Cor 15:50], without ever having believed that the Spirit exists (cf. Acts 19:2) or seeking Him or expecting to receive Him.''[35] So there are two baptisms, two gifts, by which the Holy Spirit comes to us.[36]

The second baptism involves repentance and the gift of tears,

[33]*The Discourses,* 335–338.

[34]Ibid., 312, 335–346.

[35]Ibid., 148.

[36]Ibid., 264; *The Practical and Theological Chapters,* 42.

and Symeon makes much of both of them.[37] Tears hold a particularly important role in his theology: "It has never been heard that without tears a soul that has sinned after baptism has been cleansed from the defilement of sin."[38]

Living in the Holy Spirit involves the commandments and the virtues. There is no illumination without purification, and no purification without repentance, tears, and keeping the commandments. In the life of virtue, there are two "capital virtues," humility and love.[39] The greatest of all virtues is that of love.[40]

All asceticism is in vain unless it culminates in love. Love is the criterion of true discipleship. Only it qualifies one to be called a Christian. Love of neighbor is a culmination of life in the Spirit just as is the illumination the Spirit brings.

> When we are commanded to consider our neighbor as ourself, this does not mean for just one day, but all through life. When a man is told to give to all who ask, he is told to do this for all of his days. If a man wants people to do good to him, he himself will be required to do good to others.
>
> When a man really considers his neighbor as himself, he will never tolerate having more than his neighbor. If he does have more, but refuses to share things generously until he himself becomes as poor as his neighbor, then he will find that he has not fulfilled the commandment of the master. He no longer wants to give to all who ask, and instead turns away from someone who asks of him while he still has a penny or a crust of bread. He has not treated his neighbor as he would like to be treated by him. In fact, even if a man had given food and drink and clothes to all the poor, even the least, and had done everything else for them, he has only to despise or neglect a single one and it will be reckoned as if he had passed by Christ and God when He was hungry and thirsty.[41]

Symeon's life and theology are most marked by his love of God, but one can also easily see that love of God is inseparable from

[37]*The Discourses,* 54, 70–89, 90, 158–162, 313–315.

[38]Ibid., 313.

[39]Ibid., 236–237.

[40]Ibid., 41–46, 155–156.

[41]*The Practical and Theological Chapters,* 102.

love of neighbor. Love is the goal of Christian life. It follows upon the gift of the Spirit and is integral to the deification that the Spirit effects. Deification is rooted in the incarnation and, thus, ultimately in the doctrine of the Trinity.

Catherine of Siena

Italy as we know it did not exist at the time of Catherine of Siena (1347–1380). In the north there were the independent states: Milan, Genoa, Venice, Pisa, Lucca, Siena, and Florence. In the center were the papal states and to the south the kingdom of Naples and Sicily.

In the north, economic interests led to rivalries between Milan and Florence. Florence boasted the wealth of her merchants and banking families. Siena was also in the hands of rich merchants and was often at odds with Florence. Florence itself was at war with the Pope from 1376 to 1378. The Black Death was another major factor that affected social and economic life in fourteenth-century Italy.

The papal states themselves experienced internal tensions. During most of Catherine's life the papacy was located in Avignon. Clement V (1305–1314) moved to Avignon in 1309. The Avignon popes included, in addition to Clement, John XXII (1316–1334), Benedict XII (1334–1342), Clement VI (1342–1352), Innocent VI (1352–1362), Urban V (1362–1370), and Gregory XI (1370–1378). Urban V had returned to Rome in 1367 only to return to Avignon again in 1370. Gregory XI brought the papacy back to Rome in 1377.

In 1378 there occurred the Great Western Schism. The Avignon papacy of 1309 to 1377 must not be confused with that schism, which produced two lines of popes, one line residing in Rome and the other in Avignon. The schism was not brought to a close until 1417. On April 8, 1378, Urban VI was elected to follow Gregory XI. On September 20 Clement VII was elected, the first antipope.

The fourteenth century was not only a century filled with death, popes, and Italian political conflicts. It was also a century of intense mysticism throughout Europe, among Catherine's Dominican brothers to the north, in the Rhineland (Eckhart, Tauler, Suso), among the laity in the movement known as "the friends of God," and in England (Julian of Norwich, Richard Rolle, and the author of *The Cloud of Unknowing*).

Caterina di Giacomo di Benincasa was born in Siena in 1347, the twenty-fourth of twenty-five children. At about age eighteen, Catherine received the Dominican habit as one of the Mantellate, women, often widows, who wore the habit and were affiliated with the Order of Preachers but lived in their own homes and engaged in "social work" with the sick and the poor. Catherine, according to reports, was the first nonwidow to so wear the Dominican habit. After reception of the habit, Catherine's life can be divided into four periods.[42]

Beginning in 1364 or 1365, there was a three-year period of solitude. She lived in her family's house but in her own room. This period of intense prayer and mystical living culminated with the religious experience of her mystical espousal to Jesus Christ, which inaugurated the next period in her life, one of activity.

In 1368, at age twenty-one, she became heavily involved in Siena in ministry to the sick and poor, serving at times as a nurse. She also attracted a growing group of disciples and friends. Her mystical life continued to deepen along with her active ministry. In 1370 she experienced mystical death, four hours of ecstatic union with God while her body appeared to be lifeless.

In 1374, at age twenty-seven, her activities became increasingly political as well as social and spiritual, and she became even more of a public figure. Her first journey to Florence was in 1374. In 1375 she was in Pisa attempting to persuade that republic not to join the antipapal league. In Pisa she received the stigmata. Catherine's mystical life never diminished as a result of her active involvements. From 1376 to 1378 Florence was at war with the papal states, and this conflict became a focus of Catherine's concerns.

In 1376 she journeyed to Avignon at the request of the Florentines, gullible and naive about her peacemaking mission. One of the concerns of her three-month stay and meetings with Pope Gregory XI was to encourage and support his decision to return

---

[42]For excellent introductions to Catherine's life and works, see Suzanne Noffke, "Introduction," in Catherine of Siena, *The Dialogue*, trans. Suzanne Noffke, Classics of Western Spirituality (New York: Paulist, 1980) 1–22; and Mary Ann Fatula, *Catherine of Siena's Way* (Wilmington, Del.: Michael Glazier, Inc., 1987). Both contain further bibliographical references.

to Rome from Avignon. With Gregory's return in 1377 the Avignon papacy came to a close, but Catherine's involvement in secular and ecclesiastical politics did not. In 1378 Catherine was in Florence again on another peace mission on behalf of the Pope. During the latter part of 1377 and into 1378 Catherine wrote "her book," the *Dialogue.* Her prayer continued to intensify, as did her ministries of spiritual guidance, preaching, writing, working for peace, and being of assistance to the Pope.

For a fourteenth-century Italian woman, her activities would have led more than the devil to describe her as "Damnable woman!"[43] She was relentless both in prayer for the Church and her own disciples as well as in her continuing ministries.

In 1378 the final period of her life began, which was spent entirely in Rome. On March 27 Gregory XI died. On April 8, Urban VI was elected. On September 20, the antipope was elected and the schism began. In late November Urban VI summoned Catherine to Rome, where she remained until her death, praying and pleading the cause of Urban. On April 29, 1380, at age thirty-three, she died.

Catherine's writings are composed of her *Dialogue,* the major statement of her teaching, written during 1377 and 1378 and finished before her trip to Rome; twenty-six prayers, dated between 1376 and 1380, as well as prayers that can be gleaned from her letters and the *Dialogue;* and 382 letters, an impressive correspondence to members of her family, friends and disciples, kings, popes, bishops, as well as prostitutes, soldiers, and many others.[44] Although the *Dialogue* is Catherine's main statement as a preacher and teacher, one comes to know her better as a person through her beautiful prayers and courageous correspondence.

Catherine's style can be dense and repetitive, but what is most noteworthy is her use of images. As Suzanne Noffke writes: "Her pages are studded with metaphors and compounded metaphors. She repeats, yet always with some new layer of relationship. She

---

[43]Catherine of Siena, *The Dialogue,* ch. 66, p. 125. References to *The Dialogue* will be to the Noffke translation, n. 42 above.

[44]Cf. *The Letters of Catherine of Siena,* trans. and introduction by Suzanne Noffke, vol. 1 (Binghamton, N.Y.: Medieval and Renaissance Texts and Studies, 1988), the first of four volumes that will eventually comprise the only complete English translation to date of Catherine's letters. Also see Mary O'Driscoll, "Catherine the Letter Writer," *Dominican Ashram* 3 (1984) 107–113.

explodes into ecstatic prayer. She teaches. Always she teaches."[45] For Catherine, the sinner is a stinking beast[46] and the selfish will a stinking garment.[47] The Trinity is a deep sea.[48] And she speaks of the four winds of prosperity, adversity, fear, and conscience.[49] Metaphors are prominent in her Christology.

Noteworthy about Catherine are her active life and her mystical spirituality—Noffke calls her a mystic activist.[50] She also manifests the mystic's preoccupation with love and the Dominican preoccupation for truth.

That which most stands out in Catherine's spirituality is God's compassionate, ineffable, merciful, incomprehensible, unutterable love.[51] All these adjectives are hers. This tremendous love of God stands out even more clearly in her prayers than in the *Dialogue*. God is both truth and love for Catherine: These are the most common ways in which she addresses the Lord.[52] God has fallen in love with creation,[53] and in one of her more striking images, Catherine addresses God in the *Dialogue* as "O mad lover!"[54]

---

[45]Suzanne Noffke, "Introduction," *The Dialogue,* 10.

[46]*The Dialogue,* ch. 6, p. 35.

[47]*The Prayers of Catherine of Siena,* trans. and ed. Suzanne Noffke (New York: Paulist, 1983) no. 11, p. 87. References to the prayers will first indicate the number and then the page in the Noffke translation.

[48]*The Dialogue,* ch. 167, pp. 364-365.

[49]*The Dialogue,* ch. 94, p. 174.

[50]Noffke, "Introduction," *The Dialogue,* 9. François Vandenbroucke calls Catherine a mystic and apostle, *The Spirituality of the Middle Ages,* vol. 2 of A History of Christian Spirituality, Louis Bouyer and others (New York: Seabury, 1968) 411. Also see Ursula King's study of the "mysticism of action" in Teilhard de Chardin, *Towards A New Mysticism: Teilhard de Chardin and Eastern Religions* (New York: Seabury, 1980).

[51]See *The Prayers.* All these qualities of God's love are found just by reading the first three prayers, pp. 13-40. One can continue with the others, however, and see the frequent descriptive addresses to God as love. Also see, e.g., letter 27, *The Letters of S. Catherine of Siena,* 1:97-99.

[52]"Inseparable from this integration [between prayer and active ministry] is the question of Catherine's central motif. There are critics who say it was Truth, others who contend it was Love. Both are in fact right. For Catherine God is *la prima dolce Verità* (gentle first Truth) and God is *pazzo d'amore* (mad with love) and *essa carità* (charity itself)." Noffke, "Introduction," *The Dialogue,* 8. Also see *The Dialogue,* chs. 98-109, pp. 184-204. A particularly well integrated and ecstatically expressed reference to both love and truth is *The Dialogue,* ch. 134, pp. 273-276. On truth, see *The Prayers,* no. 21, pp. 193-194.

[53]*The Prayers,* no. 3, p. 37; no. 10, pp. 78-80; no. 13, pp. 108 and 113; no. 17, p. 148. *The Dialogue,* ch. 153, p. 325; ch. 167, p. 365.

[54]*The Dialogue,* ch. 30, p. 72; ch. 153, p. 325; ch. 167, p. 364. Also see ch. 108, p. 202,

The unforgiveable sin for Catherine is refusing God's mercy—to consider one's sin to be greater than God's mercy.[55] So boundless is God's love!

Catherine's spirituality is deeply rooted in a very clear Christology: God's love is primarily made manifest in Christ crucified. Her spirituality is both Christocentric and Trinitarian. The underlying Christology is clearly stated in the first of her extant prayers, which comes from Avignon during her three-month stay there in 1376, when she was attempting to persuade Pope Gregory XI to return to Rome.

> And you, Jesus Christ,
> our reconciler,
> our refashioner,
> our redeemer—
> You, Word and Love,
> were made our mediator.
> You turned our great war with God
> into a great peace.[56]

Christ is particularly mediator and redeemer, as we shall see as we look at some of her images for him. Christology is central for Catherine, but her Christology is soteriological in character. Christ is always Christ crucified.[57] In that sense, hers is a theology or spirituality of the cross. But it is always a cross that reveals God's unspeakable love.

Catherine's understanding of the sacrifice of the cross of Christ is what would have been fairly traditional in the West after Anselm (1033-1109). In *Cur Deus Homo,* Anselm developed the theory of atonement associated with satisfaction. In contrast to the more prominent theory prior to Anselm, in which the devil had some claim to humanity, Anselm developed the theory that sin,

---

where she addresses God as "O fire of love!" On many occasions God is an abyss of charity. See ch. 138, p. 284; ch. 141, p. 291; ch. 153, p. 325; ch. 167, p. 365. Altogether there are fifty-two references to "abyss of charity": twenty-six in the letters, sixteen in *The Dialogue,* and ten in *The Prayers.*

[55]Ibid., ch. 37, p. 79.

[56]*The Prayers,* no. 1, p. 17.

[57]For just a few of the many references to Christ crucified, see *The Dialogue,* chs. 1, 4, 66, 75, 78, 96, pp. 25, 29, 125, 137, 145, 179. Also *The Prayers,* no. 24, pp. 207-209. There are 1,241 such references in all, 1,185 of them in the letters.

as an infinite offense because it offends an infinite God, required a human being who was also God, since only God could satisfactorily atone for the infinite offense perpetrated by humankind. In addition to this theology of satisfaction, however, Catherine also uses the images associated with the earlier ransom theory of atonement, the divinity of Christ used as a hook under the bait of our humanity to catch the devil, who bites on more than it can handle.[58]

The perspective of sin as an offense against an infinite God is Catherine's primary starting point. God speaks to her thus: "Do you not know, my daughter, that all the sufferings the soul bears or can bear in this life are not enough to punish one smallest sin? For an offense against me, infinite Good, demands infinite satisfaction."[59] A finite suffering or penalty cannot justly atone for sin. The offense was infinite in character. Yet God's mercy longs for such a satisfaction to be taken care of so that humankind may be justified before God, or God justified in God's continuing love for us. Again God speaks:

> For my divine justice demanded suffering in atonement for sin. But I cannot suffer, and you being only human, cannot make adequate atonement. . . .
>
> And so I satisfied both my justice and my divine mercy. For my mercy wanted to atone for your sin and make you fit to receive the good for which I had created you. Humanity, when united with divinity, was able to make atonement for the whole human race—not simply through suffering in its finite nature, that is, in the clay of Adam, but by virtue of the eternal divinity, the infinite divine nature. . . .
>
> So the pus was drained out of Adam's sin, leaving only its scar, that is, the inclination to sin and every sort of physical weakness like the scar that remains after a wound has healed.[60]

This does not imply, of course, that our sufferings in no way make atonement for sin. Indeed, we are all called to make satisfaction for sin. Our sufferings, however, only have value in terms of

[58]*The Prayers,* no. 13, p. 109; no. 19, p. 176.

[59]*The Dialogue,* ch. 3, p. 28.

[60]Ibid., ch. 14, pp. 51–52. In the same vein see ch. 75, p. 139; ch. 135, p. 278. Also *The Prayers,* no. 9, pp. 73–74; no. 20, p. 189.

atonement if they are joined with loving charity, true contrition, and contempt for sin. A central doctrine in Catherine's spirituality is that suffering alone, *without desire,* cannot atone for sin. For suffering does not atone for sin by reason of the finite pain but by reason of the contrition of the heart. True contrition, that is, the desire of the soul for God, makes satisfaction. It is that which makes one pleasing in God's eyes.[61]

Catherine's spiritual doctrine has an interesting twist at this point. Although a human person, as a finite human being, cannot make the infinite satisfaction due God, nevertheless a person can have *infinite desire.* One almost thinks here of Karl Rahner's theological anthropology of the person's transcendental openness to the infinite. For Catherine, human desire and longing can be infinite. Human satisfaction for sin rests on true contrition, and true contrition is desire for God, and human desire can be infinite: "Because those who have such sorrow have infinite desire and are one with me in loving affection (which is why they grieve when they sin or see others sinning), every suffering they bear from any source at all, in spirit or in body, is of infinite worth, and so satisfies for the offense that deserved an infinite penalty. True, these are finite deeds in finite time. But because their virtue is practiced and their suffering borne with infinite desire and contrition and sorrow for sin, it has value."[62]

Catherine's doctrine on desire is undoubtedly rooted in her own religious experience. The human person's infinite desire (which is itself a gift of God, as is all authentic religious experience) can make satisfaction for sin. Evidently, however, all of this still could not make full atonement for the sins of all humankind.[63] Only the sacrifice of Jesus Christ does that. Hence the cross of Christ is the supreme sign of God's mercy and infinite love; only it redeems the world.

Catherine lived at a time that made her very conscious of the sin of the world, sin that had seriously blemished the Church as well. The hideous reality of sin, eternal damnation, and the jus-

---

[61] *The Dialogue.* See in particular ch. 3, p. 28; ch. 4, p. 32; ch. 7, p. 37; ch. 12, p. 45; ch. 14, p. 51.

[62] Ibid., ch. 3, p. 28. On Catherine's teaching on desire, one may want to consult what she says about the gift of tears, chs. 88-97, pp. 161-183.

[63] Ibid., ch. 14, p. 51.

tice of God were very real to her.[64] Her beloved Church was infested with leprosy![65] She could thus not avoid a consciousness of God's justice and what it implied. She could not help but be aware of the cry for justice. "People have no excuse, then, because they are constantly being reproved and shown the truth. Therefore, if they do not change their ways while they have time, they will be condemned when the second reproof comes. This will be at the end point, which is death, when my justice will shout, 'Arise, you who are dead, to be judged.' "[66]

Catherine was quite conscious of the reality of sin and the demands placed on God's justice, but even more so was she taken aback by God's mercy. She prays:

> O immeasurable love!
> O gentle love!
>
> . . . .
>
> I know that mercy is your hallmark,
> and no matter where I turn
> I find nothing but your mercy.[67]

And in her *Dialogue:* "O mercy! My heart is engulfed with the thought of you! For wherever I turn my thoughts I find nothing but mercy! O eternal Father, forgive my foolish presumption in babbling on so before You—but Your merciful love is my excuse in the presence of Your kindness."[68]

Catherine is so intoxicated with God's merciful love that it appears to her as if God almost needs us.

> O eternal Father! O fiery abyss of charity! O eternal beauty!
> O eternal wisdom, O eternal goodness! O eternal mercy! O hope
> and refuge of sinners! O immeasurable generosity! O eternal
> infinite Good! O mad lover! And you have need of your crea-

---

[64]For some of Catherine's references to the reality of sin and damnation, see *The Dialogue,* ch. 15, p. 54; ch. 35, p. 76; especially ch. 38, pp. 80–81.

[65]Ibid., chs. 13–14, pp. 49–50. One entire section of *The Dialogue* is conscious both of the need not to be judgmental and yet of the tremendous corruption of the Church, chs. 110–134, pp. 205–276.

[66]Ibid., ch. 36, p. 78.

[67]*The Prayers,* no. 9, p. 69; also see p. 72 of same prayer.

[68]*The Dialogue,* ch. 30, p. 72. Also see chs. 37 and 134.

ture? It seems so to me; for you act as if you could not live without her, in spite of the fact that you are Life itself, and everything has life from you and nothing can have life without you. Why then are you so mad? Because you have fallen in love with what you have made![69]

Yet she knows that God does not need God's creatures: "You, deep well of charity, it seems you are so madly in love with your creatures that you could not live without us! Yet you are our God, and have no need of us."[70]

In her prayer, and in response to her intercessory prayer, however, Catherine is aware that God is affected and influenced by us. God tells her, "Your weeping has power over me,"[71] and "You have bound me,"[72] and "But I have told you that my wrath would be softened by the tears of my servants, and I say it again."[73] Catherine was a great believer in intercessory prayer and believed that God's just anger could be attenuated through prayer. Yet these ways in which God allows for an influence by creatures do not imply that God changes ("I am Your unchangeable God")[74] but that God comes and is responsive ("I will not draw back from any creature who wants to come to me").[75] In God's eternal triunity, there is no time. It is only time that makes God's responsiveness appear as change.

The reason Catherine's thought is so Christological is because Jesus Christ is the supreme demonstration, manifestation, and revelation of God's intoxicating love. Jesus Christ crucified is the perfect image of the mad lover! It is in and through Christ that we come to God and come to know God. Seeing the soteriological foundation for both Catherine's spirituality and her Christology, we can now look more closely at her images of Jesus or titles for him.

[69]Ibid., ch. 153, p. 325.

[70]Ibid., ch. 25, p. 63. Clear references to Catherine's awareness of God's perfect and unchangeable nature include chs. 44, p. 90; 78, p. 147; 98, p. 184. Also *The Prayers*, no. 10, p. 78.

[71]*The Dialogue*, ch. 14, p. 51.

[72]Ibid., ch. 15, p. 54.

[73]Ibid., ch. 17, p. 56.

[74]Ibid., ch. 44, p. 90. See n. 61 above.

[75]Ibid.

We referred earlier to Catherine's use of images, and this element of her style is abundantly evident in her Christology. She has a variety of names and images for Jesus, and in that sense she is in accord with the spirit of contemporary Christology, which speaks of the need for new names and titles for Christ.[76] Two things in particular stand out about Catherine's Christological images: the number of them that emphasize Christ as mediator, and the frequent qualification of the image as "gentle" *(dolce)*. Her most famous and thoroughly explored image is that of Christ the bridge. We shall return to it shortly. Then come some very traditional expressions, often qualified by *dolce:* gentle Truth,[77] gentle loving Word,[78] gentle Love,[79] gentle Son.[80] Christ is Truth, Word, Love and Son. "Truth" for Catherine is an expression that applies equally to God or to Christ, and sometimes it is difficult to know to which it refers. God is *prima Verità* (first Truth) and *prima dolce Verità,*[81] but in the *Dialogue* God often speaks of Jesus as "my Truth," and in her prayers Catherine speaks to God of "your Truth."[82] Truth and Love are the two fundamental ways in which Catherine sees both God and Christ.

Next come another set of images depicting Christ as mediator: door,[83] gate,[84] and the vine.[85] We already referred to bridge. Christ

[76]E.g., Edward Schillebeeckx, *Jesus: An Experiment in Christology,* trans. Hubert Hoskins (New York: Seabury, 1979) 62.

[77]See *The Dialogue,* ch. 89, p. 163, and n. 84 below.

[78]E.g., *The Dialogue,* chs. 24, p. 62; 53, p. 106; 90, p. 168; 100, p. 188; 121, p. 232.

[79]*The Prayers,* no. 1, p. 17; no. 5, p. 66.

[80]*The Dialogue,* ch. 27, p. 66.

[81]Examples of Truth referring clearly to God include *The Dialogue,* chs. 88, p. 161; 99, p. 187; most probably 3, p. 28; 4, p. 29. There are numerous references.

[82]Examples of Christ as Truth include *The Dialogue,* chs. 96, p. 179; 119, p. 225; 154, p. 325; *The Prayers,* no. 11, p. 87. It is not always clear. Does "First Truth" in *The Dialogue,* ch. 2, p. 27, refer to God or Christ? The interchangeability of reference for this expression reflects how Catherine saw God and Christ as one. In *The Dialogue,* ch. 89, p. 163, one finds both references: "So she travels over the bridge, following the teaching of my gentle Truth (Christ)"; "Once she has gone along the way of my only begotten Son's teaching and set her sight firmly on me, gentle first Truth (God), she comes to know what she has seen. . . ."

[83]*The Dialogue,* chs. 107, p. 201; 134, pp. 275 and 276; and 154, p. 328, where Christ is doorman instead of door. See *The Prayers,* no. 3, p. 36.

[84]*The Dialogue,* ch. 131, p. 264 and 266. Sometimes gatekeeper, *The Prayers,* no. 20, p. 189.

[85]*The Dialogue,* ch. 23, p. 61. God is the gardener, Christ the vine.

is also doctor and wet nurse.[86] As with Truth and Love, both God and Christ are also the Sun.[87] Jesus Christ is for Catherine the Sun, the wet nurse, the doctor, the vine, the gate, the door, the bridge, the gentle Son, the gentle loving Word, God's Truth, and Love. Some of the images are very biblical. Some are very much her own. All of them, however, are expressions of tremendous intimacy.

Christ "the bridge" is an image that Catherine developed at great length in her *Dialogue*.[88] As a bridge stretches from one shore to another, so Christ, through the union of the divinity and humanity, stretches between heaven and earth and is a bridge between heaven and earth.[89] The bridge unites the human and the divine. As one surveys the scene, there is the river as well as the way across the water over the bridge, and there is the river and waters underneath. This is Catherine's doctrine of "the two ways": the bridge above and the river below. Those who do not choose to cross by means of the bridge must swim on their own. "Those who do not keep to this way travel below through the river—a way not of stones but of water. And since there is no restraining the water, no one can cross through it without drowning."[90] "So I gave you a bridge, my Son, so that you could cross over the river, the stormy sea of this darksome life, without being drowned."[91] The bridge is the way of truth; the river the way of falsehood."[92] Granted that Christ, the bridge, was the way and the truth while with us on earth, what do we do now? Catherine answers this: We have Christ's teaching. "So first I made a bridge of my Son as he lived in your company, and though that living bridge has been taken from your sight, there remains the bridgeway of his teaching. . . . So now as much as before, through

---

[86]Ibid., chs. 14, p. 52; 134, p. 274. *The Prayers*, no. 19, pp. 171 and 177; and Letter 260 (Tommasèo edition), to appear in English in a later volume of the *Letters of Catherine*.

[87]*The Dialogue*, ch. 119, pp. 221-222.

[88]Although there are references to Christ the bridge throughout *The Dialogue*, there is a concentration on it in chs. 26-87, pp. 64-160. Also a summary in ch. 166, pp. 361-363. The only other reference to Christ the bridge is in letter 272 (Tommasèo), the foundation for *The Dialogue*.

[89]*The Dialogue*, chs. 22, p. 59; 26, p. 64; 29, p. 69.

[90]Ibid., ch. 27, p. 67.

[91]Ibid., ch. 21, p. 59.

[92]Ibid., chs. 27-28, pp. 66-68; ch. 42, p. 87.

his teaching as much as when he was among you, he is the way and truth and life—the way that is the bridge leading to the very height of heaven."[93]

Catherine may have had a particular bridge in mind as the basis for her image, as concrete and detailed as it is. In Florence, spanning the Arno River, is the beautiful and unique Ponte Vecchio, a bridge with walls and shops all along the sides. Catherine's bridge too had walls, a roof, a gate at the end, steps leading onto it. Christ, particularly Christ crucified, Christ's passion, is the foundation. The roof is God's mercy made possible by Christ's death and resurrection. The stone walls are stones of virtue built into the wall by Christ, for the bridge is the path of virtue. At the end is the gate through which one must pass, which is one with the bridge, which is also God's Son, both bridge and gate. Through it one enters God, the sea of peace.[94] "By my power the stones of virtue were built into walls on no less a foundation than himself, for all virtue draws life from him, nor is there any virtue that has not been tested in him. . . . So, you see, the bridge has walls and a roof of mercy."[95]

Of all the parts of the bridge, the stairs receive the most discussion, to some degree complicated since they have several referents: (1) parts of Christ's body, (2) the stages of spiritual growth, and (3) the memory, understanding, and will.

The bridge of Christ's teaching is reached by three stairs or steps. These are a figure for Christ's body: his nailed feet, his open side, and his mouth.[96] The first stair, the feet, symbolizes the affections of the soul. Those who climb it put away love of vice and sin. By means of the first step people climb onto the second and reach Christ's side. Here they can see into his inmost heart and love and then begin to feel love themselves. They desire to put on virtue. Having put away a love of vice and put on a love of virtue, they now climb onto the third step. This is the mouth of Christ, or spiritual peace, as one's love rises beyond imperfect love to perfect love.

[93]Ibid., ch. 29, p. 70.

[94]"Sea of peace" is a frequent Catherinian image for God. See *The Dialogue,* chs. 27, p. 67; 42, p. 87. Also see *The Prayers.*

[95]*The Dialogue,* ch. 27, p. 66.

[96]For the three stairs interpreted as an image of Christ's body, see ibid., chs. 26, pp. 64–65; 78, p. 145; 86, p. 158; 166, pp. 361–362.

One can already see in Catherine's unfolding of the stairs as symbolic of Christ's body three spiritual stages (although at times she also speaks about four stages): the imperfect, the perfect, and the most perfect state of unitive love.[97] The first step is that of a mercenary, the second that of a servant, the third that of a child or of a friend. In other words, one goes from mercenary love to a more freely motivated love to filial love. Those move to the first step who are motivated by fear. They set aside vice, but not out of love. Fear is enough to get them onto the first step but not enough to get them across the bridge. But the fear of damnation can get them onto the step by which they can pass to the second stage of more perfect love and love of virtue. Yet this love is still not completely perfect, for these servants love because they are still partially motivated by the delight and comfort they experience in their love for God or neighbor. Their love is not yet pure. "Unless their desire for perfection makes them recognize their imperfection, it is impossible for them not to turn back. To have eternal life it is essential to love without regard for one's own interest. Fleeing sin for fear of punishment is not enough to embrace virtue for one's own profit. No, one must rise from sin because sin displeases me, and love virtue for love of me."[98]

If people do not give up but persevere in prayer, good works, and strengthening virtue, they come to the third state, which is described in two ways—filial love and love of friendship. The third stair actually comprises two loves, a love of friendship and a filial love, the latter being the most perfect love for Catherine.[99] On this third step, however, we love God for God's own sake and not because of what God gives us (step two) or out of fear (step one). We are no longer mercenaries or servants but both friends of God and children of God. These two loves are both different expressions of the perfect love of the third stair and can also be related to Catherine's distinguishing a fourth stage from the third

[97]For the elaboration of this image, see ibid., chs. 56–63, pp. 110–120; 72–74, pp. 134–137; 166, pp. 361–362.

[98]Ibid., ch. 60, p. 114.

[99]Friendship with God sometimes seems associated more with the second step or stage (*The Dialogue*, ch. 63, p. 118), and sometimes more with the third step or stage (ibid., ch. 72, p. 134). Friendship with God is probably best seen as developing; its culmination or perfection is with the third step or stage even if it has already begun with an earlier, less perfect love. Filial love is even more perfect than love of friendship; see *The Dialogue*, ch. 63, p. 118.

stage, although these two remain inseparable. This distinction is also related to the inseparability of love of God and love of neighbor for Catherine, as we will see later.

> And this brings her to the fourth stage. That is, after the third stage, the stage of perfection in which she both tastes and gives birth to charity in the person of her neighbor, she is graced with a final stage of perfect union with me. These two stages are linked together, for the one is never found without the other any more than charity for me can exist without charity for one's neighbors or the latter without charity for me. The one cannot be separated from the other. Even so, neither of these two stages can exist without the other.[100]

The three stairs symbolize three parts of Christ's body and, in turn, three stages in the spiritual life or three degrees of love. The three stairs also symbolize the common Augustinian and medieval understanding of the three powers of the soul: memory, understanding, and will.[101] All three powers of the soul must be brought into play in perfect love. We find Catherine loving with all three powers in her prayers as well as in the *Dialogue.*

The three powers of the soul reflect the life of the Trinity and are the basis for the creature's being the image and likeness of God. Catherine's references to these three are frequent. All three powers must be united in perfect love: "I have explained the image of the three stairs for you in general in terms of the soul's three powers. These are three stairs, none of which can be climbed without the others if one wishes to go the way of the teaching, the bridge, of my Truth. Nor can the soul persevere without uniting these three powers as one."[102] We thus see the extended use Catherine makes of the image of a bridge for Christ crucified with its stairs, walls, roof, path, gate, and river underneath. It is the core image of her Christology.

Catherine does not refer to Jesus Christ as Mother, as her contemporary in England, Julian of Norwich, did. For Julian, the

---

[100]*The Dialogue*, ch. 74, p. 137.

[101]Ibid., chs. 26, p. 65; 50–54, pp. 102–109; 79, p. 148; 144, p. 299; 166, pp. 361–362. Also see letter 259 (Tommasèo), translation coming in *Letters of Catherine*, volume forthcoming.

[102]Ibid., ch. 52, p. 105.

second person of the Trinity is our Mother. Jesus is our true
Mother, and she speaks readily of Mother Jesus, Mother Christ,
and the motherhood of Christ. "As truly as God is our Father,
so truly is God our Mother," and the heavenly Mother is the second person of the Trinity and Jesus Christ.[103] Julian also speaks
of Christ, the Mother, as a nurse: "The sweet gracious hands of
our Mother are ready and diligent about us; for he in all this work
exercises the true office of a kind nurse, who has nothing else to
do but attend to the safety of her child."[104] Although Catherine
does not use such strong maternal images for Christ, she too spoke
of Christ as a wet nurse: "And he [the only-begotten Son] did
as the wet nurse who herself drinks the medicine the baby
needs. . . . My Son was your wet nurse, and he joined the big-
ness and strength of his divinity with your nature to drink the
bitter medicine of his painful death on the cross so that he might
heal and give life to you who were babies weakened by sin."[105]
Catherine did use the image of mother for the Holy Spirit: "Such
a soul has the Holy Spirit as a mother who nurses her at the breast
of divine charity."[106]

Christ, the bridge, is able to join humanity (us) to divinity (God)
because Christ himself is both human and divine. "His divinity
is kneaded into the clay of your humanity like one bread," she
wrote.[107] At this point Catherine is almost Eastern in her thought.
The doctrine of the incarnation is the other side of the coin of

---

[103]See Julian of Norwich, *Showings,* trans. Edmund Colledge and James Walsh, Classics
of Western Spirituality (New York: Paulist, 1978) 295 and 296. For Julian's depiction of
Christ the Mother, see chs. 58-63 of the long text of the *Showings,* pp. 293-305 of above
translation. For further references along this line see J. Edgar Bruns, *God as Woman, Woman
as God* (New York: Paulist, 1973); André Cabassut, "Une dévotion médiévale peu connue:
la dévotion à Jésus notre mère," *Revue d'Ascétique et de Mystique* 25 (1949) 234-245; and
Edmund Colledge and James Walsh, eds., *A Book of Showings to the Anchoress Julian of
Norwich* (Toronto: Pontifical Institute of Medieval Studies, 1978). Also see Caroline Walker
Bynum, *Jesus As Mother: Studies in the Spirituality of the High Middle Ages* (Berkeley, Calif.:
University of California Press, 1982).

[104]Julian of Norwich, *Showings,* ch. 61, p. 302.

[105]*The Dialogue,* ch. 14, p. 52.

[106]Ibid., ch. 141, p. 292. This is the only direct reference to the Holy Spirit as mother.
Catherine also uses mother as an image for charity, prayer, the Church, the pope, and the
Holy Spirit (once in *The Dialogue*), but the Holy Spirit and charity are often equated. Cather-
ine also speaks of nursing at the breast of Christ crucified (cf. letter 356, Tommasèo).

[107]Ibid., ch. 26, p. 65; *The Prayers,* no. 18, p. 164. She also speaks of the divinity being
grafted onto our humanity. *The Prayers,* no. 17, pp. 147-153.

her doctrine of union with God, or deification. Her Christology and her spirituality are two sides of one reality. Her theology is done on her knees. Her Christology grounded her spirituality; her spirituality was the fruit of her Christology. The humanity and divinity of Christ only pointed in the direction of the union with God to which we, too, are called and which has been made possible by Christ crucified. We now turn to her spiritual doctrine, which completes her Christology.

Catherine's idea is that we have been created in the image and likeness of God and we are called to be other Christs. We have been made images of God through our threefold faculties of memory, understanding, and will.[108] She prays, "You made us in your image and likeness so that, with our three powers in one soul we might image your trinity and your unity."[109] We have been so created, but we have sinned. By following the path of Christ, however, we can be re-created and become like Christ through the union of love: "But beyond the beauty I have given the soul by creating her in my image and likeness, look at those who are clothed in the wedding garment of charity, adorned with many true virtues: they are united with me through love. So I say, if you should ask me who they are, I would answer, said the gentle loving Word, that they are another me; for they have lost and drowned their own will and have clothed themselves and united themselves and conformed themselves with mine."[110]

We have already discussed the three stages of the Christian life in connection with the three stairs of the bridge. Those who enter onto the bridge move toward a most intense union with God through Christ: "For once souls have risen up in eager longing, they run along the bridge of the teaching of Christ crucified and arrive at the gate with their spirits lifted up to me. When they have crossed over and are inebriated with the blood and aflame with the fire of love, they taste in me the eternal Godhead, and I am to them a peaceful sea with which the soul becomes so united that her spirit knows no movement but in me."[111] Catherine's im-

---

[108]See *The Dialogue*, chs. 12, p. 46; 13, pp. 48–49; 51, p. 103; and *The Prayers*, no. 1, p. 16; no. 4, p. 42; no. 11, p. 90; among other references. Also see Thomas Aquinas, *ST*, I, q. 93, a. 5.

[109]*The Prayers*, no. 4, p. 42.

[110]*The Dialogue*, ch. 1, p. 26. Also see ch. 96, p. 181.

[111]Ibid., ch. 79, p. 147.

age for God and the mystical union is often the sea of peace.[112] This metaphor leads to one of her most striking images for union with God: "For then the soul is in God and God in the soul, just as the fish is in the sea and the sea in the fish."[113] The union with God is also described as more intimate than the union between soul and body.[114] Although Catherine does not use the word deification, this doctrine, so central to Eastern theology, is clearly the effect she describes of the union with God through grace. "You, God, became human and we have been made divine!" she states several different times.[115]

If we move along the bridge through the gate into the sea of peace, we are following the path of virtue. Although Catherine speaks about many of the virtues, there are three in particular that are central to her spiritual teaching: charity, discernment *(discrezione),* and humility. One image she uses for these three is that of a tree. Charity is the tree, which must be rooted or planted in the soil of humility. Discernment is a branch of the tree, or rather an engrafted shoot. "So the tree of charity is nurtured in humility and branches out in true discernment."[116]

Charity is the most perfect of the virtues; nothing is more perfect.[117] Charity gives life to all the virtues; without charity they cannot exist. Charity for Catherine is both love for God and love for neighbor. In fact, these two loves are one and the same thing.[118] Catherine is quite clear on this point: Love for God cannot exist without love for one's neighbor and love for one's neighbor cannot exist without love for God.[119] Love of neighbor takes precedence in Catherine's spirituality as in her life over seeking spiritual consolations.[120] The crowning of true mysticism manifests itself in love of neighbor. This is what God most desires. Cather-

---

[112]Ibid., ch. 54, p. 108. Also *The Prayers,* no. 2, p. 25.

[113]*The Dialogue,* chs. 2, p. 27; 112, p. 211. Also *The Prayers,* no. 20, p. 188. These are the only references. There are none in the letters.

[114]Ibid., ch. 19, p. 57; 79, p. 148.

[115]Ibid., chs. 13, p. 50; 15, p. 53; 110, p. 205; *The Prayers,* no. 11, p. 92.

[116]*The Dialogue,* ch. 10, p. 42. Also see ch. 9, pp. 41–42.

[117]Ibid., ch. 160, p. 346.

[118]Ibid., chs. 7, p. 36; 55, p. 110.

[119]Ibid., chs. 64, p. 121; 74, p. 137; 78, p. 144.

[120]Ibid., ch. 69, p. 130–131.

ine is even stronger in her emphasis on the importance of not judging: There is no one who can judge the hidden heart. Nothing in the world can make it right to sit in judgment of others. Compassion is what one must have and leave the judging to God.[121] On these points Catherine continues often and at length. They flow from the heart of the gospel. If one has true charity it bears fruit in many other virtues as well. "These three glorious virtues— patience, courage and perseverance—are rooted in true charity and have their place at the very top of that tree. . . ."[122] Charity remains the tree, but humility is the only soil in which it will grow.

The whole of Christian life must be grounded in holy humility and true self-knowledge.[123] "Never leave the knowledge of yourself. Then, put down as you are in the valley of humility you will know me in yourself, and from this knowlege you will draw all that you need."[124] One sees in this statement two elements in humility—true self-knowledge, and knowledge of God within the self. Catherine's self-knowledge is fundamentally a theological knowledge of ourselves. "Self-knowledge alone is not enough: it must be seasoned by and joined with knowledge of me within you."[125] "As the soul comes to know herself she also knows God better, for she sees how good he has been to her," and almost vice versa, "Just as you can better see the blemish on your face when you look at yourself in a mirror, so the soul who in true self-knowledge rises up with desire to look at herself in the gentle mirror of God with the eye of understanding sees all the more clearly her own defects because of the purity she sees in him."[126] This doctrine of Catherine's leads to one of her more striking in-

---

[121]Ibid., chs. 100–106, pp. 190–198. Also see the section emphasizing nonjudgment before the sins of the clergy are revealed to her, chs. 110–120, pp. 205–231. Also see *The Prayers*, especially no. 9, pp. 69–74.

[122]*The Dialogue*, ch. 77, pp. 141–142.

[123]This is true for many spiritual writers. E.g., see Johannes Tauler, sermons 8, 22, 35, in *Spiritual Conferences*, trans. and ed. Eric Colledge and Sister Mary Jane (Rockford, Ill.: Tan Books, 1978) pp. 39–47, 51–57, 65–68. Sermon 35 also available in Johannes Tauler, *Sermons*, trans. Maria Shrady, Classics of Western Spirituality (New York: Paulist, 1985) 117–123.

[124]*The Dialogue*, ch. 4, p. 29. Also see chs. 9, p. 40; 66, p. 125; 93, p. 171; as well as nn. 127–131 below for further reference to humility and self-knowledge.

[125]Ibid., ch. 86, p. 158.

[126]Ibid., ch. 13, p. 48.

tuitions as she addresses God: "I am the one who is not, and you are the one who is."[127]

One comes to this humility by shutting oneself up in "the house or cell of self-knowledge."[128] Catherine did not have her own cell in the sense that cloistered nuns in a monastery might, nor even her own house. Living in her parents' home and often enough on the road or in the world, she had to form her cell within. This was her refuge, where she knew herself to be the sinner she was so conscious of being and where she knew the inexpressible heights and depths of God's love for her, the cell from which her love of God and love of her neighbor were to burst forth. The *Dialogue* begins thus: "A soul rises up, restless with tremendous desire for God's honor and the salvation of souls. She has for some time expressed herself in virtue and has become accustomed to dwelling in the cell of self-knowledge in order to know better God's goodness to her, since upon knowledge follows love."[129]

Humility, true self-knowledge, and charity, true love of God and neighbor, are the sources from which all the other virtues spring. Earlier I mentioned how patience, courage and perseverance—three very Catherinian virtues—are rooted in the tree of charity, which in turn is rooted in the soil of humility. So likewise obedience is grounded in both, and obedience turns out to be the sister of patience. "This is why charity, the mother, has given obedience patience as a sister and has so joined the two together that the one can never be lost without the other. . . . Obedience has a wet nurse, true humility, and the soul is as obedient as she is humble and as humble as she is obedient."[130]

Of all the virtues that spring forth or are nursed forth from humility and charity, however, a special place goes to the virtue of discernment. There is no substitute for the role it plays in the life of virtue. Discernment is true knowledge and prudence in spiritual matters. Catherine herself manifests a discerning spirit,

[127]*The Prayers,* no. 11, p. 95; also see nos. 20, p. 186; 21, p. 193; 10, p. 82; and *The Dialogue,* ch. 134, pp. 273–274.

[128]*The Dialogue,* chs. 1, p. 25; 63, pp. 118 and 120; 64, p. 122; 65, p. 122; 73, p. 135; 166, p. 363.

[129]Ibid., ch. 1, p. 25.

[130]Ibid., ch. 154, p. 328.

is given insight into true discernment as a response to her prayer, and teaches some fundamental principles of discernment.[131]

The absence of spiritual consolation is not necessarily a sign of the absence of God. God withdraws spiritual consolations in order to perfect our love because we become too attached to them. Attachment to the comfort and feelings can prevent a person from moving from Catherine's second stage to the third stage of most perfect love. Spiritual consolation can even be more important to someone than love of neighbor, and then it has become an obstacle to growth in love—which is what the spiritual life is about.[132]

Another of Catherine's principles of discernment is that the devil can deceive by taking on an appearance of light. The devil does this to catch people, to get hooks into them.

> This, then, is how the soul can tell whether she is being visited by me or the devil: in my invitation she will find fear at the beginning; but in the middle and at the end, gladness and a hunger for virtue. When it is the devil, however, the beginning is happy, but then the soul is left in spiritual confusion and darkness.[133]

The Lord instructs Catherine further in such matters, as well as delineates for her in response to her request the five stages of tears.[134]

Catherine's Christology is soteriological, personal, and truly theological in character. Soteriological in that it is a theology of Christ crucified; her most developed Christological image, Christ the bridge, is a theology of the cross. It is personal in that her Christology is experientially based and rooted in her prayer and ministry as well as in the Scriptures and classical theology. Her style is not "Scholastic" even if some of her content is. Although academic theology may at times disparage such a personal Christology, we need to call to mind Karl Rahner's call for an

---

[131]For Catherine's teaching on discernment and her principles of discernment, it is best to read her entire *Dialogue*. Specific references include chs. 9–11, pp. 39–45; 49, pp. 100–102; 106, pp. 198–201, in addition to n. 134 below.

[132]Ibid., chs. 60, pp. 113–116; 69–70, pp. 130–132.

[133]Ibid., chs. 71–72, pp. 133–134.

[134]On tears, see ibid., chs. 87–97, pp. 160–183. On further principles of discernment, see ibid., chs. 102–109, pp. 193–204.

existential Christology to supplement his own historical and transcendental approaches and the need for a Christology to be grounded in "the personal relationship of a Christian to Jesus Christ."[135]

Catherine's Christology, however, is not only personal and mystical, it is also theological in the best sense.[136] One might too narrowly label her thoughts and writings as "spirituality," though spiritual they are. They are also theology, if, of course, one properly understands that term. The separation between theology and spirituality, doctrine and Christian life, is a false one. That *spiritualité*, or ascetical and mystical theology, or the theology of the Christian life be severed from Christian doctrine is to be lamented. During the first centuries of the Church, even through the Middle Ages, in East and West, it would have been inconceivable to think of the history of theology and history of spirituality as distinct. In the patristic period, the great theologians of the Church were known as much for their spiritual doctrine as for anything else. And in the East today the two are still as inseparable as are the doctrines of incarnation and deification. It is true that Catherine was a mystic, a spiritual and holy woman, but she was also a theologian, even if of a different sort than the Scholastics. To refer back to Symeon, she was a true theologian— a mystic—someone with the experience of God.

A Concluding Theological Reflection

Symeon the New Theologian makes us aware of the nature of all true theology, and of what it is that makes "new theology" to be in continuity with earlier forms of theology—the gift of the Spirit. Theology is spirituality, and vice versa.

Symeon's is ultimately a theology and experience of the triune God. There is no theology of the human apart from a theology of Jesus Christ and no theology of Jesus Christ apart from a theology of the Trinity. For Symeon, God is light. God is Father, Son, and Spirit. Each of the three *hypostases* is light. The Father is the house, the Son is the door, and the Spirit is the key. Symeon's

[135]Karl Rahner, *Foundations of Christian Faith*, trans. William V. Dych (New York: Seabury, 1978) 305–311.

[136]Mary O'Driscoll, "Catherine the Theologian," *Spirituality Today* 50 (Spring 1988) 4–17.

life and theology are driven by the desire to know and love God. One's knowledge of God is experiential, as in his teaching concerning two baptisms and the resurrection of the soul here and now in this earthly life. Every Christian is called to the contemplative or mystical life.

The doctrine of the Trinity grounds the doctrine of the incarnation, which in turn is the base for the doctrine of deification. The incarnation, for Symeon, reveals God's Word as being God's Son. And we too are sons and daughters of God, gods, although our divinity and deification is by adoption and grace. The divine indwelling is effected by the Holy Spirit. The inseparability of incarnation and deification affirms the inseparability of Christology and pneumatology. Symeon's theology can rightly be called a theology of the Holy Spirit. The Holy Spirit is even more prominent than in Catherine's mysticism.

As is true of so many mystics in the West, the core virtues in the Christian life for Symeon are humility and love, where love is the inseparable love of God and love of neighbor, although at times in Symeon the love of God seems to be given greater attention.

Catherine of Siena's theology is also both traditional and innovative. Rooted in the classical soteriological concepts of satisfaction and ransom, she sees Christ crucified as the supreme exemplification of God's love. The essence of Catherine's theology is that God is both love and truth. God is the mad, intoxicated, and intoxicating lover!

Jesus Christ, God's Word and Son, is mediator and redeemer. Catherine's Christology is classical in content but innovative in its expression or form. Even extended and graphic images cannot do full justice to the human experience of God's love made manifest in Christ. Jesus is a bridge, door, gate, doctor, wet nurse, and vine. Jesus is divinity kneaded into the dough of our humanity. This doctrine of the incarnation has its flip side in the spiritual theology of deification. Although Catherine does not use the word, we too are divine! Such is Catherine's constant awareness of God's intimacy with us.

This intimacy with God is at the center of Catherine's theology of God and her theology of the human person, her theology and anthropology. The human person embodies an infinite desire for God, which unfolds and becomes perfected in the spiritual journey toward union with God. The journey reaches its goal in that moral and mystical life in which love of God and love of neighbor are inseparable and mutually reinforcing. The life of virtue, made possible by Christ's grace, culminates in union with God, the sea of peace. It is grounded in the soil of humility or the cell of self-knowledge, which knowledge is also a theological or mystical knowledge of the self, of God in us. Catherine's theology, Christology, and anthropology are all varying expressions of God's incomprehensible intimacy, as is her pneumatology. Again with the use of a graphic image, Catherine speaks of the Holy Spirit as our mother.

Catherine is so taken aback by God's infinite love that it almost appears as if God needs us. While this is not actually the case, God is clearly affected by us. How could it be otherwise for one whose love is so infinite, intimate, and passionate? O mad lover! This is where the mystery of God in Christ gives way before human language, which is never adequate. The mystery is borne by the mystic, who attempts to convey in mystical and passionate language her experience and knowledge of God. Catherine's mystical activism, religious experiences, and use of poetic images all reveal her own infinite desire to be one with her intoxicating, divine lover. Her theology reveals both the powers and limits of language. Can our experience and understanding of God be even inadequately expressed in anything other than mystical language?

What Symeon and Catherine both exemplify in their own ways is the intrinsic relationship between theology and life, that all theology is a theology of Christian life and experience, and that mystical theology and language cannot be separated from theology proper. Mystical theology, focused on the inseparable love of God and love of neighbor, is the theology of Christian living, which in turn is grounded in our experience and knowledge of God. Theology is experiential knowledge—an experiential faith seeking a language with which to express itself.

All Christology must somehow be rooted in our human experience of God, our personal relationship with Jesus Christ, and our participation in the mystery of the death and resurrection of Christ. A reflection on this experience of relationship with Jesus Christ in the light of Christian tradition clarifies and authenticates our experience of life in Christ. But this reflection cannot be separated from the question of human language. Some theologians, or Christians, those we may more often describe as mystics than in some other way, manifest a need or preference for the language of mysticism within which to express their experience and understanding of God. Mystical language is not irrational or impractical, but it is experiential, passionate, and poetic. Although no human language can do justice to the mystery of God, mystical language and theology seems less inadequate. Its merit is that it points to mystery—and the awareness of mystery is what can often be lost in doing theology. It is ultimately mystery with which the theologian is concerned, and Christian theology is concerned specifically with the *mystery* of the life, death, and resurrection of Jesus Christ. Thus Christology cannot be severed from mysticism, and vice versa. Mystical Christology is one of the supreme manifestations of the Christian tradition of theology. To this Symeon, Catherine, and many others give witness.

SUGGESTED READINGS

Primary Sources

Catherine of Siena. *The Dialogue.* Ed. and trans. Suzanne Noffke. The Classics of Western Spirituality. New York: Paulist, 1980.

_____. *The Letters of St. Catherine of Siena,* vol. 1. Ed. and trans. Suzanne Noffke. Binghamton, N.Y.: Medieval and Renaissance Texts and Studies, 1988. The first of four volumes, which will comprise the 382 letters.

_____. *The Prayers of St. Catherine of Siena.* Ed. and trans. Suzanne Noffke. New York: Paulist, 1983.

Symeon the New Theologian. *The Discourses.* Trans. C. J. de Catanzaro. The Classics of Western Spirituality. New York: Paulist, 1980.

_____. *Hymns of Divine Love.* Trans. George A. Maloney. Denville, N.J.: Dimension Books, 1976.

_____. *The Practical and Theological Chapters, and the Three Theological Discourses.* Trans. Paul McGucken. Kalamazoo, Mich.: Cistercian Publications, 1982.

Secondary Sources

Ashley, Benedict. "Guide to Saint Catherine's Dialogue." *Cross and Crown* 29 (1977) 237-249.

Bell, Rudolph M. *Holy Anorexia*. Chicago: University of Chicago Press, 1985. See the review by Donald Goergen, *Spirituality Today* 39 (1987) 367-369.

Bouyer, Louis, Jean Leclercq, and Francois Vandenbroucke. *The Spirituality of the Middle Ages. A History of Christian Spirituality* vol. 2. New York: Seabury, 1968. See especially pp. 407-446, 548-590.

Bynum, Caroline Walker. *Jesus As Mother: Studies in the Spirituality of the High Middle Ages*. Berkeley, Calif.: University of California Press, 1982.

_____. "And Woman His Humanity: Female Imagery in the Religious Writing of the Later Middle Ages" in *Gender and Religion: On the Complexity of Symbols*, pp. 257-288. Ed. Caroline Walker Bynum, and others. Boston: Beacon Press, 1986.

_____. *Holy Feast and Holy Fast: The Religious Significance of Food to Medieval Women*. Berkeley, Calif.: University of California Press, 1987.

Congar, Yves. *I Believe in the Holy Spirit*, 3 vols. Trans. David Smith. New York: Seabury, 1983.

Fatula, Mary Ann. *Catherine of Siena's Way*. Wilmington, Del.: Michael Glazier, Inc., 1987. An excellent introduction.

Foster, Kenelm. "St. Catherine's Teaching on Christ." *Life of the Spirit* 16 (1962) 310-323.

Gardner, Edmund G. *Saint Catherine of Siena: A Study in the Religion, Literature and History of the Fourteenth Century in Italy*. London: E. P. Dent and Co., 1907.

Jorgensen, Johannes. *Saint Catherine of Siena*. Trans. Ingeborg Lund. London: Longmans, Green, and Co., 1939.

Kieckhefer, Richard. *Unquiet Souls, Fourteenth Century Saints and Their Religious Milieu*. Chicago: University of Chicago Press, 1984. Not a study of Catherine in particular, but an excellent study of the fourteenth-century spiritual climate with frequent references to Catherine.

Krivocheine, Basil. *In the Light of Christ, Saint Symeon the New Theologian (949-1022)*. Trans. Anthony P. Gytheil. Crestwood, N.Y.: St. Vladimir's Seminary Press, 1986. The best introduction available in English.

Maloney, George. *The Mystic of Fire and Light: St. Symeon the New Theologian*. Denville, N.J.: Dimension Books, 1975.

Noffke, Suzanne, ed. *The Text and Concordances of the Works of Caterina da Siena*. Madison, Wis.: The Hispanic Seminary of Medieval Studies, 1987.

O'Driscoll, Mary. "Catherine the Theologian." *Spirituality Today* 40 (1988) 4-17.

Raitt, Jill, ed. *Christian Spirituality, High Middle Ages and Reformation*. Vol. 17 of *World Spirituality*. New York: Crossroad, 1987.

Raymond of Capua. *The Life of Catherine of Siena*. Trans. J. Conleth Kearns. Wilmington, Del.: Michael Glazier, Inc., 1980.

Spirituality Today 32 (1980). Five articles on Catherine by Jeremy Finnegan, Marie Walter Flood, Suzanne Noffke, Mary O'Driscoll, and Marie Stephen Reges.

Tavard, George. "The Christology of the Mystics." *Theological Studies* 42 (1981) 561-579.

6

Thomas Aquinas
and the Language of Philosophy

Thomas Aquinas (1225–74) stands alongside Augustine as one of the greatest theologians in the Catholic tradition. In some ways his theology is well known. In other ways, he may be seldom read. As Augustine's theology had been influenced by Neoplatonism, Thomas' theology, while still carrying an Augustinian flavor, was more influenced by the philosophy of Aristotle. Within the extensive pluralism of the medieval world, Thomas was a moderate realist. He always sought to maintain a balance between faith and reason, or revelation and philosophical inquiry. Reason meant philosophy was not to be spurned but was rather to be put at the service of faith—a faith always seeking to understand and articulate itself better.

Thomas Aquinas was primarily a theologian, but a theologian who saw the values of clarity, precision, and noncontradiction within philosophical inquiry as being of importance to the work of theology. Thomas relied heavily upon Scripture, and he was a mystic and poet in his own right. Yet his preference in doing theology was for the language of reason or philosophy. True, toward the end of his life when Thomas discontinued writing, he found himself in the grips of mystery that philosophical language itself was unable to grasp. Yet Thomas preferred the language of philosophy in theological discourse. Mystical language may do greater justice to the incomprehensible mystery of God, but philosophical language is necessary if one desires intellectual clarity and intelligibility.

One form of discourse need not be seen as superior to the other. Both serve valid purposes. To dismiss mystical theology is to risk losing the sense of mystery to which all theology is directed. But to dismiss philosophical theology is to risk putting faith at odds with human reason, intelligence, and nature, to run the risk of faith being characterized as irrational, to run the risk of faith becoming intellectually unacceptable.

Thomas Aquinas, in fact, uses both the language of mysticism and the language of philosophy, but when he is functioning most explicitly as a theologian, it is to the language of rational discourse that he turns. In him we have a theologian of outstanding intellectual precision.

We cannot discuss here all the emphases in Thomas' Christology. Rather, we turn to that area—his theology of the hypostatic union—wherein Thomas makes an original contribution to the Catholic tradition and is seen as putting all the resources of philosophical thought at the service of his desire to understand and articulate better the Catholic faith.

Readers will find this discussion and the language of Thomas to be a contrast to the passionate outpourings of Symeon and Catherine. But if we persevere in attempting to understand Thomas, we will find another kind of profundity, in which the power and limits of reason give witness to the depth of Thomas' faith and love for God. Thomas, in accord with the Dominican tradition of which he was so great a part, primarily wanted to be of service to the proclamation of the gospel.

The Metaphysics of the Hypostatic Union

We shall survey here Thomas' theology of the incarnation as presented in the *tertia pars* of his *Summa,* questions 1–59, in so far as this elucidates his understanding of the hypostatic union. Thomas traces the word "nature" or *natura* to *nativitas* (birth) or *nascitura* (to be born) (III, 2, 1), which words imply "coming forth from a source."[1] They speak of the origins of something. So likewise the word "nature" refers to the origins or source of

---

[1] Cf. James A. Weisheipl, "The Concept of Nature," *New Scholasticism* 28 (1954) 377–408.

the activities of a being. This inner source is either matter or form. The word "nature" is analogical, for it refers to form, the active principle from which behavior and properties originate, and matter, the passive principle or source. Nature does not denote a static thing in itself but the source from which something proceeds (*a quo,* from which). By extension, nature also analogously denotes what that thing essentially is, and nature comes to be identical with essence (*quod quid est,* that which something is), the "whatness" of a species. Nature answers the question, what is it? Nature is not an *it (quod est),* but rather that by which something is what it is *(quo est).* A nature isn't a thing; a thing has a nature. Thus, Thomas concludes that the union of the divine and human natures in Christ does not take place in one of the natures, for a nature is not a thing, not something substantial, not an *ousia* to which or into which something can be united. The basis of the union of the two natures cannot be one of those natures (III, 2, 1).

What then is the basis of the union? It is the person *(persona).* *"Persona aliud significat quam natura"* ("Person" means something other than "nature," III, 2, 2). And what does "person" mean? Nature is not an it; as such, *qua* nature, it does not exist. With respect to creatures, it is not their nature to exist, it is not of their essence to exist, their essence and their existence *(esse)* are two different principles. It is only true of God that God's nature is to exist; in God there is no such distinction. Nature, then, does not imply as such a particular, concrete, existing reality. A concrete, existing reality is an *ousia,* a *substantia,* a substance, in the primary sense of that term. "Substance," in its primary sense, implies that something exists. A substance is a concrete, definite, existing reality. A substance *(substantia, ousia)* has existence. It is also called a "supposit" *(suppositum).* All these words have the sense of that which supports, or stands under, or subsists.

For Thomas, the word "person" *(persona)* implies substance in its primary sense, an *ousia,* a subsistent being, but it also implies a particular kind of substance, a substance with a particular nature, namely an intellectual nature. Thomas follows here Boethius' classical definition: an individual substance of a rational nature (III, 2, 2; I, 29, 1–2). Person implies an intelligent and free subsisting existent. In Christian thought in the Middle Ages the Greek word *hypostasis* was translated as *persona,* although it can also have the wider meaning of supposit (III, 2, 3). A person or *hypostasis* is a concrete existing reality that has a particular kind of nature. A *hypostasis* or *persona* is an *ousia* or *substantia*, but not all substances are persons. All persons, however, are substances. *Ousia* or *substantia* or *suppositum* are terms with a wider meaning than person.

If nature answers the question of what it is, person answers the question of who it is. In creatures we distinguish between a person (a supposit or substance or *quod est*) and a nature (*id quo*, that by which it is what it is). That, then, in which the union takes place is not a nature, but has to be an *ousia* or *substantia* or *suppositum*. But since we have to do here with an intelligent being, we can be more specific. It is the *hypostasis* or *persona*, the person. The union takes place in the person. And who is the *persona* or *hypostasis* in the case of Jesus? It is the *persona* or *hypostasis* of the Word (III, 2, 2).

The ultimate reality or subject in which or in whom the union takes place is the *hypostasis*. It is a hypostatic union. The *hypostasis* of the Word is the bottom line, the ultimate, self-subsisting reality that underlies in Jesus both a divine nature and a human nature. Although, in Jesus, the ultimate subsisting reality is the divine word with its own divine nature, and since it could not be otherwise and there still be a true and genuine incarnation, nevertheless the human nature remains complete, intact. It is simply that its ultimate ontological basis is not a created *esse* or act of existence. But Christ, or a human being, comprises both a body and a soul (III, 2, 5). Christ is a human being as others are human beings. He is a member of the same species. The word "human" applies to him and to others in a univocal way (*Christus dicitur homo univoce cum hominibus aliis,* III, 2, 5). He is one of us.

In the language of medieval Scholasticism, was the union of the human nature with the divine person a substantial union or an accidental one? Strictly speaking, a hypostatic union is a substantial union, but not exactly; it is a unique union, the only one of its kind. Thus it does not fit ordinary categories (III, 2, 6).

The union is certainly not accidental. An accident can be present or absent without its subject ceasing to exist. Now the Son of God became human in time, thus the pre-existent Son has subsistent existence prior to his union with the human nature, prior to the incarnation, and the human nature is not essential to the

Word as subsisting Word. Yet, once assumed, the human nature is essential to the incarnate Word.

Although the human nature is not an independent *ousia* of its own, it is an essence and not an accident. Christ does not, however, as a human being, have an existence independent of the divine Word, whereas the Word is subsistent apart from this assumption of the human nature. Yet the incarnate Word would not be the incarnate Word apart from the human nature. As Thomas says, "Whatever comes to something already complete in being comes as an accident, *unless* it is drawn into becoming part of that complete existence" (III, 2, 6, ad 2). There is no other example of this type of substantial union, in which one element in the union pre-exists the other element essential to it, and yet there is no substantial change by which it becomes something else. It remains the divine *hypostasis,* which now subsists in two natures.

Because the union between the *hypostasis* of the Word and the human nature it unites to itself begins to be at a particular period of time, the union is described as created (III, 2, 17). It did not exist from all eternity, although the Word itself did so exist, but not as united to the human nature. The union is not only a created reality, it comes about by grace (III, 2, 10), both in the sense that it is God's will freely doing it and in the sense that it was done without any preceding merits on the part of the nature assumed (III, 2, 10-11); not in the sense, however, that Christ's habitual grace was the medium for the union, as in our union with the Godhead (III, 6, 6). In that sense, the union was not a union through grace but a personal or hypostatic union. Perhaps it is better to say that the grace of the union is not the same thing as habitual or sanctifying grace. We are united to God by the union of habitual grace; this, however, is not the basis upon which the union of the two natures in Christ is accomplished. The basis there is the grace of the union, or the person of the Word assuming a human nature. It is a different kind of union. One is incarnation, the other divinization.

In accord with the Council of Chalcedon, Thomas makes clear that there are two distinct, complete natures in Christ, but only one person *(persona, hypostasis)*. Although this makes logical sense, it has created problems for us moderns because the word "person" does not have the same meaning for Thomas and for us. Thomas is in no way denying a human psychology in Christ; this is implied for medievals when they posit a human soul in Christ, the seat of the human psychological activities. "Personality" for us is a psychological word or reality; it connotes uniqueness, individuality, sociability, the basis for interpersonal relationships. None of this is lacking to Jesus for Thomas. But the word "person" for Thomas does not mean the psychology of the person but rather the ontology of the person. Thomas is not here concerned about the psychological subject of Christ's human actions but the metaphysical basis of his existence. Thus, it is probably just as clear to keep the word *hypostasis* rather than translate it. *Hypostasis,* as we have seen, is in the order of *ousia* or *substantia;* it is a *substantia* with an intellectual nature.

The question must be put: Is there a *hypostasis* in Christ Jesus other than the *hypostasis* of the Word? For Thomas there simply cannot be, and this in no way means that Jesus is lacking anything that pertains to human nature. We will see Thomas' final solution shortly. For now, as Thomas points out (III, 4, 2), if the human nature had a *hypostasis* of its own, either the *hypostasis* would be destroyed in the union or there would be two *hypostases* in Christ. "The assumed nature does not lack its own proper *hypostasis* because of any defect that pertains to the perfection of the human nature, but because something beyond human nature is added, namely, a union to a divine person" (III, 4, 2 ad 2). The *hypostasis* of the Word suffices as a *hypostasis* for the human nature. There is no need whatsoever for two *hypostases.* Two *hypostases* could imply two "persons" or two separate individuals. One would have no union at all, unless it were to be a union of habitual grace, which would make Jesus an adopted son. But even then there would be only one *hypostasis;* it would simply be the *hypostasis* of a man Jesus who was not an incarnation but who was open to divinization. The nonhypostatic character of the human nature does not diminish the humanity of Christ; it simply means that its ultimate ontological basis is the Word. "Therefore it is not proper to say that the Son of God assumed a man" (III, 4, 3), as if that man Jesus had an independent *hypostasis* of his own as human. Rather the Son assumed a human nature, and the effect of the union was the man Jesus. From a temporal point of view, "The Word of God united to itself all at once a complete human nature" (III, 6, 1): became incarnate.

The incarnation does not involve a time sequence; the assumption of the whole and all the parts was simultaneous (III, 6, 6).

In Christ, then, we have a union in which a divine person, the person of the Word or Son, takes to himself a human nature. This union can also be considered under the heading of grace, or as grace, for it is a divine gift. As grace, the hypostatic or personal union is also called the "grace of union" (III, 2, 10; 6, 6; 7, 13). The question is thus raised about the relationship between the grace of union *(gratia unionis)* and Christ's habitual grace *(gratia habitualis)*.[2] For Thomas, the grace of union or hypostatic union is distinct from Christ's habitual grace. It does not fall under the same genus, and it has a priority (III, 7, 13). It both logically and ontologically precedes Christ's habitual grace, although not necessarily temporally. "The presence of God in Christ is understood according to the union of a human nature to the divine person. Hence the habitual grace of Christ is understood as following upon this union, just as light follows the sun" (III, 7, 13).

Early Scholasticism had debated the relationship between the grace of union and habitual grace. For some, the grace of union was habitual grace, as disposing the humanity of Christ for the hypostatic union (*Sentences* III, 13, 3, 1). Thomas rejected this notion; for him Christ's humanity was not disposed for the hypostatic union by any prior, created grace (*Quodlibet* IX, 2, 1, ad 3; *De Veritate* XXIX, 2). For him the grace of union was simply the same thing as the hypostatic union, and as such ontologically distinct from habitual grace. The hypostatic union was not a consequence of Christ's habitual grace, not even as predisposed by the latter (III, 7, 13 ad 2). The grace of union, however, did not make superfluous the habitual grace, which followed upon the grace of union as a perfection of Christ's human nature. Habitual grace was required for Christ's *human* soul to know and love God as intimately as possible (III, 7, 1). The question is the relationship between Christ's essential, substantial being and his accidental, human perfection. Although Thomas made the distinction, he did not thereby imply that Christ's habitual grace was in any way lacking. In fact, Christ had the fullness of habitual grace (III, 7, 9).

---

[2]In later Scholasticism grace came to be associated with sanctification and the expression "sanctifying grace" became more common than "habitual grace," which was still Thomas' expression.

Thomas' primary contribution to Christology was his understanding of the manner of the union between the divine and the human in Christ, his particular understanding of the hypostatic union. Although with Cyril of Alexandria and later with the Council of Chalcedon, the union was conceived to be in the *hypostasis,* the philosophical understanding of that hypostatic union remained to be worked out. Theologians understood it differently. Thomas articulated his understanding in the significant question 17 of the *tertia pars,* which evidences the ongoing theological development in his own thought.

Thomas had begun his *Summa* in 1266 while in Rome. He was in Paris as regent master for a second time from early 1269 until late April of 1272. Thomas finished the *secunda secundae* during his second Parisian regency, and he may have even begun the *tertia pars* before leaving Paris. Thomas' last disputation in Paris was his *De unione verbi incarnati,* which antedates question 17 of the *tertia pars.* We do not know how much of the *tertia pars* Thomas wrote before leaving Paris for Naples; James Weisheipl suggests only the first few questions.[3] Question 17 would then have been written later, after Thomas left Paris for Naples, where he composed most of the *tertia pars,* during 1272 and 1273, and where he discontinued his writing.

Question 17 comprises only two articles, whether Christ is one *(unum)* or two, and whether in Christ there is only one *esse* or act of existence. The entire question concerns itself with the unity of Christ.

There is, of course, in Christ, a certain duality; this is that of the two natures. On this basis, can Christ be said to be more than one thing? Christ is both God and a human being. Is Christ not therefore two things? Even if one affirms that there is only one person *(persona, hypostasis)* in Christ, can it not be said that Christ is not two persons but still two things? Thomas replies no in the first article of question 17. Christ is not only *unus* (one person) but also *unum* (one supposit).

Both article 3 of the *De unione* and article 1 of question 17 pertain to Christological language and grammar, about which we will say more when we discuss the *communicatio idiomatum* in the

[3] James A. Weisheipl, *Friar Thomas D'Aquino: His Life, Thought, and Works* (Garden City, N.Y.: Doubleday, 1974) 307–314.

next section. The particular problem (forced upon us by the Latin language in a way that would not be true of the English language) is whether Christ is one or two when using the neuter gender (English does not convey the theological point made by Scholastic theology, in which Latin can distinguish between *unus* and *unum*).

In *De unione* and the *Summa* (III, 2, 3 and 6), Thomas had inquired whether there was only one supposit in Christ. This may strike us as strange. Accustomed to Thomas' Christology, where person and supposit are practically synonymous for Christology, if Christ is only one person *(persona)* then he is only one supposit *(suppositum)*. Yet there were those in the twelfth century who held the opinion that Christ was one person but two supposits.

This particular issue, whether Christ as human is *aliquid* (something, something substantial, a supposit), is closely related to another issue, the unity in Christ, and both issues have a previous history in the Scholastic theology of the twelfth and thirteenth centuries. These are the two issues facing Thomas in his question 17. The question of the inner unity of Christ is related to the famous three opinions passed on by Peter Lombard in his *Sentences* (III, 6). Thomas had written of these as well (III, 2, 6). We must turn our attention to them briefly.

The central issue in a theology of the incarnation in the twelfth and thirteenth centuries was that of the mode of union of the Word or Son with human nature. Lombard presented this issue in terms of three opinions held by his contemporaries.[4] We shall refer to these opinions by the now commonly accepted names, the assumptus theory (Lombard's first opinion), the subsistence theory (Lombard's second opinion), and the habitus theory (the third opinion), although these names were only first introduced early in the twentieth century. The opinions, but not the modern names, would have been known by the Scholastic theologians. According to Walter Principe, "To a considerable extent, then, the history of the theology of the mode of union in Christ as that theology developed in the second half of the twelfth century and

[4]Cf. Karl Adam, *The Christ of Faith*, trans. Joyce Crick (New York: Pantheon Books, 1962) 218–221; Nicholas M. Haring, "The Case of Gilbert de la Porrée Bishop of Poitiers, 1142–1154," *Medieval Studies* 13 (1951) 1–40; Walter H. Principe, *William of Auxerre's Theology of the Hypostatic Union*, vol. 1 of *The Theology of the Hypostatic Union in the Early Thirteenth Century* (Toronto: Pontifical Institute of Medieval Studies, 1963) 64–78.

the first half of the thirteenth century is the history of the attitude of theologians towards these three opinions and of the particular conclusions they elaborated in connection with these.''⁵

The three opinions were not three systematically elaborated opinions but rather three general groupings or tendencies. Within each, individual theologians differed.

The first opinion, the assumptus theory, emphasized the identity of the *homo assumptus* (the human being assumed or taken to oneself) and the *persona assumens* (the person assuming). The person of the Logos assumes a human being. But the assumption leads to a complete identity between the two. The two natures remain distinct, yet Christ as human was omniscient and omnipotent because of the intensity of the union between the two. ''The Word of God is embodied in the man; the man Jesus is the visible manifestation of the invisible Word of God. The man Jesus, taken up into God, is selfsame and identical with the God that takes him up.''⁶ The human being assumed possesses everything that the divine person possesses, not by virtue of its nature but by virtue of this assumption.

This theory, which ends in an almost identification of the two, the one assuming and the one assumed, nevertheless starts with that which was assumed as being an individual human being. It is not simply a human nature that was assumed but a human substance, an *aliquid* (something), an independent reality. This later led opponents of the theory to see in this theory a doctrine of two subjects or supposits, although not two persons. One of the last theologians to defend the assumptus theory was Peter of Capua, whose *summa* was written about 1200. Opponents were to consider the theory as semi-Nestorian. Thomas so considered it (III, 2, 6). In the thirteenth century it was an opinion associated with a doctrine of one person but two subjects or supposits in Christ.

We can thus see that the issue about the character of the union became closely related to the other issue, whether Christ as human is *aliquid,* something, a supposit, a distinguishable but not separable issue. Proponents of the first opinion came to argue that Christ was *aliquis homo* (had some sort of subsistence as a human

⁵Principe, *William of Auxerre's Theology of the Hypostatic Union,* 10.
⁶Adam, *The Christ of Faith,* 218.

being). Opponents argued that Christ as human was not *aliquid* (his humanity did not have some subsistence of its own), for such would imply *duae personae*. In medieval Christology after Lombard there were both the issue of the three opinions or theories on the union and also the issue of the *aliquid/non est aliquid* of the assumed nature. In the beginning, proponents of the second and third opinions argued the *non est aliquid* position, but many who advocated the subsistence theory also held the *aliquid* position (Simon of Tournai, Evarard of Ypres, Master Martinus, Radulphus Ardens, Peter Cantor, Praepositinus, Stephen Langton, Godfrey of Poitiers).[7]

The second opinion or subsistence theory held that the divine person supported or bore the human nature, not an individual human being. The Logos bears both the divine nature as well as our common human nature. This opinion is, in its origins, a Platonic realism in which the universal has a real existence prior to concrete things. Thus, human nature as such has its subsistence in the Logos, which did not assume an individual human nature but a universal human nature. Through the power of the Logos this common human nature became this one concrete individual, but it was still human nature as such that Christ bore. The incarnation is not the result of an assumption by the divine person but rather follows from the subsistence of the human nature in the divine person.

The habitus theory, or third opinion, can best be understood by contrasting it with the assumptus theory. In the assumptus theory, Christ as human is *aliquid;* in the habitus theory Christ as human *non est aliquid*. Given the immutability of God, the divine person cannot assume something new into its very being. The unity cannot lead to an identity. In one sense, in the assumptus theory, the unity in Christ is emphasized at the expense of his duality, although it begins strangely with a human *aliquid* and was criticized as Nestorian. Some of this reflects the fact that the opinions were not static but developing. The assumptus theory began by emphasizing the identity between *assumens* (the one assuming) and *assumptus* (the assumed) but gradually came to be identified more with the distinction between the two, whereas in the habitus theory, the distinction is there from the beginning. The immutable Logos cannot assume into itself a human being. There is more of an awareness of the duality. The divinity and humanity persist side by side. Hence the catchword of this opinion, *habitus* (clothing, appearance). The Logos puts on humanity as someone puts on clothing. "When putting on apparel, we do not become the apparel, but are merely apparelled. And thus God too does not become man, but only puts on the garment of humanity."[8]

In using this analogy and in order to maintain a real union in Christ, a unity that is closer than the union of body and soul in Christ, the proponents of the habitus theory maintained that the Logos is united to the human nature not as a whole but to its parts. It is united to body and soul separately, and not to body and soul as already united. Before the body and soul of Christ were united to constitute a human *aliquid,* the Logos united to itself a body and a soul separately. Thus we can see that Christ as human is in no way *aliquid.* The Logos is garmented not with human nature, nor with a human being, but rather with the separate parts of human nature separately.

We can perhaps summarize these three theories, which does not do justice to the individual exponents of them, nor to their ongoing development in the twelfth and thirteenth centuries, by saying that (1) the assumptus theory held that the Son assumed a human being, that the *homo assumptus* was an *aliquid,* that one could distinguish two supposits in Christ although only one person, that of the Logos, the *persona assumens;* (2) the subsistence theory approaches a deeper union in Christ in that the *humanum* subsists in the Logos, has no existence apart from the *subsistentia* of the Logos but that which is assumed is not a human being (a *homo assumptus*) but human nature as such, although this theory opened itself to variation, with some later maintaining that Christ as man is *aliquid* and others (earlier) maintaining that Christ as man *non est aliquid;*[9] (3) the habitus theory used the analogy of the Son being clothed as with a garment, which involved be-

[8]Adam, *The Christ of Faith,* 219.

[9]This issue of *aliquid* is also related to Pope Alexander III's condemnation in 1170 and 1177 of the *non est aliquid* opinion, which led later theologians to weave a subsistence theory together with an *aliquid* position. See Principe, *William of Auxerre's Theology of the Hypostatic Union,* 67–68.

ing clothed with the body and the soul separately, such that, as human, there was no human *aliquid* in Christ.

We thus find in the background three opinions, the question of whether Christ as human is *aliquid,* or whether Christ is truly *unum,* and whether the nature of the *unum* (oneness) in Christ is accidental. As we have already seen, Thomas rejects both the assumptus theory and the habitus theory and understands them to be Nestorian. He writes, "Clearly, then, of the three opinions cited, the second, that there is one hypostasis of God and man, should not be classified as an opinion, but as the teaching of Catholic faith. Similarly, the first, that there are two hypostases, and the third, that the union is accidental, are not to be termed opinions, but heresies condemned by Councils of the church" (III, 2, 6). As we saw previously, Thomas rejected the interpretation of the union in Christ as an accidental one; such was his interpretation of the habitus theory. Yet the assumptus theory, in affirming that Christ as human is *aliquid,* seems also to destroy the unity in Christ. If Christ as human is hypostasis or supposit, then Christ is two; this is Nestorian. The truth for Thomas lies somewhere in between these two opinions. Thus it is that he tackles the question of the unity of Christ in the two articles of question 17.

The first article asks whether Christ is *unum.* If one were to distinguish "person" and "supposit," such that there was in Christ not only two natures but also a human as well as divine supposit, albeit one person, one would then argue that Christ was *unus* (one person) but not *unum* (because two supposits). For Thomas, however, as article 6 of question 2 and article 1 of question 17 make clear, there is no human supposit in Christ, for *suppositum* cannot be separated from *persona.* Christ is *unus* and *unum,* and two only in reference to the two natures. The human nature in Christ is not a supposit, which would make it a quasi-person. Christ is a single supposit, a single *aliquid,* subsisting in two natures.

There is duality in Christ with respect to his two natures. Yet, if one speaks properly, it must be said that Christ is one, because the two natures are predicated of Christ only as they are considered to be in a subsisting subject, and it is this unity or oneness of the subsisting subject that is the most proper way to speak of him. Thus, "Because we place in Christ only one person [*persona*] and one supposit [*suppositum*] . . . it follows that we say that not only is Christ *unus* (one) in the masculine gender but also that he is *unum* (one) in the neuter gender" (III, 17, 1). And, "Although Christ possesses a duality of natures, he cannot be said to be two, because he nevertheless does not possess a duality of supposits" (III, 17, 1 ad 6).

In question 17, article 2, Thomas then makes his major contribution toward understanding Christ's unity. What it comes down to is that in Christ there is but one *esse,* one act of existence. As Thomas says, *one thing* implies *one act of existence.* This statement, however, implies Thomas' metaphysical background, his contribution to Christian philosophy of the distinction between essence and existence, that only in God are essence and existence one (I, 3, 4). It is of God's essence to exist, and it is not of the essence of any finite nature as such to exist. The actual existence of finite creatures, then, does not belong to created natures, but to the supposit, which has *esse,* or the act of existing. Thus Thomas has at hand his earlier distinction between *esse* and *essentia.* The *unitas* in Christ flows from the fact that there is only one *esse,* one act of existing, which is the *esse* of the Son, the *Logos,* an eternal act of existence, which is identical with the divine nature itself and which in the incarnation becomes the *esse* that supports, stands under, and is the unique act of existence underlying Christ's human nature. There is no human nature of Christ, no man Jesus, apart from its/his existence in the *esse* of the Son. It is in this sense that Jesus *is* the Son; his very *esse* is the *esse* of the Son, his very "isness" is the "isness" of the Son: Jesus *is* (his "isness" is) the Son. Thomas' Christology, too, comes down to a contemplation on the meaning of *to be.*

Thomas writes (III, 17, 2): "If therefore in Christ there were two acts of existence, and not only one, Christ would be two and not one." But Thomas has already argued that Christ is only one, both *unus* and *unum.* The underlying bottom line, subject, or *ousia* in Christ, that which possesses existence, has an *esse* of its own, is the Son. If the human nature were united to the Son, not hypostatically or personally or substantially but, rather, accidentally, then one could attribute to Christ two acts of existence, one pertaining to his divine nature and another pertaining to his human nature. But then Christ would not *be* God. He would be a graced or divinized man. It is at the level of *being* that God and humankind have become one in Christ. But, as Thomas argued earlier (III, 2, 5, and 6), the union in Christ is hypostatic or personal *(kath hypostasin* or *secundum personam)* not *per accidens.* "Consequently, with his human nature he does not acquire a new personal existence, but simply a new relation of his already existing personal existence to the human nature. Accordingly, this person is now said to subsist not only in his divine nature but also in his human nature" (III, 17, 2). There is, in the Thomas of question 17, only one *esse* in Christ, the divine *esse*, by which and in which the human nature subsists.

Thomas' opinion in the *tertia pars* of his *Summa* shows a development in his own thinking on the incarnation. For, when he was disputing the *De unione verbi incarnati* before leaving Paris in 1272, he had not yet come to the insight he expresses in question 17. His understanding in the two works is somewhat different. In the *De unione,* article 4, Thomas is still groping toward an adequate solution, and there he allows Christ to have a human *esse.* We can see the inadequacy of Thomas' solution at that time: "There is, however, another *esse* of the supposit, not in so far as it is eternal, but in so far as it became human in time. . . . Nevertheless it is not the principal *esse* of the supposit, but a secondary one" *(De unione,* 4, *utrum in Christo sit unum tantum esse).* In the *Summa,* however, only several months later, Thomas changed his mind: The human nature in Christ cannot have an *esse* of its own. Its *esse* is the *esse* of the eternal Word, in which it subsists and has its being. "The eternal *esse* of the Son of God, which is the divine nature, becomes the *esse* of the man, inasmuch as the human nature is assumed by the Son of God into the unity of his person" (III, 17, 2, ad 2).

Thomas' distinction between *esse* and essence lies at the heart of his final understanding of the theology of the hypostatic union. His theology here cannot be seen as typical of the Middle Ages. Just as in the New Testament and among the Fathers there were diverse and individual Christologies, so the Middle Ages were as pluralistic as all previous ages. Other medieval positions did not distinguish essence and *esse* in creatures, and thus the Scotists, nominalists, and Suarezians interpreted the hypostatic union differently. Not all theologians then or now necessarily agree with the opinion to which Thomas finally came.

Thomas' stress on the unity of Christ is also reflected in his discussion of Christ's conception (III, 33). It is not Thomas' biological presupposition but rather his theological concern that is of significance in this discussion. Thomas thought of the conception of Christ as taking place in three stages, the movement of blood to the place of generation, the formation of the body from this material, the growth of the body to proper size. Only the middle stage is, properly speaking, conception, for the first is simply preparatory to it and the third a consequence of it (III, 33, 1). The middle phase, the actual conception of Christ, took place instantaneously, through the infinite power of the Holy Spirit. The body of Christ was formed by the Spirit and assumed by the Son in an instant. For it was not fitting that Christ assume anything other than a completely formed body, which he assumed in the very instant that it was formed (III, 33, 1). Not only was the body completely formed by the Holy Spirit at that moment when the incarnation took place, but in that same instant of conception Christ's body was animated by a rational soul (III, 33, 2).

All this is by way of contrast to ordinary conceptions, for Thomas followed Aristotle's teaching on the successive animation of a foetus.[10] The formation of Christ's body, its animation, and its assumption by the Son all took place simultaneously and instantaneously. Underlying this, of course, we can see Thomas' concern that there be no other hypostasis or supposit in Christ than the divine hypostasis. There was no other supposit in Christ. The flesh of Christ was not first conceived and *then* assumed; the flesh did not pre-exist as if subsistent in itself before being assumed by the Word (III, 33, 3).

Thomas' interpretation of the conception of Christ is partially his response to Adoptionism: The conception, which consists in the Word being hypostatically united to the flesh, is not an adoption but an incarnation. "We speak properly when we say that God was made man, not when we say that a man was made God" (III, 33, 3; also III, 16, 6 and 7). The eternal Son did not assume a man *(homo assumptus)* but a human nature. "The mystery of the incarnation is not considered an ascent, as if something pre-existing advanced up to the dignity of the union . . . but rather a descent by which the perfect Word of God assumed to himself the imperfection of our nature" (III, 33, 3, ad 3). Christ's miraculous conception and his being the Word of God incarnate

---

[10]Cf. Aristotle, *De Generatione Animalium,* II, 1 and 3.

through the hypostatic union are closely connected for Thomas. The virginal conception is *how* the Word became flesh and dwelled among us.

It is to his lectures on chapter 1, verse 14, of the Gospel of John, also from the period of his second Parisian regency, that one ought to go to hear Thomas proclaim his faith. In a fairly typical, Scholastic fashion, Thomas finds in the text of Scripture the refutation of all the Christological heresies.

> It should be noted that this statement, *the Word was made flesh,* has been misinterpreted by some. . . . For certain ones have presumed that the Word became flesh in the sense that he or something of him was turned into flesh. . . . One of these was Eutyches. . . . Therefore, one must say in opposition to Eutyches, *the Word was made flesh,* that is, the Word assumed flesh, but not in the sense that the Word himself is that flesh. . . . There were others who, although they believed that the Word was not changed into flesh but assumed it, nevertheless said that he assumed flesh without a soul. . . . This was the error of Arius, who said that there was no soul in Christ, but that the Word of God was there in place of a soul. . . . It is plain that flesh does not acquire the specific nature of flesh except through its soul. . . . So if the Word did not assume flesh with a soul, it is obvious that he did not assume flesh but *the Word was made flesh;* therefore, he assumed flesh with a soul. And there were others who, influenced by this, said that the Word did indeed assume flesh with a soul, but this soul was only a sensitive soul, not an intellectual one; the Word took the place of the intellectual soul in Christ's body. This was the error of Apollinaris. . . . The Word assumed human nature in order to repair it. Therefore, he repaired what he assumed. But if he did not assume a rational soul, he would not have repaired it. . . . Therefore, *the Word was made flesh,* i.e., assumed flesh which was animated by a rational soul. . . . A question arises as to why the Evangelist did not say that the Word assumed flesh, but rather that *the Word was made flesh.* I answer that he did this to exclude the error of Nestorius. He said that in Christ there were two persons and two sons. . . . But if this were so, it would mean that God did not become man, for one particular *suppositum* cannot be predicated of

another. Accordingly, if the person or *suppositum* of the Word is different than the person or *suppositum* of the man, in Christ, then what the Evangelist says is not true, namely, *the Word was made flesh*. . . . If you ask how the Word is man, it must be said that he is man in the way that anyone is man, namely, as having human nature. Not that the Word is human nature itself, but he is a divine *suppositum* united to a human nature.[11]

On the Predication of Properties

The *communicatio idiomatum* has a long history going back to the post-apostolic age. It was traditional in the Church's way of speaking about Christ before it had a clearly articulated theological foundation for itself. It was traditional before it became orthodox. It historically became a test of orthodoxy, for a right way of speaking manifested a right understanding. Language articulates the understanding of faith, which cannot be separated from its expression. Language has historically been central to the theological task. How to express the unity of God who is Father, Son, and Spirit? Nicea introduced *homoousios*. So in Christology: how does one speak about Jesus Christ? The history of the *communicatio* is parallel to the history of Christology itself.

Although we could not yet call it a consciously chosen form of Christological language, the way of speaking in which human qualities or properties were attributed to the one subject of the union in which there was an exchange of predication between the human predicates and the divine subject, we already find this way of speaking in the second century. Ignatius speaks of the blood of God and the suffering of my God (Ign. *Eph.* 1, 1; Ign. *Rom.* 6, 3). A hymn to Christ in the Sybilline Oracles, the middle of the second century, says, "O blessed tree, on which God was hung" (VI, 26). And in the West, Tertullian had written early, "There are, to be sure, other things quite as foolish which have reference to the humiliations and sufferings of God. Or else, let them call a crucified God wisdom. . . . The Son of God was crucified; I am not ashamed because men must needs be ashamed" (*De Carne Christi,* V, 1-4).

---

[11]See Thomas Aquinas, *Commentary on the Gospel of St. John,* trans. J. A. Weisheipl and F. R. Larcher (Albany, N.Y.: Magi Books, 1980) lecture 7, pp. 83-89.

The *communicatio* is most clearly manifest in Alexandrian theology, and it is Alexandrian Logos theology that eventually provided the theological basis for it. This is true in both Athanasius and Cyril. The *communicatio* was a sign of orthodoxy for Cyril and a reason for rejecting the theology of Nestorius. The Antiochene theology was less able to provide a theological foundation for the *communicatio,* which was part of the tradition of the Church, the Church's way of speaking and worshiping. The *theotokos* title had emerged in the middle of the third century and was simply expressing the Church's faith or understanding of the ultimate reality that Christ was. Thus, the *theotokos* affair forced the need for a theological basis for the *communicatio,* and as a result of it the *communicatio* became orthodox for the faith.

For a "divisive Christology" is less of a theological basis for an "exchange of predication" than is a "unitive Christology." One of the effects of Ephesus was to vindicate a way of speaking about Christ that had been traditional since the second century and before but not thought through. Although Ephesus, in its defense of *theotokos,* vindicated the *communicatio* and made it a part of orthodox teaching, it remained for Chalcedon to provide a theology for it. The properties or attributes of the two natures could be exchanged as long as they were being applied to the concrete individual who was one *hypostasis.* One could not say the divine nature suffered, but one could say that the Son of God suffered; one could not say that the human nature was omniscient, but one could say that Christ was. The attributes could not be attributed to the other nature but could be attributed to the person, the subject of predication. Not until Chalcedon effected a distinction between *physis* and *hypostasis* did the Church have a theology that explained its *praxis.* One of the permanent contributions of Ephesus and Chalcedon was to formulate a technical Christological language. Nestorius' error was to call into question the *communicatio,* which expressed the Church's faith. The issue was bigger than appeared on the surface and not merely semantic. For one could predicate both divine and human qualities of the one subject. If Christ was *one subject,* then Mary was *theotokos.* The Church's traditional way of speaking, we might say, was based on intuition, an intuition that was only clearly theologized when forced to clarify itself in the Cyrillian-Nestorian conflict. Leo's *Tome* makes it clear that this was the Church's way of speaking, the Church's understanding.

Christological language is technical language, and one must understand both the meaning of terms and the canons of proper use, not because the mystery can be reduced to semantic questions but in order to preserve the mystery from faulty formulations. The basis of the *communicatio* is twofold: (1) The two natures in Christ are not to be confused; thus one cannot attribute to one nature an attribute of the other, such as in saying that the divine nature dies, or the human nature is eternal. Also, even if the person (a concrete noun rather than an abstract noun) is the subject of predication, but so qualified as to refer to one nature, one cannot exchange predications. Thus, neither could one say that Christ, as man, is eternal; or that Christ, as Word of God, suffered and died. The two natures are not to be identified or confused in one's way of speaking about Christ. (2) Predication of attributes of either nature can take place when the subject is the person (an unqualified, concrete noun), since one person is the real subject of both natures. This is simply a recognition of the hypostatic union. Thus, one can say that Christ is uncreated (because this is true of his divine nature), and one can say that Christ is created (because this is true of his human nature). Contrary properties can be attributed to the one person, but not of the other nature. What we have said applies to affirmative statements only. Negative statements are of a different sort. Thus, something that can be denied of one nature cannot simply be denied of the person, because the person subsists in both natures. One can say that the divine nature does not die, but one cannot say that Christ did not die. This is simply an application of an understanding of the Chalcedonian distinction between *hypostasis* and *physis*. Because there is but one hypostasis, no matter by what title or name one designates him, one can say "God's uniquely begotten Son was crucified" and "Jesus Christ is Creator of heaven and earth." The proper noun "Jesus" more commonly denotes Jesus as man. Strictly speaking, the Theopaschite formula is orthodox (one of the Trinity was crucified, or, God suffered), but it became a Monophysite slogan, by which it was implied that the one divine nature suffered because of a lack of distinction between *hypostasis* and *physis*.

Thomas Aquinas was simply manifesting the tradition of the

Church when he was attentive to how one speaks properly concerning Christ. The metaphysics of the union must be respected in Christological language. All twelve articles of question 16 of the *tertia pars* of his *Summa* manifest his sensitivity to the Church's tradition concerning the *communicatio* or predication of properties.

Is the statement "God is a man" a true statement? Yes, it is. For the word "God" stands for the person of the Son, the subject of the sentence, and the ontological subject of the union; and the Son subsists in a human nature as well as a divine nature. That man is the Son of God (III, 16, 1-2).

Can Christ, strictly speaking, be called a man of the Lord? No. Because "Christ," as a concrete noun and subject, signifies the ontological subject of the union, namely, the person or *hypostasis* of the Son. Thus, Christ is Lord and God. It is more proper to say that he is Lord than to say he is "of the Lord." It is true that Christ is a man, but Christ is a man who is Lord, not a man who is of the Lord. Thomas does admit that one can speak loosely and say that Christ can be called a man of the Lord by reason of his human nature. Thus, speaking less properly, one could say that Christ, as man, is a man of the Lord, or that Jesus, signifying by this Christ as man, is a man of the Lord (III, 16, 3). Thomas' clearest statement of the rules of Christological language are in articles 4 and 5 of question 16, but he is sensitive to these rules throughout his Christology (III, 9, 1, ad 3; 20, 2).

Thomas elucidated still another principle. One's language about Christ ought to be qualified if a statement could be misleading or connote heresy. Thus the statement "God was made a man" is valid (III, 16, 6), but the statement "Christ is a creature" is not (III, 16, 8). Strictly speaking, the latter statement is true. Yet it readily connotes an Arian position and is thus misleading. The statement is not so much false as careless. Thus, lest it lend support to a false understanding of Christ, the statement should be qualified.

> Not even the expressions we use should conform to those of heretics lest we seem to favor their error. The Arian heretics said that Christ was a creature, and less than the Father, not only by reason of his human nature, but also by reason of his divine person. Thus it ought not be said without qualification

that Christ is a creature, or less than the Father; but only with a qualification, such as "according to his human nature." Those things, however, which cannot be suspected of being attributed to the divine person as divine, can be stated of Christ without qualification by reason of his human nature, as we say without qualification that Christ suffered, died, and was buried (III, 16, 8).

Hence it would be more correct to say "Christ, as human, is a creature" (III, 16, 10).

In a similar vein and in another place, conscious of misleading statements (and we might call to mind the eighth-century Adoptionist heresy), Thomas cautions against the statement "Christ, as man, is an adopted son of God" (III, 23, 4). Although Hilary seems to feel free to speak in that vein, Thomas replied that Hilary's language in that instance is *impropria locutio* (improper speech). Sonship, strictly speaking *(proprie),* pertains to *hypostasis* or person and not to nature. In Christ, however, there is only one person, and that person is Son of God by nature. "In no way can he be called an adopted son" (III, 23, 4). Even to qualify the statement in this instance would not prevent misunderstanding.

There is no need for further examples.[12] We can see that theology, and Christology in particular, implies a careful use of language. There is a Christological logic that is the counterpart of Christological metaphysics. Some situations may legitimate a bold or less precise expression, but theological statements must respect how language expresses mystery. It is not a question of "mere semantics," but a question of how best to articulate the faith. The basic principles of the *communicatio* have a strong basis in tradition because they express the orthodox Christian faith. What we say expresses what we believe.

A Concluding Theological Reflection

Thomas clearly had pastoral concerns in his theology. He wrote the *Summa theologiae* for theological beginners and the *Summa*

---

[12]It is a worthwhile exercise to consider in greater detail all the statements Thomas discusses in III, 16. In some ways they are a test of whether or not one has understood Thomas' theology of the hypostatic union as articulated in questions 2–6 and 17.

contra gentiles for preachers and missionaries. Thomas was also a mystic and poet, and his experience of God profound, as witnessed in his liturgy for Corpus Christi. Yet what is most immediately apparent about Thomas' theology is its philosophical character, depth, and precision. Although this may not always be easily appreciated, it is significant. One cannot study Thomas carefully without learning the importance of Scripture, the need for balance in formulating opinions, the art of distinguishing, the obligation to do justice to both faith and reason, the value of clarity, the importance of language, and that intellectual laziness in a theologian is unacceptable.

Not every theologian is called upon to be a philosophical theologian, but some are, and they perform a valuable service. A mystical language may be more bold and expressive, but philosophical language is also necessary if theology is to remain intelligible, intellectually credible, and capable of discussion in the public forum. Philosophy opens theology to the world and helps prevent theology from becoming only private, subjective, and ecclesially narrow. Philosophical discourse, whatever the philosophical starting point may be, helps to articulate the faith. It is for this that Thomas stands out. His theology of the hypostatic union is only one example. Whether the language of hypostatic union is the best way in which to talk about the incarnation today is a different issue, but Thomas brought clarity, depth, and originality to the discussion—which clarity, depth, and originality contemporary theology also needs to pursue.

Not every theologian in the time of Thomas or after has accepted his theology of the hypostatic union. But it still remains a valid question, whether it has in fact been surpassed. It may not be our primary concern, or it may not serve our pastoral needs today, but when one attempts to understand the particular union that Jesus Christ is, one cannot do better than going to Thomas to grapple with the issues involved—and one will come away with a deeper appreciation of the mystery of Christ for having done so.

By the careful use of language, both out of respect for philosophical inquiry and also out of a deep faith, Thomas was able to address theologically the uniqueness of Jesus Christ. This uniqueness lies within the unique kind of union that the hypostatic union is. There simply is no other union of its kind.

Just as the act of creation itself is a unique kind of causation for Thomas and there are no other instances of causation of exactly the same sort, whereby the finite proceeds from the infinite, so the incarnation is also a unique act of God in which God assumes a human nature.

For Thomas, there are not two distinct pre-existing realities, which at a certain moment are united. There is only one preexistent reality, the pre-incarnate eternal Word or Son, who assumes a particular human nature at a given moment of history. It is a unique act of God as far as we know. It is not that a human being, an *aliquis* or even *aliquid,* assumed a divine nature, but that God assumed at a certain moment in history a human nature. This hypostatic union, or union that takes place in the *hypostasis* or person of the Word, is an assumption by that Word of a human nature by which assumption the Word subsists in two natures. The human nature that was assumed, which was the Word incarnate, Jesus Christ, never had an existence, an *esse,* of its own apart from the Word. Jesus Christ *is* that Word, that Word incarnate. That human nature was created and assumed by the Word at one and the same time. That human nature is *the humanity of the Word*. This is Thomas' theology of the hypostatic union.

SUGGESTED READINGS

Primary Sources

Albert and Thomas, Selected Writings. Ed. and trans. Simon Tugwell. Classics of Western Spirituality. New York: Paulist, 1988.

Thomas Aquinas. *Commentary on the Gospel of St. John.* Trans. J. A. Weisheipl and F. R. Larcher. Albany, N.Y.: Magi Books, 1980.

_____. *Commentary on St. Paul's Epistle to the Ephesians.* Trans. M. L. Lamb. Albany, N.Y.: Magi Books, 1966.

_____. *Commentary on St. Paul's Epistle to the Galatians.* Trans. F. R. Larcher. Albany, N.Y.: Magi Books, 1966.

_____. *De unione verbi incarnati.* No English translation. Vol. 13 of *Opera Omnia* (Vivés), or vol. 2 of *Quaestiones Disputatae* (Marietti).

————. *Summa contra gentiles*. Trans. Pegis, Anderson, Bourke, and O'Neil as *On the Truth of the Catholic Faith,* 5 vols. New York: Doubleday, 1955-1957.

————. *Summa theologiae*. Trans. along with Latin text in 60 vols. New York: McGraw-Hill, 1964-1976.

————. *Compendium of Theology*. Trans. Cyril Vollert. St. Louis: B. Herder, 1947.

Secondary Sources

Adam, Karl. *The Christ of Faith*. Trans. Joyce Crick. New York: Pantheon Books, 1962.

Chenu, M. D. *St. Thomas d'Aquin et la théologie*. Maitres Spirituels. Paris: Seuil, 1977.

————. *Toward Understanding St. Thomas*. Trans. Albert Landry and Dominic Hughes. Chicago: Henry Regnery Co., 1964.

Copleston, F. C. *Aquinas*. New York: Penguin Books, 1955.

Farrell, Walter. *Only Son*. New York: Sheed and Ward, 1953.

Gilson, Etienne. *The Christian Philosophy of St. Thomas Aquinas*. Trans. L. K. Shook. New York: Random House, 1956.

————. *Dante and Philosophy*. Trans. David Moore. New York: Harper & Row, 1949/1963.

————. *Reason and Revelation in the Middle Ages*. New York: Charles Scribner's Sons, 1938/1966.

Goergen, Donald. "Albert the Great and Thomas Aquinas on the Motive of the Incarnation." *The Thomist* 44 (1980) 523-538.

Murphy, Thomas, "St. Thomas' Intuition in the De Unione." *Heythrop Journal* 7 (1966) 301-309.

Pieper, Josef. *The Silence of St. Thomas*. Trans. John Murray and Daniel O'Connor. New York: Pantheon Books, 1957.

Potvin, Thomas. *The Theology of the Primacy of Christ According to St. Thomas and Its Scriptural Foundations*. Fribourg, Switzerland: University Press, 1973.

Principe, Walter H. *William of Auxerre's Theology of the Hypostatic Union*. Vol. 1 of *The Theology of the Hypostatic Union in the Early Thirteenth Century*. Toronto: Pontifical Institute of Medieval Studies, 1963.

————. *Alexander of Hales' Theology of the Hypostatic Union*. Vol. 2 of *The Theology of the Hypostatic Union in the Early Thirteenth Century*. Toronto: Pontifical Institute of Medieval Studies, 1967.

_____. *Hugh of Saint-Cher's Theology of the Hypostatic Union*. Vol. 3 of *The Theology of the Hypostatic Union in the Early Thirteenth Century*. Toronto: Pontifical Institute of Medieval Studies, 1970.

_____. *Philip the Chancellor's Theology of the Hypostatic Union*. Vol. 4 of *The Theology of the Hypostatic Union in the Early Thirteenth Century*. Toronto: Pontifical Institute of Medieval Studies, 1975.

Ruello, Francis. *La christologie de Thomas d'Aquin*. Theologie historique 76. Paris: Beauchesne, 1987.

Sertillanges, A. M. *St. Thomas Aquinas and His Work*. Trans. Godfrey Anstruthers. London: Aquin Press, 1957.

Weisheipl, James A. *Friar Thomas D'Aquino, His Life, Thought and Works*. Garden City, N.Y.: Doubleday, 1974.

Woshienko, Nicholas. *Christ's Human Knowledge According to the Theology of St. Thomas*. Ph.D. diss. Boston University, 1979.

7

Martin Luther
and the Language of a Pastor

In the sixteenth century the Reformation gave birth to another
major division within Christianity, which still affects the Christian Church in our own day. In addition to Byzantine Eastern
Orthodox Christianity and Roman Western Catholic Christianity,
there developed a third major Christian tradition, Protestant, with
its origins in northern Europe. The new development evidenced
once again the tendency of the Christian tradition toward diversification, manifest in the New Testament period, in the tension
between Alexandria and Antioch, and among the Nestorian, Orthodox, and Monophysite Churches. The Reformation itself
shows the same tendency of the Christian tradition to diversify.
Martin Luther and John Calvin are distinct theologians, even if
both are sons of the Reformation, and one can even say the same
of Luther and Philip Melanchthon. The Reformation gave birth
to many new strands of Christian theology. For purposes of sim-
plification one can group them into four: the Lutheran, Reformed,
Anabaptist, and Anglican traditions.

Martin Luther (1483–1546) was the most significant theologian
of the sixteenth century. Luther's theology, like Augustine's, was
intimately interwoven with his life and experience. The great theme
of Luther's theology was his contrast between a "theology of
glory" and a "theology of the cross," between a "legal" knowledge of God and an "evangelical" one, between the "left-handed"
knowledge of God and "right-handed" knowledge, between

works and grace, between law and gospel. "The gospel proclaims nothing else but salvation by grace, given to man without any works and merits whatsoever" (*Sermon,* [1522], *LW,* 51:112).[1]

Luther's theology was not metaphysical, philosophical, or rational. It was rather, as one can readily see, dialectical, with a greater concern for proclamation than for rational distinctions. It was not a dialectic of complementarity but of existential opposition due to sin and the bondage of the human will and reason. It was, as Luther said, a theology of the cross of Christ. Its theological concern was salvation.

Luther's theology was a theology of the Word, not in the sense of the Alexandrian Logos theologies, but rather in the sense of the Word of God *as proclaimed.* The Word is a reality with interrelated levels of meanings: The Word is the eternal, second person of the Trinity; the Word is Christ, the incarnate Word; the Word is the gospel, which is the heart of the Word as written in the Scriptures or as proclaimed and heard in the Church. The Word is Christ; the Word is Scripture; the Word is the proclamation of the gospel. The Word of God is the starting point for Christology. There is an outward Word, Scripture, and an inward Word, the work of the Holy Spirit, and the two go together. God speaks God's Word in our hearts through the power of the Spirit; but the Spirit does not speak apart from the outward Word. Nor does the spoken or proclaimed Word enter into our hearts apart from the Spirit. Word and Spirit go together.

Although the Spirit works in and through the Word, the Spirit does so freely. The Spirit is not controlled by the preacher. The preaching of the Word and the hearing of the Word are rather dependent upon the Spirit and await the activity of the Spirit, who chooses to work in and through God's Word. The Spirit does not speak the inward Word apart from the proclamation or hearing of the outward Word, and yet this Spirit is not bound by that outward Word but remains free.

With respect to Christology proper, and the doctrine of the incarnation, Luther is quite traditional. The same can be said of his teaching on the Trinity. God is both one and three, in accord

---

[1] References in the text to the writings of Luther come from the translation entitled *Luther's Works* (abbreviated *LW*), ed. Jaroslav Pelikan (vols. 1–30) and Helmut T. Lehmann (vols. 31–55), published by Concordia and Fortress. The references indicate volume and page (e.g., 51:112).

with the ancient creeds, which are in accord with Scripture. Likewise, according to Luther, the doctrine of the two natures in Christ is in accord with Scripture. Yet, in contrast to medieval theologians, Luther does not attempt to penetrate the mode of union in the incarnation through reason. The incarnation is an enigma and remains such. The Creator has become a creature; reason must give way to faith.

Luther's Christology manifested both an "Alexandrian" and an "Antiochene" element, Antiochene in its emphasis on the humanity of Christ, Alexandrian in its awareness of the unity of Christ. Luther made clear use of the *communicatio idiomatum,* and it provided the basis for his doctrine of Christ's real and bodily presence in the Eucharist. Jesus, in his human life, partook of the divine attributes. Jesus was omniscient, omnipotent, and omnipresent. Christ's self-emptying does not mean that he left behind his divine characteristics; rather, self-emptying refers to the character of his earthly life. Jesus on earth continued to possess the qualities of God but also continued to set them aside in order to be one with us. He set aside the use of the divine attributes, although they remained available to him. Luther accepted the traditional two-nature doctrine, but approached the implications of it in accord with the enigma that it is. For Luther, Christ was simply both divine and human. He possessed the divine majesty as a human being, and in him God shared in human suffering.

Except for an emphasis on the paradoxical or enigmatic character of the two-nature doctrine, Luther's Christology itself was traditional and followed Chalcedonian lines. The *novum* (newness) in Luther's Christology was its shift to the centrality of the doctrine of salvation and its corresponding *pro me* (on my behalf) structure (*LW* 34:111). In the East, Christology and soteriology had been held together with the complementarity between the Greek doctrines of incarnation and deification. In Western theology since Augustine and the Pelagian controversy, the dialectic between sin and grace had been formative of Western thought. Luther experienced Catholic practice prior to the Reformation with its theology of merit as obscuring the doctrine of salvation by grace, which doctrine he placed as the uncompromising center of the theological task. In Western soteriology, the predominant Anselmian emphasis on the objective fact of salvation had obscured its personal character. Thus Luther interpreted the intensely *pro me* character of salvation as constitutive of the doctrine of salvation. In Christ, God has been revealed as being *for us*.

Luther's soteriological Christology is both Johannine and Pauline. John 14:9 ("Whoever sees me has seen the Father") was one of its bases; we come to know God through Christ (*LW* 24:56-64). And what we come to know is how God feels about us, that God is unqualifiedly for us. To know Jesus is to know his Father and his Father's love. The way to come to know the Father is through Jesus' humanity, which is in the foreground of Luther's Christology. "If you can humble yourself, adhere to the Word with your heart, and hold to Christ's humanity—then the divinity will indeed become manifest" (*LW* 23:102).

God's love is not an abstract affirmation of faith. Such objectifying faith is not saving faith. True faith, faith that saves, recognizes God's love *for me*. Johannine Christology teaches us that we know the Father through the Son. We come to God through Christ, and that to which we come is God's love for us. God's love is salvific on our behalf: such is the central content of Luther's Christology.

The *novum* in Luther's Christology lies here, not in faith's objective knowledge of Jesus Christ as formulated in the classical Christologies, which he accepts, not in some theological articulation of who Christ is "in himself," but rather in the saving knowledge of who Christ is "for me." For Luther, Christological orthodoxy is not necessarily true faith. In Christ, God has been revealed as personally involved with us. It is not a metaphysical understanding or objective knowledge but a personal knowledge that is decisive.[2] Thus, Christology is primarily soteriology.

In what, then, did the work of Christ consist? First is the fact that Christ's work was a satisfaction paid to God. In Christ, God was reconciled. In this respect Luther followed Anselm.[3] God's grace comes to us apart from any merit on our part. Yet God's anger at sin and God's sense of justice are not to be simply dismissed. Some satisfaction is due to God that justifies God's mercy

[2]Cf. Donald Goergen, *The Death and Resurrection of Jesus* (Wilmington, Del.: Michael Glazier, Inc., 1988) pp. 183f. on objective and personal knowledge.

[3]Gustaf Aulen interprets Luther's theology of atonement as not belonging within the Latin theory of satisfaction in *Christus Victor* (New York: Macmillan, 1969). Althaus refutes Aulen's interpretation. See Paul Althaus, *The Theology of Martin Luther* (Philadelphia: Fortress, 1963/1970) 218-223.

toward us. This was accomplished through a wonderful exchange, through a substitution in which Jesus took our place. Satisfaction takes place not through our bearing the burden of our sin but through Christ's having done so. In Luther's soteriology, Christ is a "satisfaction" and a "substitution." God's righteousness is revealed, as is God's mercy and love. Christ's sufferings and death on our behalf were genuinely human. Although sinless, he accepted the punishment due sin—for our sakes.

Second, Christ effected a victory over the demonic powers. Luther's soteriology had much in common with the pre-Anselmian, ransom view of the atonement, which pictured Christ in combat with the devil. In this sense, Christ's work carried with it not only the note of expiation but also victory and freedom from bondage. In this aspect of Christ's work, his death and resurrection were closely tied together. For Christ was victorious not only over Satan but also over death.

And finally, Christ's work is effective *for me* when it is appropriated in and through faith. Christ's work in and of itself took place "outside of us" and "in history"; it is an objective, accomplished reality. Yet it does not reach us apart from faith. Salvation in Christ has its "objective" side, but is not objective alone; it is subjectively owned through faith by which *we* are saved. All have been saved in Christ by grace, but through faith.

> Christ's victory is not a metaphysical event of the kind which would enable us to say that since the time of his victory the demonic powers are no longer present. Rather, it is a victory in the sense that the victory depends on him and that the enemies are overcome and no longer present when he is present. We may describe the reality of his victory only with this spatial image of "where he is present" and not with the temporal image of "since" as though the world has, since Golgotha and Easter, been changed in a metaphysical sense. The demonic powers, including the wrath of God and the law, are all still there, but they are overcome in Christ; and therefore they are overcome for those in whom Christ lives through faith.[4]

Christ's historical work is accomplished anew in us through faith. Christ not only reconciles God; he reconciles *us* to God through faith. Just as Christology is primarily soteriology, so soteriology

[4]Althaus, *The Theology of Martin Luther*, 212-213.

is primarily *pro me.* Christology is the doctrine of justification by grace through faith.

What is it that saves us, or justifies us, or makes us righteous before God? Luther answers: Nothing that comes from us. God alone is the cause of our salvation. Although the law is not useless, neither is it a means to justification.

For Luther, the law has a twofold function, the one "civil" or "political" and the other "spiritual" or "theological." The first is that the law functions to preserve public order and justice. The second is an even deeper function. The law reveals God's will and our sinfulness; it functions as a condemnation, since we are not able to fulfill what the law requires. The law never functions in a way that helps to make us righteous. Righteousness or justification is grace alone, and its proclamation is the gospel, which functions by way of contrast to the law. In his doctrine of law and gospel Luther opposed both the Catholic doctrine of merit and the antinomianism (rejection of the moral law as obligatory for Christians) manifested in other currents of the Reformation. Both law and gospel have different functions, but both are part of preaching the Word. Luther himself does not use the expression, "the third use of the law," which is found in Melanchthon, the formula of Concord, and later Lutheran orthodoxy. The third function of the law is as a guide in Christian life according to which Christians ought to pattern their lives. Thus the law not only leads the Christian to a knowledge of his or her sin but also as instruction toward "good works." Although the law has serious theological and ethical meaning for Luther, its fulfillment in no way merits salvation for us. Salvation does not come from "works," but from grace and faith. Not even fulfilling the law with the help of God's grace contributes toward our salvation. There is no sense in which we can be said to merit salvation. Any form of moralism or of rationalism detracts from the true source of our salvation: faith. Only faith lets God be God, and thus only faith is true worship. Only faith is a right relationship with God.

The doctrine of justification by grace through faith is not simply one doctrine among others. It is *the* doctrine, the hinge on which everything else depends. It is the central doctrine in Christology, for it is only faith in Christ that is saving faith. There is no saving faith in God apart from Christ. Christ alone effects, reveals, and makes God's salvation present.

The word justification *(iustificatio)* has a twofold meaning for Luther. The first and primary meaning implies the judgment of God by which God forgives our sin, declares us to be righteous in his sight, and imputes justice to us. In a second and complementary sense justification also refers to our actually becoming righteous, something that remains incomplete while we are on earth. In its primary sense, justification is "extrinsic" to us. God imputes *(computare, imputare, reputare)* a righteousness to us which we in no way merit (*LW* 27:221; 34:153, 166–167). Our righteousness is not a quality inherent in us, but rather God's willingness to consider us as being righteous. Our justification is not "a work" of ours, not a righteousness "actively achieved," but a righteousness "passively received," unearned. Justification is grace alone and is received into the Christian's life by faith alone. Nor is this a faith in "objective facts" but is rather a faith that apprehends, or appropriates, or grasps Christ *(fides apprehensiva):* a faith in which one is grasped by the *pro me* character of God's grace (*LW* 34:109–114; 31:55–56; 26:129f.). It is through faith that God's grace breaks through to us. Nor is faith to be considered "a work," that is, a human work. It is rather God's work, God working righteousness in us. Through true faith, Christ is made present to us (*LW* 26:130) and becomes salvation.

The other side of the coin of justification is our becoming righteous, our transformation, even if not yet fully. Not only is righteousness imputed to us; it is effected within us. In his preface to his *Commentary on Romans* Luther writes:

> Faith, however, is a divine work in us which changes us and makes us to be born anew of God. . . . It kills the old Adam and makes us all together different men, in heart and spirit and mind and powers; and it brings with it the Holy Spirit. . . . It is impossible for it not to be doing good works incessantly. . . . Faith is a living, daring confidence in God's grace, so sure and certain that the believer would stake his life on it a thousand times. This knowledge of and confidence in God's grace makes men glad and bold and happy in dealing with God and with all creatures (*LW* 35:370–371).

Yet, in spite of the righteousness that God imputes to us and the righteousness that begins to take hold in us, we are still sinners. This fact never changes. And this is the central paradox in Luther's theocentric Christology: The person justified through faith remains *simul iustus et peccator* (righteous and a sinner at the same time).[5] There is a tension in Luther's doctrine of justification between the doctrine of imputed righteousness and the doctrine of righteousness as an eschatological reality already begun.

The cross of Christ is the source of all true knowledge about God and the human condition. For the cross symbolizes both God's graciousness and humankind's sinfulness, both the suffering of God reaching out to save us in Christ and the judgment of God on sin, both God's mercy and God's justice, both God's love and God's wrath. For the cross is the entry into the very heart of God and the reality of who we have become. Only the cross is an access to true knowledge. The cross reveals God's no to sin and God's yes to us as Christ takes our place in taking unto himself the punishment due to sin and thus unleashing God's mercy. The cross is the paradox par excellence, and only faith can grasp it. All true theology is a theology of the cross.

Luther's emphasis on the cross of Christ, the historical sufferings of Christ, and the humanity of Christ do not mean that Luther's Christology is a "Christology from below." Luther's Christology presupposes the divinity of Jesus and the pre-existence of the eternal Son. This is not something to which one comes later in the Christological endeavor. Although Luther's Christology is not "metaphysical" in the way that the "Christologies from above" were in the Latin West during the Middle Ages, yet Luther's Christology was from above, even if grounded in proclamation and dialectic rather than metaphysics and philosophy. Luther's primary concern was not the incarnation but the saving event of the cross; he had shifted soteriology to center stage. The primary affirmation of his Christology was thus: God is for us.

Except for the Eucharist, Luther gave more attention in his theology to the doctrine of justification than to any other doctrine. His teaching on the Lord's Supper, however, was to some degree forced by circumstances and history, for in his teaching on the Eucharist Luther held to a middle course between Catholics and more extreme Reformers. But Luther's theological position on the Lord's Supper was a Christological doctrine as well.

[5]Ibid., 234–245. See *Luther, LW* 27, 230f.; 12, 328.

Luther held that there were only two sacraments: baptism and Eucharist. On the Eucharist, Luther defined himself over against Catholic practice and theology. He rejected (1) the Catholic practice of not giving the cup to the laity, (2) the doctrine of transubstantiation, and (3) the teaching that the Mass is a sacrifice. Over against other Reformers, Luther held to the real presence of Christ in the Eucharist; he did not teach a "symbolic" or "spiritual" presence only. Although he affirmed the real presence of Christ, he rejected transubstantiation as a metaphysical, rational, or philosophical explanation. In accord with his emphasis on faith and consistent with his approach to the incarnation, Luther did not seek to answer *how* types of questions, which he did not consider proper theological questions but rather "works" of human reasoning. Luther preferred to let God be God. Yet in his teaching on real presence, Luther was closer to the Catholics than to Reformed theology.

As indicated previously, Luther's doctrine on the Eucharist was Christological. It was based on the ubiquity of Christ, which was a theological consequence of the incarnation and the *communicatio idiomatum*. Over against Reformers who maintained that Christ's body could not be really present in the Eucharist because it had been exalted to the right hand of God, Luther maintained that the right hand of God was not circumscribed to the heavens. Rather Christ, as God, had the capacity to be everywhere at the same time. Nevertheless, Christ could freely choose to limit his presence and thus freely chose to be present in the Eucharist. Luther's theology manifests a close connection between Christology and sacramental theology, the latter intrinsically related to the former. Christ is present to us today through Word and Sacrament.

These are the major emphases in Luther's theology. But let us look a little more closely at how his theological emphases developed and the language with which he articulated them.

The Development in Luther's Christology

Luther did not write a specific treatise on Christology as such, yet Jesus Christ clearly permeated his thought. He was already thinking "Christologically" in his early commentaries on Scripture, even on the Old Testament, as in his earliest commentary on the Psalms. Luther interpreted the psalms Christologically, that is, he attributed them to Christ, even those passages that speak so humanly of abandonment and suffering.[6] The psalms are the prayers of Christ. And Christ is God, God incarnate, God hidden in the flesh, the cause of salvation, both by virtue of his work in the past, in history, and by virtue of his work in the present, through faith. There is a twofold way in which Christ brings salvation.

Christology and soteriology are indissolubly linked for Luther. This is one of the hallmarks of his Christological thought. This link can be perceived in an early commentary on the Letter to the Romans, his second great commentary (1515–1516).[7] The theology of Jesus Christ cannot be separated from the theology of the Christian life. In this very early reflection on Romans 3:24-25, Luther affirmed that we receive salvation without meriting it *(sine meritis)*. He spoke of the merit of Christ *(meritum Christi)* but only to indicate that we are saved by Christ, on account of Christ *(propter Christum)*, and not by our own merits. Jesus Christ is the only righteousness that humanity can offer God. Because of Christ *(propter Christum)*, sin is covered up and we are forgiven. Our access to Christ is through faith *(per fidem,* or *fide)*. It is through faith that we are saved by the righteousness of Jesus Christ.

Jesus Christ is both Savior and example *(exemplar, exemplum)*. This usage, already in the early commentary on Romans, is carried further in the commentary on the Letter to the Hebrews (1517–1518), wherein Christ is both *sacramentum* and *exemplum,* both the source (or sacrament) of our salvation and an example *(Lectures on Hebrews, LW* 29:131-133, 142, 178, 216, 226). Christology and soteriology again come together: the *pro me* (for me) or *pro nobis* (for us) structure of Luther's thought. We are

[6]This hermeneutical principle does not seem to have been unique to Luther but was rather common in late medieval exegesis. See Alister E. McGrath, *Luther's Theology of the Cross: Martin Luther's Theological Breakthrough* (Oxford: Basil Blackwell, 1985) 75-81; and Jaroslav Pelikan, *Luther the Expositor,* a companion volume to *Luther's Works* (St. Louis: Concordia, 1959).

[7]For a study of the development of Luther's thought, see especially Marc Lienhard, *Luther: Witness to Jesus Christ, Stages and Themes of the Reformer's Christology,* trans. Edwin H. Robertson (Minneapolis: Augsburg, 1982); and also for the early development, see McGrath, *Luther's Theology of the Cross.*

saved on account of Christ *(propter Christum,* Christ as *sacramentum);* we are also called to imitate Christ (Christ as *exemplum).* But we do not begin the theology of the Christian life with the imitation of Christ, for such a reversal that places Christ as example prior to Christ as sacrament, as Savior, as cause of salvation, leads to a works righteousness and betrays the gospel. We only come to salvation through faith. Yet Christ is both the cause of our salvation and an example—in that order—and both of them indicate that there can be no theology of Jesus Christ that is not a theology of the Christian life. Christology must be understood as *pro nobis,* not a study of who Jesus is in himself but the proclamation of who he is for us.

The Reformation is often said to have begun with Luther's attack on indulgences and the posting of his ninety-five theses in 1517 (see *Explanations of the Ninety-five Theses* [1518], *LW* 31:79-252). Yet the German sermons of 1518–1519 and other writings of this period continued earlier emphases. Several of the sermons of this period were a reflection on the passion of Christ, a common theme in late medieval spirituality, but they began to reflect Luther's growing emphasis on the cross and the theology of the cross.[8]

The cross reveals the gravity of sin, and our knowledge of sin must not be simply intellectual but also heartfelt, or not simply objective knowledge but personal knowledge. The cross not only reveals the tragedy of sin, but also the forgiveness of sin. The *theologia crucis* (theology of the cross) reveals me as *simul justus et peccator*—both a sinner and saved at the same time.

---

[8]Luther scholars vary in their dating of the theological break and breakthrough that Luther made. McGrath, *Luther's Theology of the Cross,* makes the following points: Prior to 1514, Luther's theology can be and ought to be situated within the *via moderna* of late medieval theology and is typical of that theology (such as is exemplified by Ockham, Biel). Prior to 1514, Luther is a typical late medieval theologian. Luther's creative theological contribution begins with his effort to rethink the meaning of the "righteousness of God" and culminates in his "theology of the cross." Luther's thought between 1514–1518 manifests a continuous development rather than a dramatic shift. Yet by the end of 1515 Luther had begun his break with the *via moderna* and late medieval theology with his rethinking of the meaning of the righteousness of God, by which Luther now understood God alone as the source of justification. A righteousness that is alien to humanity *(extra nos; iustitia christi aliena)* first appeared in the lectures on Romans (1515-1516). Luther's re-thinking the meaning of God's righteousness (which is not what we ordinarily think of as righteousness) culminates by 1518 in the development of his *theologia crucis.* The cross alone gives us proper access to our knowledge of God.

A theme that continued in the sermons of this period is that of the abandonment of Jesus by God, which theme came to the foreground in a reflection on Philippians 2, and the kenosis, or self-emptying, of Jesus.[9] The subject of the kenosis is not the pre-incarnate or pre-existent Word but the incarnate Word, Jesus Christ. The kenosis is rather Christ's continual self-emptying, servanthood, even to the point of his abandonment on the cross. This theology of the cross received repeated emphasis in Luther's commentary on the Psalms of 1519–1521. Christ's passion was not only physical suffering, a common traditional emphasis, but also mental torment of the most profound sort, not the image of a person in possession of the beatific vision as in medieval theology but a Jesus feeling abandoned by God while remaining faithful to God.

The cross is the supreme paradox, and paradox lay at the heart of the way in which Luther expressed himself. Jesus is a paradox, the incarnation a paradox, and the cross a revelation of paradox as the sole path to understanding God and the Christian life. Luther's *simul* (at the same time) attempts to hold together a Jesus Christ seemingly abandoned by God and yet to whom God was fully present. The paradox of the cross goes beyond the paradox of the incarnation and the two natures of Christ. The paradox of the cross is more existential for us. The cross is soteriology, and the paradox of the incarnation apart from the cross can too easily be an effort to do a Christology of Jesus in himself, but a proper knowledge of Jesus is always *pro me* (always refers to me—soteriology).

In the treatise *On the Freedom of a Christian* (1520) Luther treats of the marriage between God and humanity—or again how our sin is exchanged for God's righteousness (*LW* 31:351-353). One can rightly say that Luther is not concerned in his Christological thinking about a philosophical or anthropological understanding of the human but is rather concerned about an existential or soteriological understanding. Christ's humanity is like ours and comes from a solidarity with sinful human beings. And this is the basis for the exchange between Christ's righteousness and our sinfulness. Christ takes to himself sin and punishment existentially felt, and at the same time imputes to us his own righteous-

---

[9] Lienhard, *Luther: Witness to Jesus Christ,* 112-113.

ness, a righteousness alien to us, the righteousness of God. This righteousness comes to us by grace through faith and leads to a new way of life in Christ.

Yet the cross cannot be understood apart from the incarnation. It is grounded in the reality of the incarnation and the two natures of Christ. In some of the sermons of 1522 and later, Luther's understanding of the incarnation comes through. For Luther, God is found only through and in the humanity of Jesus Christ, who is the only way to God (not that it is the only conceivable way but rather the way that God chose). Luther is not one to probe the why or the how of the incarnation, but, rather, he explores the significance of the fact of the incarnation apprehended through faith. In Jesus Christ, God is present in the flesh.

The incarnation is not so much an unveiling of the attributes, deity, or divinity of God, but rather the love of God—or better stated, of God as love. Whether Christ is divine (which Christ is for Luther) is not as important as what one understands by the divinity of Christ—whether one apprehends its saving character.

The divinity of Christ is that of the eternal Word but not something to be "proven." It is accessible only to faith. Here Luther begins to oppose faith to reason, another facet in his theology. Earlier, faith was opposed to works, now to reason as a way of knowing, which mode of knowing will be seen also as "a work." Here an either/or enters his theology that is significant, no longer the language of paradox (both/and), but the language of a faith that can be irrational. Luther affirms the paradox but also finds it difficult to hold together the divinity and humanity of Christ. Yet Christ's divinity is a major article of faith and his humanity our only access to God.

Luther's Christ is clearly very human.[10] In this I consider him more Antiochene in his Christology, although he has been called at times Alexandrian, Nestorian, and Docetist. The classical categories don't work for Luther. Christ's humanity is like ours in every way except for sin and grace. Christ's knowledge was not perfect. He submitted himself to the law. When Christ speaks of his pre-existence, he speaks as God; when he speaks of his ignorance, he speaks as a human being. (This is reminiscent of Theodore of Mopsuestia.)

[10]Ibid., 167–172.

The "exchange of properties" is rooted in the reality of the incarnation and the participation of the divinity in the humanity and vice versa. In Christ, "God suffered,"[11] and the humanity of this one human being touched God. Luther's probing the two natures of Christ is challenging. Yet we must recall that Luther consciously resists treating the incarnation as a problem to be solved. It is the work of Christ that is significant for Luther—the constant "for you."[12] It is not a philosophical understanding of the mystery but the proclamation of the gospel that best indicates that one has understood the incarnation. The incarnation is directed toward preaching. And the gospel is not objective or historiographical knowledge about Christ but rather a saving, personal faith knowledge of Christ as being "for me."

Although the major emphases in Luther's Christology can be detected early, even before 1517, Luther's Christology continued to develop as it was pushed further, especially in conjunction with his theology of the Eucharist as that developed amid conflict with other Protestants (1525–1528). In his theology of the Eucharist, Luther remained closer to Roman Catholicism, and it was in this context that he was pushed to develop his concept of the ubiquity of Christ.

Luther's approach to the theology of the Eucharist is similar to his approach to the incarnation. Its foundation is Scripture. We can only push so far the question of "how." It is apprehended by faith alone. "I see the clear, distinct, and powerful words of God which compel me to confess, that the body and blood of Christ are in the sacrament. . . . How Christ is brought into the bread . . . I do not know. But I do know full well that the Word of God cannot lie" (*LW* 40:176). Thus Luther defends the doctrine of the real presence while rejecting the explanation of transubstantiation. Although Luther resists explaining the doctrine of the real presence, in his controversy with Zwingli and other Protestant reformers, he is pushed to do so or at least to go further in that direction than he may have wanted to do. Luther defends (or explains) the real presence on the basis of the ubiquity of Jesus Christ. (See *Against the Heavenly Prophets in the Mat-*

[11]Ibid., 171.

[12]See J. K. Siggins, *Martin Luther's Doctrine of Christ*, Yale Publications in Religion 14 (New Haven: Yale University Press, 1970) 108–143.

ter of Images and Sacraments, [1525], *LW* 40:73f.; and *That These Words of Christ, "This Is My Body," etc., Still Stand Firm Against the Fanatics,* [1527], *LW* 37:3f.)

In his treatise *Concerning Christ's Supper* (1528) (*LW* 37:151f.), following Scholastic theology, Luther distinguished different kinds of presence and different kinds of union, for example, the "natural union" found only in the Trinity, the "personal union" found in the incarnation, and, among other forms of union, the "sacramental union" of the Eucharist wherein the body of Christ is united to the bread and wine. Luther affirms the ubiquity of the body of Christ on the basis of the union of the two natures in one person and the *communicatio idiomatum.* Where the divinity is, there the humanity must be also. This sacramental union is rooted in the hypostatic union. God is everywhere; therefore Christ in his humanity is everywhere, and therefore in the Eucharist. Even already on earth, prior to the resurrection, ascension, and glorification, Christ is omnipresent due to this divine nature. Yet the omnipresence of God (and of Jesus Christ due to the hypostatic union) does not allow one to find or seek God outside of Jesus Christ (or outside of Word and Sacrament). Here Luther distinguishes the more general presence from God's presence *for us* (Jesus Christ), to which God has freely bound himself and by which we are thus bound. We can still come to God only through Jesus Christ in spite of God's omnipresence.

Although our primary concern here is not Luther's theology of the Eucharist, and I think that in his theology of the Eucharist Luther was pushed further toward explanation than he would have preferred to go, nevertheless, his theology of the Eucharist helps us understand Luther the theologian and raises at least three questions:

1. Once Luther affirms so strongly the omnipresence of God, even though he distinguishes it from God's freely chosen presence for us in Jesus Christ but also affirms the omnipresence of Christ, has he not provided a theological basis for a natural theology or theology of creation rooted in revelation itself and Jesus Christ? Does the theology of Jesus Christ not take us in the direction of an awareness of God's wider presence in Christ? If one can ground the real presence of Christ in the Eucharist as a specific instance and form of Christ's om-

nipresence (and reject the "explanation" of transubstantiation), can one not also ground the real presence of God in Christ as a specific instance and form of God's omnipresence (and also reject the "explanation" of hypostatic union)? As Luther is pushed, do we not begin to find some inconsistencies, and is he dangerously close to providing a theological foundation that undermines some of his own theology? Luther's foundational concern, of course, is to reject a theology of "works" in order to affirm a theology of salvation by grace through faith.

2. Does not the doctrine of the omnipresence of Christ lend itself to the language of mysticism and even provide a basis for a specifically Christian mysticism? Luther is being pushed beyond what his language may allow and he himself desire. Although he fears mysticism as "a work," can mysticism not fall within the theology of grace? Is Luther himself in the end not a mystic, whose theology is deeply formed by his personal experience of God and salvation, and for whom the language of mysticism could be an asset rather than hindrance? Luther is being deeply affected by what he feels the need to deny (a theology of works) rather than the implication of what he affirms. (These implications could make him a reformed Catholic rather than Reformed Protestant.)

3. There is something uniquely pastoral about Luther's theology and its focus on the doctrine of salvation, but does Luther *theologically* have to avoid (can he avoid) philosophical theology? Does philosophical theology not also express a pastoral concern? We must grant the dangers of philosophical theology, but does not an avoidance of it also run the risk of inconsistencies that cannot be easily resolved or simply dismissed? When Luther moves from an awareness of paradox in theology to either/or (a faith opposed to reason) does not an anti-rationalism enter his theology which is not elsewhere evident?

In spite of the questions I raise, Luther did not change his mind. He maintained his commitment to God revealed in Jesus Christ and never ceased opposing both mystical theology and speculative theology. According to Luther, the ubiquity of Christ was rooted in the union of the two natures in this one person and the participation of Jesus' humanity in the divine life. Yet Luther had not explicitly affirmed the ubiquity of Christ until forced to do so during the controversies over the Eucharist. In doing so, Luther opened the door to mystical and speculative theology whether he wanted to do so or not. Likewise, in the controversy with Erasmus on free will, and in his treatise *On the Bondage of the Will* (1525) (*LW* 33), Luther opened the door to further problems.

Prior to this treatise Luther had affirmed the hiddenness of God *(Deus absconditus),* but the God who hides himself is the very God who reveals himself in Jesus Christ, hidden in the humanity of Jesus Christ so that the Godhead does not overwhelm humankind but rather can be accessible and revealed as being *for us.* But the hiddenness of God takes a new twist in Luther's rejection of free will. In rejecting free will as an explanation for damnation, Luther is again pushed and this time into a theory of double predestination and the two wills of God.

There is, on the one hand, the God of the Gospels, the God of Jesus Christ, the *Deus revelatus* (revealed God) hidden in the flesh.[13] On the other hand, there is later for Luther *Deus ipse* (God himself), the hidden God of the treatise on free will, the God whose inscrutable will undergirds damnation.[14] God's will is not arbitrary but free. The *Deus absconditus* (hidden God), about whom we cannot speculate but whose inscrutable will is still the "explanation" for damnation, does strike one as a contrast to the *Deus revelatus* in Jesus Christ, who is for us. Yet this *Deus revelatus,* Jesus Christ and salvation, are God's free decision. They cannot be deduced from the nature of God. We are only saved through faith in Christ. God willed it so. We are back to Luther's early emphasis but, left there, not completely at ease.

That the doctrine of justification by faith is the enduring emphasis in Luther's theology, that it is the central content of the gospel as distinguished from the law, and that his Christology is really derived from his soteriology rather than the other way round becomes clear again in Luther's lectures on the Letter to the Galatians (1531) (*LW* 26–27). Whether one says that it is justification by faith or Jesus Christ that is the center of this commentary

[13]The earlier Luther: *Deus absconditus* is *Deus revelatus,* the God hidden *in* his revelation, the God revealed in the *cross* of Christ, the hidden God revealed to the eye of *faith.*

[14]With the treatise on free will (1525), the *Deus absconditus* is the God who is hidden *behind* revelation apart from the revelation in Jesus Christ, the mysterious God whose will remains concealed and undisclosed, in whose will predestination is grounded.

makes no difference, for Jesus Christ is justification. That is who Jesus most truly is for Luther. That is what Jesus Christ means. Christology is soteriology. Jesus Christ *is* salvation. Faith in Jesus Christ is always *saving* faith, never a merely objective knowledge.

One of the major contrasts in Luther's theology is that between the law and the gospel. The gospel is always the affirmation of justification by faith, and yet, paradoxically, the law is necessary. Its "first use" is that it reveals ourselves to us as sinners; it is a *lex accusans* that condemns us, unveils sin to us, and prepares the way for the gospel. The law is not evil, but rather incomplete and powerless. The gospel proclaims the forgiveness of sin merited for us by the death of Jesus Christ.

In later writings, Luther continued to stress the unique character of the incarnation, philosophically impenetrable but at the heart of faith. Luther also continued to stress the communication of properties as the only adequate way for expressing this mystery in human language. But, for Luther, the communication of attributes was not a rational philosophical mode of discourse but rather the language of paradox, rooted in the reality of the incarnation and the only way of speaking that could do justice to the faith. This communication of attributes was for Luther an expression of faith, derived from faith and not an effort at philosophical precision. For Luther it was the only way to avoid Nestorianism.

The Cappadocians had spoken of the interpenetration *(peri-chorēsis)* of the divinity and humanity. The Alexandrians (Cyril, John of Damascus) in particular developed this conception, although often more in the direction of the penetration of the human nature by the divine, to the point that they ran the risk of a certain Docetism or Monophysitism. The communication of attributes continued to become more and more central in Luther's own Christology.

For Luther the communication is not merely nominal, not simply a way of speaking but an expression of the reality, and in this he is closer to Thomas Aquinas than Zwingli. Yet for Luther there is more than simply saying that what is attributed to one of the two natures can be attributed to the one person that Jesus is. For Luther there seems to be a real exchange between the two natures themselves, such as when ubiquity is communicated to the human nature of Christ and suffering communicated to the divine nature. Thus, since the incarnation, no relationship with God is possible that excludes Jesus. In the incarnation, God took to himself a human nature. Even prior to the incarnation, however, from all eternity, the Son is always determined in relationship to the incarnation. In one sense there is no *Logos asarkos* (Word not enfleshed) for Luther, and thus Luther affirmed the pre-existent humanity of Jesus and not only a pre-existent Word. There is no God apart from Christ: This is Luther's constant theme.

A Concluding Theological Reflection

When we speak of mystical theology in the sense of the theology of Symeon or Catherine, we are not speaking about mystical theology as a branch or subdivision of theology, nor even as descriptive of a theological method, but rather as a way of articulating or expressing theology, the preference for mystical language. The writings of Symeon and Catherine *are* theology, but theology for which the preferred language is that of mysticism. To a great degree then, preference for mystical language in addition to temperament flows from one's starting point or preoccupying concern for writing theology in the first place—religious experience, or one's human, intimate, and personal experiences of God, or one's compulsion or desire to express God's love and mercy. The language of mysticism is simply the best way or only way for Symeon and Catherine to talk about God.

Likewise, when we speak about the philosophical theology of someone like Thomas Aquinas, we are not speaking about a division of theology (say in contrast to biblical, historical, or pastoral theology, for Thomas' theology was all of these as well), nor about methodology as such, but again about a preference for language—a way of articulating or expressing theology, or a way of talking about God rooted in Thomas' temperament but also in his preoccupying concerns, such as the desire for clarity in theology, the value of precision in seeking truth, and the felt need to respond to the legitimate claims of reason and rationality.

Such a theology was also to a great degree contextual. It was situated within a university setting and obviously needed to respond to methods of inquiry and the kinds of questions a university setting raised. In a similar fashion, Symeon's theology was also contextual, that of a monastery, as was Catherine's, that of a contemplative in action. Thomas' theology was clearly rooted in his experience of God, but its preoccupations demanded a learned or rational theology for which philosophical language was better qualified. Thus it became his predominant way of speaking about God.

What then can be said of Martin Luther, the language with which he writes theology and speaks about God, and his starting point and preoccupying concerns? Luther's language is that of the preacher or pastor, the language of proclamation, and at times the language of paradox. As Suzanne Noffke has suggested, Catherine is always teaching. If so, Luther is always preaching. His temperament, his starting point, his concerns and preoccupations are those of a pastor. By way of contrast to mystical theology or philosophical theology, Luther's theology is predominantly pastoral theology—and, again, not pastoral theology as a subdivision of theology as a whole, nor as descriptive of a theological method, but pastoral theology in the sense of a preferred or chosen form of language that best responds to his concerns, experience of God, and perceived needs. Luther was developing a theology for the people, and his preoccupation was to proclaim salvation. This is what he saw as necessary, and what guided his primary decisions along the way. In one sense his theology was mystical, that is, rooted in his profound experience of God, and at times became philosophical, although he was not then at his best. He was at his best in proclaiming the gospel. And his theology was also contextual—the need for people to hear the word of the gospel.

Luther's preoccupying concern was the proclamation of the gospel in such a way that people, ordinary people, lay people, would *hear* the word of salvation. His concern was radically pastoral, radically soteriological, and also accounted to a great degree for the language within which he did his theology—a language the people could understand if it were a commentary on the Bible or a polemical discourse. When forced by other theologians, especially other reformers, such as in the controversy on the Eucharist or later in his life, he went beyond the way of speaking of his choice.

Luther's preoccupying concern accounts for the strengths as well as weaknesses in his theology. One can't help but get the feeling that at times Luther denied what he denied only in order to affirm more clearly, more boldly, what he wanted to affirm, and that what he denied was not always as necessary to deny as he may have thought. Yet he always wanted to put Jesus Christ, the gospel, salvation, grace, faith, in bold relief. And this is when he was at his best and when we have the most to learn from him.

Luther probably did not need to attack mysticism or reason in order to affirm salvation by grace through faith as the core of the gospel. Nor did he need to deny salvation or grace outside Jesus Christ in order to affirm the centrality of justification by faith in Jesus Christ. Yet Luther had a sense of what we have called since Vatican Council II "the hierarchy of truths" and would allow nothing that might seem to compromise the central message of the Word of God. Luther's pastoral concern made him put soteriology at the heart of theology, and his soteriological concern made him uncompromising (at times to a fault) about the need to reform theology. His cultural and historical situation may have made such a reformation necessary—for the sake of the gospel—or it may not have been necessary, but such is not a judgment easily made. Whatever excesses to which Luther's theology may or may not have gone, his language was the language of proclamation, the language of a passionate preacher, and thus one not always easily given to restraint.

There is no suggestion here that either mystical theology or philosophical theology or pastoral theology is superior or better. I would rather suggest that all are necessary and serve valid purposes. Theology as a whole would be weakened if one simply discounted or refused the language of mysticism, or the language of philosophy, or the language of proclamation. Nor does one more adequately express the gospel than another. They each serve a purpose. Mystical theology shows that theology cannot be severed from spirituality, the life of the Spirit, an experiential love of God, and be true theology. Philosophical theology shows that theology cannot contradict reason, be intrinsically opposed to rational intelligibility, or be in insoluble conflict with intelligent human nature and be true theology. And pastoral theology shows that theology must be responsive to the needs of God's people, sensitive to changes in cultural-historical contexts, and conscious of the primacy of the gospel message if it is to be true theology.

No one language for talking about God is adequate by itself

alone. No one language has the right to a monopoly on theological discourse. Indeed, all the human ways of speaking put together do not "comprehend" God, or dissolve the mystery that God is. No one concept or image of God is adequate by itself alone, nor all the concepts and images put together. God remains God, beyond our human modes of speech. Yet human speech learns and struggles to express its experience and understanding of God. It reaches out toward mystery, finds itself engulfed within what it set out to grasp, and in the very act of speaking points toward the mystery that God is.

Language about God fails when it takes itself too seriously, too literally, as final or definitive, as ultimately adequate rather than symbolic of the search for God, the thirst for God, the respect for God's own initiative in the process of God's self-revelation through history. Thus, different forms of language, different styles of theology, different theological methods, ought to respect rather than dismiss the other forms of discourse. To claim an exclusivity or superiority for one's own preferred mode of discourse is to have already betrayed the God who transcends human speech, to have revealed one's failure to understand the nature of the search, and to have trivialized the task at hand.

Granted the complementarity and necessity of varied ways of talking about God as well as of proclaiming the word of God, the Catholic tradition in theology as well as the history of Christian theology as a whole will remain indebted to Martin Luther for his challenge to the Christian tradition as he received and experienced it. Given the limitations of human speech and the propensity of human beings to generalize and absolutize their human experiences of God and preferred ways of articulating those experiences, Luther teaches us to focus on God's word rather than our own words and to make God's revelation in Jesus Christ the starting point for our human reflection on God. Thus a primacy must be given to the gospel of Jesus Christ, and the gospel of Jesus Christ does become the hermeneutical principle through which the Scriptures are to be appropriated and interpreted, and the gospel stands in dialectical tension with the ecclesial human institutions to which it has been entrusted. To some degree this does mean that the quest for "the historical Jesus" becomes a quest for the historical gospel of Jesus, but at the same time one realizes that one cannot separate the gospel of Jesus Christ from the person of Jesus himself or from the life, mission, ministry, death, and resurrection of Jesus.

Luther also gives us his own interpretation of the gospel of Jesus Christ and the word of God that it is: the centrality of salvation, grace, and faith. Thus there is no "Christology" apart from soteriology and no soteriology apart from theological anthropology. Therefore, the starting point for Christian theology ought to be soteriology, or God's concern for human beings.

Since God's concern is with human beings and God's word is directed toward human beings, so our theological concern is always a pastoral concern. In some sense, all theology ought to be pastoral theology, all theology ought to enhance the proclamation of the gospel, all theology ought to be geared toward preaching, with the realization that preaching is not by sermons alone. Luther requires that a theology of preaching comprise and undergird our theology of word, sacrament, and Christian life and praxis.

Mystical theology teaches us that preaching must do justice to our human experiences of God as well as to the transcendent mystery that God is. Philosophical theology teaches us that preaching must respect human intelligence as well as the mystery that God is. Pastoral theology teaches us that preaching must address the human condition, context, and situation—personal and social—in which human beings find themselves as well as trust the word God's very own self has addressed to that human situation. Nor should we limit human discourse about our ultimate concerns to mystical, philosophical, and pastoral forms of language, for there remain the languages of prophecy, prayer, liturgy, and literature as well. But theological discourse places one of its hands in the hands of God, God's word, and our human experiences of God and its other hand in the hands of God's people, God's world and God's creation and attempts inadequately but with integrity to articulate the meaning of that journey, that search, that struggle.

SUGGESTED READINGS

Primary Source

Pelikan, Jaroslav, and Helmut T. Lehmann, eds. *Luther's Works,* American ed., 55 vols. St. Louis: Concordia, and Philadelphia: Fortress, 1955 ff.

Secondary Sources

Althaus, Paul. *The Theology of Martin Luther.* Trans. Robert C. Schultz. Philadelphia: Fortress, 1970. A good introduction.

Bainton, Roland H. *Here I Stand: A Life of Martin Luther.* Nashville: Abingdon, 1950.

Congar, Yves. *Martin Luther, sa foi, sa réforme.* Paris: Les Editions du Cerf, 1983.

Ebeling, Gerhard. *Luther: An Introduction to His Thought.* Trans. R. A. Wilson. Philadelphia: Fortress, 1970.

Henn, William. "The Hierarchy of Truths Twenty Years Later." *Theological Studies* 48 (1987) 439-471.

Hoffman, Bengt R. *Luther and the Mystics.* Minneapolis: Augsburg, 1976.

Lienhard, Marc. *Luther: Witness to Jesus Christ, Stages and Themes of the Reformer's Christology.* Trans. Edwin H. Robertson. Minneapolis: Augsburg, 1982. A good introduction to Luther's Christology in particular.

McCue, James F. *"Simul justus et peccator* in Augustine, Aquinas, and Luther: Toward Putting the Debate in Context." *Journal of the American Academy of Religion* 48 (1980) 81-96.

McGrath, Alister E. *Luther's Theology of the Cross: Martin Luther's Theological Breakthrough.* Oxford: Basil Blackwell, 1985.

McKim, Donald K. "Recent Lutheran Studies." *Theological Studies* 48 (1987) 499-504.

McSorley, Harry J. *Luther: Right or Wrong?* An Ecumenical-Theological Study of Luther's Major Work, The Bondage of the Will. New York: Newman, and Minneapolis: Augsburg, 1969.

Pelikan, Jaroslav. *Reformation of Church and Dogma (1300-1700).* Vol. 4 of The Christian Tradition, A History of the Development of Doctrine. Chicago: University of Chicago Press, 1984.

Siggins, J. K. *Martin Luther's Doctrine of Christ.* Yale Publications in
    Religion 14. New Haven: Yale University Press, 1970.
von Loewenich, Walther. *Luther's Theology Of The Cross.* Trans. Hubert
    J. A. Bouman. Minneapolis: Augsburg, 1976.
Watson, Philip S. *Let God Be God: An Interpretation of the Theology
    of Martin Luther.* Philadelphia: Fortress, 1947/1970.

8

Lessons from Christian History

The Gospel of John offered the Church a theologically creative and quite distinctive interpretation of Jesus Christ. Its theology of Jesus was very formative of Christian theology after the first century. Its focus was on the singularity of Jesus as God's unique Son and as God's Word. The Fourth Gospel reflected not only on the post-history of Jesus following upon his death but also on the pre-history of Jesus prior to his birth. Jesus, as understood through the faith of the Johannine Christians who were Jesus' disciples though they had not experienced him in the flesh, could only be adequately grasped as a man whose ultimate origin was "from above," someone whose total story involved three distinct phases: his mission as the eternal Word, his earthly mission as God's unique Son, and his continuing post-resurrection activity and presence as Lord and God.

The degree to which Christianity is considered an "incarnational religion" shows the perduring influence of the Johannine Christian faith. Jesus is a fabric woven out of both time and eternity, both history and transcendent glory, both humanity and divinity, and in a brilliantly integrated way. In Jesus heaven and earth, God and humankind, meet.

From the Johannine Christian perspective, one cannot oppose "faith" and "history," or the "Jesus of faith" and a "Jesus of history." There is only one Jesus, the Jesus of Christian faith. For only faith reads history properly. Only faith has the eyes to see properly. The only true perspective is to know Jesus as he truly is, as God's unique Son. This is the Johannine Christology, which also became the historical Christian faith. The resurrection of Jesus and Johannine theology are two elements that make a purely historiographical perspective on Jesus inadequate.

The Gospel of John contained its ambiguities, literary and otherwise, as well as its unresolved issues—such as Jesus' subordination to the Father and his equality with God. This issue alone, the fruit of Johannine theology, would challenge Christian theology even to our day. But this was, nevertheless, the Johannine faith—intentional and paradoxical. Could anything other than paradox attempt to articulate in language what became increasingly clear to faith?

The gospel of Jesus Christ is the starting point for Christian theology. Martin Luther vividly made this point. The New Testament is the translation of this gospel into literature or Scripture. Christianity is a historical religion. It began with the history of Jesus and even the history of the Jewish and Hebrew people. But it continued to develop historically after Jesus and even after the composition of the New Testament. There is both continuity and discontinuity between the gospel and the historical Christian faith. They are not simply synonymous. More had been made explicit. History was creatively faithful to the gospel but also allowed the gospel interaction with a wider history and culture. Similarly, the Catholic tradition is not simply synonymous with the historical Christian faith, although it was perhaps the shape that the faith took during the first centuries of its embodiment in the Greco-Roman world. Nor is the Roman Church synonymous with the Catholic (or even Latin) tradition, nor the Roman Church synonymous with the Roman Church today. There is more to the historical Christian faith than the gospel of Jesus Christ alone. And there is more to the Catholic tradition than the historical Christian faith of the New Testament and the first centuries of Christian theology and conciliar clarifications. And there is more to the Roman Church as it historically develops than just the Catholic tradition of the faith. These are subtle distinctions, analogous expressions, and always questions of history and historico-cultural diversity.

Johannine theology raised for later generations the question of the precise relationship between God and Word and Jesus. All are intrinsically connected, so one cannot fully define any apart from reference to the others. Jesus is the Word, the Word incarnate or enfleshed, and yet there is "more" to the Word than Jesus alone, more than the Word's incarnation as Jesus. The Word had a long history prior to its incarnation as Jesus. Also, the Word is God, and yet there is "more" to God than the Word alone. God is both God and Word. Because Jesus truly *is* the Word, and the Word *is* God, Jesus truly *is* God. Yet there is "more" to God than Jesus, though Jesus is God revealed, disclosed, made visible. And there is more to Jesus than his oneness with God. Jesus is also *sarx,* flesh, human. After Jesus, one cannot talk about God apart from Jesus (God is always the Father of Jesus), nor can one talk about Jesus apart from God (Jesus is God's uniquely begotten Son). With Jesus, one can begin to speak of the relationship between God and the Word as a relationship between Father and Son. "Son" became one of the richest ways of talking about who Jesus is, and "Father" a way of talking about Jesus' God.

To know Jesus is to know the Father, and to know the Father is to recognize Jesus. As I said above, after Jesus, one cannot talk about God apart from Jesus, or Jesus apart from God. The story of each is so intimately and inextricably interwoven with the other. Likewise, one will not be able to talk about Jesus without talking about the Spirit, the Advocate. God sends the Son, and the Son sends the Spirit. God, Word, and Spirit are all three vitally and inextricably connected.

The history of the Christian movement involved division from the beginning, and not only from Judaism but also from within, from the "secessionists" within the Johannine community through the non-Chalcedonian Churches to our own day. Not all took the path of "the great Church," or the path of the great councils, or the path of the classic Christian tradition. How one theologically assesses these diverse paths or a particular historical development other than from the stance of the seeming superiority of one's own confessional perspective remains a significant theological issue. Christianity not only has a history, it is this history. One cannot separate out a pure essence for Christianity from the history that has shaped it and the diverse historical shapes it has taken. This is not to imply that all historical developments are of equal value or have equivalent claims on the truth.

There was and is more to Jesus than the earthly phase of Jesus' mission. In the same way there was and is more to the early Christian movement, or Christianity, than Jesus. And there was and is more to the Catholic tradition than the gospel.

In one sense the history of Christian theology began with the Gospel of John, in another sense with the letters of Paul. No event in Christendom was more monumental than the resurrection of Jesus, which event cannot be separated from the gifts of the Spirit. Easter and Pentecost belong together; we cannot have one without the other. After that first Pentecost, however, one of the next monumental moments in Christian history was its transition from orality to textuality, as Werner Kelber has pointed out.[1] After Pentecost, almost twenty years later, the proclamation of the gospel took a literary form as well, and eventually led to the Christians' New Testament. Other than the emergence of this literary or textual phase itself, however, no event was probably more momentous than the "making of the Fourth Gospel." From the death of Jesus (ca. 30 C.E.) to the Gospel of John (ca. 100), the Jesus movement had gone a long way. Yet it is significant to emphasize that the transition to textuality began a literary dimension in Christian life and history. This literary activity flourished in the second century and every century since. Christian literature was both formative of a Christian culture and formed by the cultures within which it took shape.

One of the major characteristics of Christian thought has been its diversity or variety. Certainly there has always been a common core, whether consciously thought of in those terms or not, such as the proclamation that Jesus was raised from the dead and is the Christ or Messiah or Savior. Yet variety, even though the Church at times had to place limits on it for the sake of its own identity, seems to be one of the characteristics of Christian theology. One needs to theologize or understand theologically this diversity, plurality, or variety, for it is certainly the work of the Holy Spirit. One finds diversity in the New Testament itself, as well as among Christian Jews or Jewish Christians, not to mention every succeeding generation of Christian thought. That diversity may reflect geographical, cultural, historical, national, political, economic, philosophical, linguistic, spiritual, pastoral, gender, or individual differences, but plurality there was and is.

---

[1]See Werner H. Kelber, *The Oral and the Written Gospel* (Philadelphia: Fortress, 1983).

There is no one orthodox Christian theology, even though the Church at times understandably felt the need to consolidate itself or its teachings for its own sake as well as for the sake of the gospel. This led to tendencies, traditions, families, or schools of orthodox Christian thought as well as to the delineation of unaccepted heterodox positions.

Sometimes the differences reflected existential or pastoral concerns, such as the theology of Ignatius of Antioch or, much later, of Martin Luther. Others focused on learned and philosophical needs, manifesting a desire for intelligibility, such as among the apologists of the second century, the Christian Platonists of the third century, or Thomas Aquinas in the thirteenth century. Still others simply made the effort to articulate personal religious experience within the cultural confines of that experience, such as in the mystical theology of Gregory of Nyssa and the long tradition that mystical theology would represent. The fact of diversity in Christian thinking as well as the fact of concrete historical decisions made by the Christian tradition along the way are part and parcel of Christianity's history. Somehow both had to do with the work of the Holy Spirit. How "unity" as well as "diversity" are both the work of the Holy Spirit remains a theological issue.

There were some directions that Christian thought could have taken, and at times did take, that were judged to be false, such as Adoptionism, Docetism, and Gnosticism. They did not do justice to the major direction historically taken by the Christian faith. Other paths would not be as clearly set aside, such as those taken by the Nestorian and Monophysite Churches. Still other paths manifested a diversity that remained central to the fullness of Christian thought, such as Orthodoxy and Catholicism, and the later Reformed tradition. But even the Catholic tradition alone, as it moved into the Western European medieval world, retained its capacity to embrace plurality as an expression of its catholicity.

Variety in theology also reflects the variety of valid hermeneutical or exegetical approaches to the New Testament material, for example, the typology of Justin, the allegorical methods of Alexandria, the more literal or philological exegesis of Antioch.

The Fourth Gospel introduced a theology of the Logos into Christian history, even though the Logos was not the central theological concept in that Gospel. Nevertheless, the history of Christian theologies of Jesus eventually gave it a central role, not only due to the influence of the Fourth Gospel as well as the influence of Neoplatonic thought but also due to the need to work out a theology of the triad that the one God is.

From a Christological perspective alone, the Fourth Gospel turned over to Christian theology some unfinished business. Two crucial issues in particular were the need for a more refined theology of the Logos and the need for a more articulate theology of the humanity of Jesus. The former would be taken up by Justin Martyr in the second century, but it was particularly the contribution, preoccupation, or even limitation of the great Alexandrian tradition. Its resolution would eventually lead to a theology of the Trinity, the Nicene faith, and the theology of Athanasius as its best exponent within the Alexandrian tradition. The second need, for a theology of the humanity of Jesus, would find itself more closely tied to the concerns of theological anthropology. It had already been defended in its fullness by Ignatius of Antioch and became the contribution, preoccupation, or even limitation of the great Antiochene tradition. The destinies of a Christian theology of God and a Christian theology of the human would be inevitably interwoven because of the Christian theology of Jesus.

Theology and language are inseparable, though language creates its own problems for theology. Sometimes Christological language is a very technical theological language that has developed in the course of the Church's history. At other times the language must, by the very purpose of theology itself, be pastoral, the language of the people, and not the technical vocabulary of trained historians or theologians. There always needs to be both with a mutual respect, one for the other. Sometimes theology must become technical in order to clarify itself better. At other times it must be pastoral in order to speak its understanding to the wider faithful. The history of Christological language involves the history of the *communicatio idiomatum,* or proper way of talking about Jesus that does justice to the two poles within which Jesus is being understood. Some exchange of predication goes back as far as Ignatius of Antioch, as does the anticipation of the *theotokos* doctrine. But this early use of language was almost more intuitive or faith-inspired than theologically refined. Only the history of the conflicts and consensus in Christology would gradually refine the Church's way of speaking about Jesus such that it would be helpful rather than confusing. We must always recognize that some of the Church's theological language is technical language, some is mystical language, and some is pastoral.

Theology can never be abstracted from history (culture, geography, politics, socio-economics, personality, gender), nor reduced to it. Theology is an expression of the Holy Spirit at work in history. Due to Jesus and an incarnational faith, the two are inseparable (the Holy Spirit and history) and yet neither can be reduced to the other.

Some valuable theological themes to which Christian theology gave birth included:

1. Jesus as one who reveals God, as the revelation of God, a theme already present in the Gospel of John and Ignatius of Antioch;
2. the divine indwelling, already present in Ignatius of Antioch, and then prominently emphasized later in the Antiochene school;
3. deification, going back at least to Justin Martyr and Irenaeus (although he does not explicitly use the word);
4. Justin's emphasis on the Logos as present in all humanity, particularly in human philosophy (Greek) and other religions (Jewish) and not confined to Jesus alone, who nevertheless was its supreme or full manifestation;
5. emerging principles for biblical hermeneutics, such as the typological interpretation (going back as far as Justin and Irenaeus);
6. Jesus as a Second Adam, with its basis in Pauline theology and given explicit development by Irenaeus;
7. Irenaean and later emphasis on the *imago Dei* theme from Scripture;
8. the "work" of Jesus presented through the metaphor of ransom in Irenaeus;
9. a sense of catholicity (Ignatius) and tradition (Irenaeus) as basic to Christian theology;
10. Clement's theology of the Word, or theology of God. He distinguished between the "abyss" (or "bosom of the Father") and the "Logos," and successive stages in the life of the Logos. The Logos was one with God in the bosom of the Father; the Word became Son by "delimitation" *(perigraphē)*

with creation (the first manifestation or incarnation of the Word/Son); the Logos continued to be active through the prophets (a "second incarnation"); and, finally, the fullness of the incarnation is found in the child of the Logos, Jesus. Whether one accepts Clement's particular theology of the Logos or not, it is interesting to note that the Logos has a history because it is the Logos that is involved with creation and history, and there is always more in some sense to the theology of the Logos than the theology of Jesus alone. Clement's theology of the Logos, like that of the Fourth Gospel, is also a theology of revelation. God is both utterly transcendent (the "abyss") and revealed.

Whatever may be said of the complete acceptability or orthodoxy of Origen's theology, which is a question one could raise about Clement or any other theologian for that matter, it must be admitted that Origen was a theological genius from both biblical and speculative points of view. He contributed significantly toward a proper theology of the Trinity. He knew the term *trias*, and he spoke of three *hypostaseis*. God was one and three. Origen's main contribution to the theology of the Logos (or of the Trinity) was his affirmation that the Logos/Son is clearly eternal, clearly divine, *homoousios* with the Father (a word used, maybe coined, by Origen). At the same time there remains in Origen a pre-Nicene subordinationism that still needed to be resolved. But the theology of the Logos was developing, becoming gradually clarified, was approaching a better understanding. Origen's doctrine of universal salvation was not unrelated to his theology of the Logos and theological anthropology, and it is something that continues to challenge Christian thought.

What we sometimes call heresy or radically inadequate Christian thought often serves a valuable purpose. It may be a road that needs to be tried before we know where it leads. It may be necessary in order to stimulate the process of clarification. Or, at times, it may serve as a needed corrective to theology even if later recognized as unacceptable in terms of its adequacy to the Christian faith. Arius at least served the purpose of forcing the Church to clarify and advance its theology of the Trinity. He was the primary stimulus for the classic Nicene expression of the faith. Although he had taken Origenism in a radical direction by picking up its subordinationism and thus became a non-Origenist in the process (for Arius the Logos/Son was God by grace, not nature, not *homoousios*), he nevertheless may also have forced not only a clarification but a corrective in developing Christian theology by enabling a shift from a more speculative theology (Clement, Origen) to a more pastoral theology of the Trinity (Athanasius), thus making us aware of the possibility at least that some theological issues (the Trinity) may not always be speculatively soluble and that the primary purpose of theology is after all pastoral.

For Athanasius, God was both transcendent and self-revealing. The Logos was not an intermediate being between God and the world, but fully God; not subordinate, but fully divine, as is the Spirit. The one God is Father, Son, and Spirit. Athanasius was also concerned about *our* salvation (a pastoral concern, as soteriology inevitably is). Only a proper theology of God could properly undergird a theology of salvation. For Athanasius, salvation was deification *(theopoiēsis),* the predominant way of understanding salvation in the Greek East and still one of the several prominent images for salvation (along with other theologies articulated more fully later, e.g., resurrection, justification, liberation). But deification would always require a doctrine of incarnation. The two would go hand in hand. There could be no adequate theology of salvation apart from an adequate theology of the Trinity. The theology of the Trinity was first and foremost a pastoral concern. "God was made one of us that we might be made God" (Athanasius, *On the Incarnation,* 54).

Athanasius also gave us another foundational Christological statement, which can be seen as a contrast to the theology and image of indwelling that would be developed in the Antiochene tradition. It was a Christological statement that reflected the primary concern and contribution of the Alexandrian tradition, namely, an emphasis on the unity, or oneness, of Jesus Christ: "The Word was made human and did not come into a human being" (Athanasius, *Discourse Against the Arians,* 3, 10). The Word became flesh (Alexandrian perspective, *Logos-sarx*) and dwelled among us (Antiochene emphasis, *Logos-anthropos*).

Although Athanasius' theology of the humanity of Christ (a weakness in Alexandrian theology in general) was less than adequate by later standards, his Nicene theology of Jesus clearly opposed any form of Adoptionism (what the Alexandrians feared about the Antiochenes). Adoptionism became a dead end for the historical and developing Christian faith. Jesus was God becoming one of us, not God entering into one of us and one of us becoming God. The latter is true of the rest of us, but Jesus is uniquely God. Thus Athanasius can comfortably call Mary *theotokos*. If the Word is *homoousios* with God, and if Jesus and the Word are one (not two), then Mary is *theotokos* because Jesus is truly God—God made flesh.

Apollinaris, like Arius, had a contribution to make. He clarified the Achilles' heel of Alexandrian theology: its failure to do full justice to the humanity of Christ, to the human soul or human psychic functioning of Christ, its inadequate theological anthropological basis for the theology of Christ. Apollinarian theology clearly could not be and would not be the direction Christian thought about Jesus would take. Yet Apollinaris in one sense only put the Alexandrian weakness out in full view of the Christian world—and it was rejected. The path to the future could not be through Alexandria alone. For Apollinaris, for Jesus to be one, his human nature must be incomplete, but this simply would not do. Jesus had to be both one and fully human, in such a way that his oneness with God did not impair his identity as one of us. How can one perceive both the unity of Christ and the humanity of Christ without one being emphasized at the expense of the other? This is one of the fundamental Christological questions we learn from history. For Apollinaris, Christ was one *physis,* but this would not do adequate justice to Jesus. Jesus was one *hypostasis* also. In fact, Apollinaris introduced this word into Christological language. We are becoming aware of the need for a more technical or precise Christological vocabulary if we are to do justice to Jesus, while at the same time we are recognizing the inadequacy of all language in the face of mystery. We realized earlier the need for theology to remain fundamentally pastoral, but we also now see the need for it also to be precise—even if no one theology can always be both. Both are needs of the community of the faithful. With Cyril we will continue to see the need to clarify more precisely how the wider Church will use or be able to use words like *physis* and *hypostasis* when talking about Christ. Their meanings in Alexandria (practically synonymous) will not necessarily be the meanings in the wider, universal, Catholic Church. It will take conciliar theology to adapt them for use by the Church catholic as Nicea had done with *homoousios*.

The Christology of the Antiochene school is often described as a Logos-anthropos framework, but it may be just as helpful to say that the strength of the tradition was its theological anthropology and, thus, also its theology of the humanity of Jesus. One has to appreciate their contribution as one tries to bring together the divine Logos and human Jesus into one concrete existing being. Already with Eustathius of Antioch, there was an awareness of this theology of the divine indwelling, and Jesus as a specific instance of this. God indwells Jesus as God dwells in a temple. Jesus is God's temple. In this image, the humanity of Jesus was intact from the beginning. Thus in Antiochene theology, more than in any Alexandrian theology, there was significance given to the human soul of Christ. It was the subject of Christ's sufferings.

For the Antiochenes, there were two aspects to Christ: *Logos* and *anthropos* (a human being). The challenge was whether they could hold the two together as well as the Alexandrians, but the challenge for the Alexandrians was whether they could do justice to the twofold character of Jesus. Renewed Theodorian studies and revisionism in Nestorian studies have helped us to appreciate the Antiochene gift and preoccupation. Jesus was first and foremost fully human. This could not be compromised. Thus, in Jesus there was a moral union of wills because in every human being perfection comes from a moral union between the divine will and human will. Jesus' humanity lacked nothing that human beings lacked. Thus his *human* perfection consisted in the moral union—which was not the cause but the effect of the union of the two natures *(physeis)*. The Antiochenes were Dyophysites because only a doctrine of two natures in Jesus would leave Jesus with a complete human nature. Likewise, anthropologically, the human person is an image of God (a theme prominent in Irenaeus), and thus Jesus' humanity was also an image of God. For Theodore of Mopsuestia, it was also possible for Christ to sin although he did not. Salvation for Theodore involved Jesus' human obedience. Redemption was accomplished by what Christ had accomplished. The challenge, however, is clear. If Jesus was a fully human being, *anthropos,* a being assumed by the Word, how could this avoid the Alexandrian suspicion of an implicit Adoptionism that hung over the Antiochenes like a shadow. It was clear that Antioch was saying no to Docetism and Alexandria no to Adoptionism, but it was not always clear how to steer a balanced course between them—or whether there was yet a Christological language to do so.

In all of the theological developments in the third, fourth, and fifth centuries, one can see the need for both theological *development,* often carried forward by individual theologians, and theological *consolidation,* often effected by a body of bishops or a more general council of the Church. Both were essential to the development of doctrine.

There were distinctive contributions made to Christology by the developing Latin theology of the West, which contributions were less the object of conflict and tension than in the East. Language, as we have emphasized frequently, is central to the work of theology. One cannot underestimate the significance of a transition to doing theology in Latin rather than in Greek, or in some other language. One's language is the medium within which one must work.

Theology in the West was less speculative in its origins, not necessarily more practical or applicable or soteriological, but less allegorical. These differences should be seen as neither strengths nor weaknesses but rather as a richness that came with diversity. Tertullian contributed words like *trinitas, substantia,* and *persona* to Trinitarian and Christological development. God is one *substantia,* three *personae.* Christ, however, could be better understood as two *substantiae* and one *persona,* the second *persona* of the *trinitas.*

Hilary was as opposed to Arianism in the West as Athanasius was in the East. Both Tertullian and Hilary were able to give theological significance to the human soul of Christ. Hilary also recognized both the "duality" and the "unity" of Christ in his theology of incarnation. At the same time, he had developed a kenotic theology of the incarnation as well, not, however, in the sense of later nineteenth-century kenotic theologies. The divine Logos was the subject of the incarnation even as Jesus acted on earth, and Jesus' humanity was permeated by the divinity while on earth. But the kenosis was in the Logos' voluntary acts to suspend Jesus' divinized humanity so that Jesus might suffer as we suffer. Hilary gives us both a theology of kenosis and a three-stage theology of Jesus. Perhaps the Latin contribution to Christology was most apparent in Leo's letter to Flavian and its Latin emphasis on the twofold consubstantiality of Christ. For Leo, Jesus was son of God and son of Mary, and he adopted an Eastern formula: "consubstantial with the Father, consubstantial with the mother."

The history and theology of general councils, their socio-political and religious character, their innovative role in the life of the Church, all deserve greater attention. They appeared at critical points in the life of the Church and enabled the Church to move to a new agenda. They made choices, and thus some theological options were set aside. They helped the Church to consolidate itself, to set limits, which put some closure on debates but gave new starting points. The Church could not live with unlimited diversity. Diversity, due to historical, cultural, and linguistic differences, was necessary to be faithful to the gospel. But unlimited diversity would betray or destroy the gospel. The Church had seen the need for some consolidation of itself already in the second century with the formation of a New Testament canon. The general council was a new way in a later period of history to respond to this periodic need for self-clarification. The Council of Nicea represented a new structure in the Church, a new way of responding to the issues of the time, a new way of speaking. A council did not endorse a particular theology or theological method but set the outside limits within which speculative debates would take shape.

Nicea said no to Arianism and Trinitarian subordinationism and yes to "the Logos" being of the same substance *(homoousios)* as the Father. Constantinople gave another no to Arianism, and said no to Apollinarianism and the pneumatomachi, affirming the full divinity of the Spirit and the human psychology of Jesus. Ephesus said no to "Nestorianism," leaving us with the question today of whether Nestorius was in fact a Nestorian. Ephesus thus affirmed not only the oneness of Jesus Christ but also thereby the title of *theotokos* for Mary. It thus gave ground to a certain way of speaking about Christ that was expressed by the *communicatio idiomatum.* Chalcedon said no to Eutychean Monophysitism, affirmed the Antiochene tradition's Dyophysitism (two *physeis*) and the Alexandrian or Cyrillian emphasis on one *hypostasis,* which were in accord with Christology in the West as expressed by Leo I. *Physis* and *hypostasis* were made distinguishable, nonsynonymous, technical theological terms, as had happened with *homoousios* at Nicea.

The Chalcedonian solution can be seen today in the light of its limitations, but at the time it was a brilliant reconciliation of insights seeking synthesis. Yet it was not immediately accepted, nor was it uniformly interpreted. The Monophysite Christology of Severus of Antioch and the Monophysite Churches continued to hold as sacred Cyril's phrase: "the one incarnate nature of God the Logos." Also, though Chalcedon had spoken clearly that Christ was one *hypostasis,* it had not spoken about the one *hypostasis* in such a way that this *hypostasis* was the selfsame pre-incarnate *hypostasis* of the Logos within Trinitarian theology, although this is almost assumed today to be what Chalcedon taught. It was rather the post-Chalcedonian, Leontius of Jerusalem, in the sixth century, who formally identified or clarified the *hypostasis* of the union affirmed at Chalcedon with the pre-incarnate *hypostasis* that is the eternal Logos. In some ways this may seem a helpful theological clarification of Chalcedon, in other ways as a development. At any rate, it led to the theology of Chalcedon being later understood as the enhypostatic character of Jesus' human nature. Its *hypostasis* was the *hypostasis* of the Logos. But even here there would be many varying medieval opinions or interpretations in the West.

As one further pursues the study of Byzantine, medieval, and Reformed Christology, other significant themes emerge that are helpful in constructing a contemporary Christology, themes which have their roots in the patristic period but which are also given particular emphasis later:

1. the close relationship between Christology and pneumatology and the awareness that the resurrection of Jesus cannot be theologically separated from the Pentecostal gifts of the Holy Spirit;
2. the close relationship between religious experience and theology, between one's spiritual experience of God and one's reflection about God, between Christian life and Christian theology, with the awareness that spirituality and theology are intimately interwoven and inseparable;

3. the distinction between "Word" and "Son," in that the Word was not revealed to be a Son and God a Father until the incarnation (cf. Symeon the New Theologian), or that the Word is not properly called Son until the incarnation (cf. Marcellus of Ancyra);

4. the close relationship between the doctrine of the incarnation and that of salvation, the theology of the latter rooted in that of the former, as we see in the doctrine of deification in particular;

5. Jesus Christ experienced and interpreted as a salvific and therefore ever-present event, with salvation being variously but primarily interpreted as deification (or sanctification or transformation), or justification (or forgiveness or reconciliation or redemption), or resurrection from the dead (or life eternal), or more prominently in contemporary times as liberation (into human wholeness), these images or interpretations not being exclusive of each other;

6. the intrinsic relationship between love of God and love of neighbor in the teaching of Jesus and in spiritual theology, in such a way that we cannot have one without the other, nor is one more important than the other, the two being indissolubly united in Christian life;

7. the cross, the central Christian symbol in the West, as the supreme manifestation of God's love, however it be theologically interpreted further, and this is true for someone like Catherine of Siena as well as for Martin Luther, for both of whom Christology is ultimately a theology of the cross, that is to say, of God's mercy and love;

8. the awareness or appreciation of the fact that (so clear in someone like Aquinas) the "hypostatic union" was one of a kind, a unique union, in that sense analogous to the act of creation itself, which was also a unique kind of causation, and that for Thomas, unlike earlier medieval theologians, the "hypostatic union" implied in Christ one "act of existing," namely, that of the eternal Word, which does not diminish Christ's full human nature, since for Thomas nature or essence does not imply existence;

9. Christian orthodoxy, in its rejection of Docetism but more specifically Apollinarianism, having affirmed a complete

human psychology as operative in Jesus, who is completely human, having all that human nature implies—body, psyche, and human spirit;

10. different kinds of theological language, and that one cannot separate theology from the language within which it is expressed. The appreciation for Christological language or way of speaking and the formulation of predicates in Christology is reflected in the history and significance of the *communicatio idiomatum*.

A reflection on the relation between theology and language also makes us aware:

a. that some forms of Christological speech are technical speech or technical theological language, although not all talk about Jesus Christ is necessarily technical;

b. that besides technical speech appropriate to an explication of the Christological tradition of the Church and philosophical theology, there is language more appropriate to proclamation, the language of the preacher or pastor. There is also language more appropriate to articulating personal and intimate religious experience, the language of mysticism. Finally there is as well the language more appropriate to drawing out the socio-economic or political implications of the Christ-event, the language of political theology;

c. that while reserving the right, necessity, and even frequent justification for Christological language that is not technical or precise, neither should one disparage the need for technical theological discourse, given the need for rationality and intelligibility. In this, Thomas Aquinas' discussion of language (*Summa*, III, 16) serves as a helpful example.

Catholic Christology, while remaining faithful to tradition, will always be in need of reconstruction in the light of the ongoing history of people's human experiences and particularly their experiences of God, in response to the needs of other cultures or new periods of history, and in order to make the historical Christian faith intelligible to people whose concerns, preoccupations, struggles, joys, ways of speaking, languages, and hopes are ever new. Following its historical pattern, the Catholic tradition in

Christology must respect the need and tendency for theologies to be diverse, the need to consolidate after particular debates and to set limits as well as to establish new starting points in the process. The tradition must also respect that particular theologies will have at times national, ethnic, cultural, and individual perspectives. There is the Catholic tradition in Christian theology but no one Catholic theology in itself that is normative for the tradition. At the same time, Catholic theology must recognize with Orthodox theology that it comes forth from a conciliar history that itself needs continuing re-evaluation and re-appropriation.

Any reconstruction of Christology today accepts limits within which it works, namely, those of Docetism and Adoptionism. These have been sufficiently shown in history to be false paths into the future. The Synoptic Gospels give us a fairly ascertainable picture of the earthly Jesus and give witness to a faith rooted in the experience that Jesus was raised from the dead. The Gospel of John gives us a highly developed and literarily constructed theology of Jesus as God's Son. That human Jesus, who is God's divine Son, the eternal Word of God enfleshed, was raised from the dead and bestowed the gift of the Spirit.

Generations of Christians and centuries of faithful and brilliant Christian thinkers continued to struggle with what the New Testament was proposing—someone utterly human and utterly one with God as a source of salvation.

The Antiochene tradition in Christology was sensitive from the start to any form of Docetism, recognized the need for a solid theological anthropology if one were to do justice to the anthropology or humanity of Jesus, and ultimately made its contribution to Christology through Chalcedon by its insistence on an adequate theology of the humanity of Jesus—and thus one could not back away from two natures in Jesus Christ.

The Alexandrian tradition, which stamped the history of Christology with the need for an adequate theology of the Word if there was to be an adequate theology of Jesus, recognized Jesus as God's Word. And if Jesus *is* God's Word, it is important not to sever Jesus' unity with God or Jesus' oneness as a person. Jesus is ultimately one being existing in two natures. The Alexandrian tradition would always say a strong no to Adoptionism.

Chalcedon helped us to affirm Jesus' oneness of being by asserting that Jesus *is* one *hypostasis* (which need not exclude pre-

Chalcedonian Cyrillian Monophysitism) who *subsists* in two *physeis* or natures (which ought not be interpreted as a form of "Nestorianism"). Thus Eutychean Monophysitism and "Nestorian" Dyophysitism became technical theological parameters that clarified further for philosophical theology what Docetism and Adoptionism were all about if they were to be truly avoided. The contribution of Chalcedon was primarily a contribution to the making of theological language. It distinguished for the Catholic Church *hypostasis* and *physis*. Nicea's contribution, too, had been to the history of theological discourse by making *homoousios* the only orthodox interpretation of the Gospel of John.

But theological precision and technical theological language, while extremely necessary, are not the only concerns of theology. Theology, and a theology of Jesus, must be primarily pastoral—as the Second Vatican Council called to mind. It must also be mystical or spiritual—as Orthodoxy has always affirmed in its insistence on the unity between doctrine and life. A theology of Jesus is judged as more or less adequate or inadequate in the light of its ability to communicate the gospel and salvation—as the soteriological starting point of the Reformation makes clear.

We cannot fail to mention that talk of salvation must always be placed in the context of the concerns and needs of our world and our period of history to which the gospel is being proclaimed and for whom our theology is being constructed. A theology of Jesus must be confessionally, professionally, and socially responsible. It must also be pastorally sensitive, spiritually grounded, and seriously intelligible. Having learned something from history, the task of reconstruction awaits us in the next volume of this series.

General Bibliography

SUGGESTED READINGS

Altaner, Berthold. *Patrology.* Trans. Hilda Graef. New York: Herder and Herder, 1960.

Brown, Harold O. J. *Heresies: The Image of Christ in the Mirror of Heresy and Orthodoxy from the Apostles to the Present.* Garden City, N.Y.: Doubleday, 1984.

Congar, Yves M.-J. *A History of Theology.* Trans. Hunter Guthrie. Garden City, N.Y.: Doubleday, 1968.

Daniélou, Jean. *The Theology of Jewish Christianity.* Vol. 1 of *The Development of Early Christian Doctrine Before the Council of Nicaea.* Trans. John A. Baker. Chicago: The Henry Regnery Co., 1964.

_____. *Gospel Message and Hellenistic Culture.* Vol. 2 of *The Development of Early Christian Doctrine Before the Council of Nicaea.* Trans. John A. Baker. Philadelphia: Westminster Press, 1973.

_____. *The Origins of Latin Christianity.* Vol. 3 of *The Development of Early Christian Doctrine Before the Council of Nicaea.* Trans. David Smith and John A. Baker. Philadelphia: Westminster Press, 1977.

Daniélou, Jean, and Henri Marrou. *The First Six Hundred Years.* Vol. 1 of *The Christian Centuries.* Trans. Vincent Cronin. New York: Paulist, 1964.

Frend, W. H. C. *The Rise of Christianity.* Philadelphia: Fortress, 1984. An excellent history of the Church. See review essay by D. Moody Smith, *Journal of the American Academy of Religion* 54 (1986) 337–342.

Gonzalez, Justo L. *A History of Christian Thought,* 3 vols. A very readable history of theology. Nashville: Abingdon, 1970–1975.

Grillmeier, Aloys. *Christ in Christian Tradition: From the Apostolic Age to Chalcedon (AD 451)*. Rev. ed. Trans. John Bowden. The best history available of Christology itself. London: Mowbrays, 1975.

_____. *Christ in Christian Tradition: From Chalcedon to Justinian I*, pt. 1. Trans. Pauline Allen, and John Cawte. Atlanta: John Knox, 1987.

Jedin, Hubert, and others, eds. *History of the Church*, 10 vols. Trans. from the German. New York: Seabury and Crossroad, 1980–1982.

Kelly, J. N. D. *Early Christian Creeds*. 2nd ed. London: Longmans, Green, and Co., 1960.

_____. *Early Christian Doctrines*. 2nd ed. New York: Harper & Row, Publishers, 1960.

Knowles, David, and Dimitri Obolensky. *The Middle Ages*. Vol. 2 of *The Christian Centuries*. New York: Paulist, 1969.

Pelikan, Jaroslav. *The Emergence of the Catholic Tradition (100–600)*. Vol. 1 of *The Christian Tradition: A History of the Development of Doctrine*. A very competent and commendable series. Chicago: University of Chicago Press, 1971.

_____. *The Spirit of Eastern Christendom (600–1700)*. Vol. 2 of *The Christian Tradition: A History of the Development of Doctrine*. Chicago: University of Chicago Press, 1974.

_____. *The Growth of Medieval Theology (600–1300)*. Vol. 3 of *The Christian Tradition: A History of the Development of Doctrine*. Chicago: University of Chicago Press, 1978.

_____. *Reformation of Church and Dogma (1300–1700)*. Vol. 4 of *The Christian Tradition: A History of the Development of Doctrine*. Chicago: University of Chicago Press, 1984.

_____. *Christian Doctrine and Modern Culture (since 1700)*. Vol. 5 of *The Christian Tradition: A History of the Development of Doctrine*. Chicago: University of Chicago Press, 1988.

Quasten, Johannes. *Patrology*, 4 vols. Vol. 1: *The Beginnings of Patristic Literature*. Vol. 2: *The Ante-Nicene Literature After Irenaeus*. Vol. 3: *The Golden Age of Greek Patristic Literature*. Vol. 4: *The Golden Age of Latin Patristic Literature from the Council of Nicaea to the Council of Chalcedon*. Ed. Angelo di Berardino, trans. Placid Solari. Utrecht-Antwerp: Spectrum, 1964–1966. Vol. 4, Westminster, Md.: Christian Classics, 1986.

von Campenhausen. *The Fathers of the Greek Church*. Trans. Stanley Godman. New York: Pantheon Books, 1959.

_____. *The Fathers of the Latin Church*. Trans. Manfred Hoffman. Stanford, Calif.: Stanford University Press, 1969.

Glossary

ADOPTIONISM. Ordinarily refers to the heretical tendency in the early Church to interpret Jesus as less than fully divine, as an adopted son of God rather than as the natural Son of God or as the eternal Son incarnate, often associated with Paul of Samosata or earlier Judeo-Christian theology that interpreted Jesus as a human being particularly favored by God. For the Spanish Adoptionists of the eighth century, see chapter 4.

COMMUNICATIO IDIOMATUM, or the communication of properties. A way of speaking in Christology whereby the properties of one nature (either divine or human) can be predicated of the person of Jesus Christ but not of the other natures. For example, one cannot say that divine nature suffers or that human nature is omniscient, but one can say that Jesus Christ suffers and is omniscient. These principles for proper speech vary with theologians or theological schools.

DOCETISM. The heretical tendency in Christian theology that denied the full humanity of Jesus and the full reality of Jesus' bodiliness and sufferings, maintaining that Jesus only seemed to be human. The word comes from the Greek word *dokein* (to seem).

DONATISM. Donatus divided the Latin Church in North Africa in the fourth century. The dispute was concerned with whether baptized Christians who had surrendered to demands during the time of persecution, especially that of Diocletian, those who were *lapsi,* could be restored to communion with the Church, about which possibility Donatists were rigorist, and thus they rejected it. Also, the Donatists taught that the validity of a sacrament was dependent on whether the minister of the sacrament was in the state of grace.

GNOSTICISM. Primarily refers to the heretical Gnosticism of the second to fourth centuries, which existed in various forms but in general taught a doctrine of salvation rooted in a secret knowledge *(gnosis),* the radical distinction between the unknown and transcendent true God and the evil God or God the Creator, the rejection of the goodness of the material world and bodiliness, a Docetic picture of Jesus, and the belief in a pre-mundane fall, which accounts for the present human condition.

HOMOOUSIOS. The Greek word that came to express the Nicene interpretation of the relationship between the Father and the Son and the orthodox understanding of the relationship of the persons in the Trinity. It means "of the same substance," or consubstantial, inferring the equality and divinity of the Son and the Father, in contrast to Arianism.

MANICHEISM. A heresy associated with Mani of Persia (ca. 215–275), who taught an absolute dualism between spirit and matter, the evil of the material world, and a strict asceticism as the only path to salvation, which path could only be pursued by a small number of elect. It surfaced again in the Middle Ages as Albigensianism.

MILLENARIANISM. An eschatological teaching concerned with the second coming of Christ that maintained that Christ upon his return would reign on earth with his followers for a period of a thousand years before the full heavenly reign of God would be established, or that the saints of God would rule on earth for a thousand years before the return of Christ.

MODALISM. A heretical form of Monarchianism which maintained that God is three only in the sense that God manifests three faces, or modes, of acting with respect to the world, but not that God's very being is triune.

MONARCHIANISM. An early Christian emphasis on the oneness of God (one rule). In an orthodox sense, this is compatible with Christian monotheism. More often used to refer to heretical Monarchians who denied the reality of the Trinity in their emphasis on God as one or reduced the Trinity to modes of acting (see modalism).

MONOPHYSITISM. The doctrine that there is one nature *(physis)* in Jesus Christ. After Chalcedon's definition of two natures, Monophysitism would be considered a heresy that did not do justice to the full humanity of Jesus; also the path taken by the non-Chalcedonian Churches for whom Monophysitism emphasized the oneness of Jesus Christ as taught earlier by Cyril of Alexandria. One ought distinguish between an orthodox, pre-Chalcedonian, Cyrillian Monophysitism; and a post-Chalcedonian Monophysitism of the Oriental non-Chalcedonian Churches; and Eutychean, heretical Monophysitism.

PHILO OF ALEXANDRIA. An Alexandrian Jewish philosopher and older contemporary of Paul, influenced by Middle Platonism, who emphasized the transcendence of God, the need for intermediaries between God and the human world, and allegorical methods for exegesis of the Hebrew Scriptures.

PELAGIANISM. A heresy primarily to affect the West, taught by Pelagius, a British monk, who maintained that human beings could, apart from grace, do good and thus merit salvation. Opposed by Augustine, it seemed to deny the full effect or reality of original sin.

PLATONISM, MIDDLE PLATONISM, AND NEOPLATONISM. Platonism refers to the philosophical doctrine of the ancient Greek philosopher Plato (ca. 428–347 B.C.E.) and the philosophical tradition influenced by his thought. Significant among Platonic doctrines is his teaching concerning another world, where ideal forms have eternal concrete existence of which this world is but a shadow. Middle Platonism refers to the second major period of influence in the history of Platonic thought, the second century C.E., which had a strong impact on the developing Christian theologies. Neoplatonism, or Platonism as developed by Plotinus (ca. 205–270 C.E.), was another major period of Platonic influence and deeply affected the theology of Augustine (354–430).

SABELLIANISM. A form of modalism associated with Sabellius (early third century) who taught that there was no real ontological distinction between Father and Son; these were only different names for the one God. Thus, by way of conclusion, the "Father" also suffered and died on the cross since there was no real distinction between them, hence also "Patripassianism," the teaching that the Father also suffered. See modalism.

STOICISM. A philosophical school founded by Zeno (335–263 B.C.E.), which influenced heavily the history of Christian thought, especially the Latin tradition, through the philosophies of Seneca (ca. 4 B.C.E.–65 C.E.) and Cicero (106–43 B.C.E). It held a conception of the Logos as the world-soul in which every person participates, the relationship of "the rational" and the "natural" and thus the law of nature, as well as an asceticism necessary to live a rational moral life.

Index of Proper Names